Gender in Science
Fiction Films,
1964–1979

Gender in Science Fiction Films, 1964–1979

A Critical Study

BONNIE NOONAN

McFarland & Company, Inc., Publishers

Jefferson, North Carolina

LIBRARY OF CONGRESS CATALOGUING-IN-PUBLICATION DATA

Noonan, Bonnie, 1949–
Gender in science fiction films, 1964–1979 : a critical study /
Bonnie Noonan.
p.   cm.
Includes bibliographical references and index.
Includes filmography.

ISBN 978-0-7864-5974-2 (softcover : acid free paper) ∞
ISBN 978-1-4766-2210-1 (ebook)

1. Science fiction films—History and criticism.
2. Sex role in motion pictures.   3. Women in motion pictures.
4. Men in motion pictures.   I. Title.

PN1995.9.S26N64 2015   791.43'615—dc23   2015018926

BRITISH LIBRARY CATALOGUING DATA ARE AVAILABLE

On the cover: Jane Fonda in *Barbarella: Queen of the Galaxy*,
1968 (Paramount Pictures/Photofest)

Printed in the United States of America

*McFarland & Company, Inc., Publishers
Box 611, Jefferson, North Carolina 28640
www.mcfarlandpub.com*

For Timm Madden,
of course…

Thank you to my discerning colleagues
Leslie Gale Parr and Robin Goldman Vander.
Thank you as well to my lifelong friends Janice Bezou,
Milton Boylan, Jimmy Otis, and Ersy Schwartz.

Table of Contents

Preface

I loved working on *Women Scientists in Fifties Science Fiction Films* (McFarland, 2005). The films that I explored in that book contributed greatly to my ideas of growing up female in the 1950s in that they expanded parameters, imagined possibilities, and created prototypes I could dream about emulating. They used concepts of the wonderfully optimistic science of the Fifties as a basis for the intersection of speculation and reality through which exciting new realities could be manifested. I saw *Them!* and imagined myself an entomologist, the only observer with enough training to descend into the film's nest of gigantic, mutated, flesh-eating ants. I saw *This Island Earth* and imagined myself a nuclear physicist, "just a step" behind the other reigning nuclear physicist of the era, the film's hero, Dr. Cal Meacham. I saw *World Without End* and imagined myself assistant to the head scientist of an underground Earth of the future. I saw *Beyond the Time Barrier* and imagined myself an interplanetary pilot who had broken through the time sphere during her third flight from Earth to Venus. I saw *Attack of the 50 Foot Woman* and imagined myself ... huge.

Eventually, writers ran out of bugs to enlarge or ways to alter human bodies. Actual space travel became reality, necessitating as well more reality-based representations of science. The science fiction film genre of the Fifties began to morph, radiating outward through various trajectories, becoming at times more serious, at times more spectacular. My interest in science fiction during this time of change, however, was primarily spent watching *The Outer Limits* on television (premiering in 1963 and ending in 1965), a series that I see as the true repository of the Fifties "B" science fiction film genre.

I did not see *Robinson Crusoe on Mars* when it was first released in 1964, even though it was directed by Byron Haskin, director of 1953's *The*

War of the Worlds, 1955's *Conquest of Space,* 1958's *From the Earth to the Moon.*[1] Of course I did eventually see the film and can see now that it served as a link between the science fiction traditions of the Fifties and the modernization of those traditions that followed, particularly with respect to gender: Where the lead female figures in the science-fiction films of the Fifties embodied various characteristics from supportive wife to commanding scientist, the female lead in *Robinson Crusoe* had become a monkey named Mona as men struggled to survive on their own in a hostile environment.

I did not see John Frankenheimer's *Seconds* when it first came out in 1966, in part because *Seconds* was not particularly successful at the box office. Perhaps its poor promotion and reception were partially due to the fact that the film explored the pressures on middle-aged men to remain young during an era when youth was beginning to be valued as never before. One could even argue that the evolution of hero as boy begins with the movie's hero Tony Wilson, played by Rock Hudson, an actor who must have known he could not for very much longer go on playing the post-pubertal ingénue of *Pillow Talk* (1959) and *Lover Come Back* (1961) (both of which I did see immediately on release). In *Seconds,* Wilson is granted "new life in a younger body."[2] The adoration of male youth poignantly explored in this film is even more problematically explored in *Logan's Run* (1976), where "no one is allowed to live past the age of thirty" and culminates quite naturalistically in Steven Spielberg's *E.T. The Extra-Terrestrial* (1982), one of the most popular films in the genre, with Henry Thomas's quintessential boy-hero, Elliot.

I did not see François Truffaut's *Fahrenheit 451* immediately on its release in 1966, though I had, of course, already read Ray Bradbury's novel. I did see *Fantastic Voyage* with "Raquel Welch in a wet suit" in 1966 on a family outing to the movies. I did not see *One Million Years B.C.* in 1966, but I do remember seeing the poster of a glorious Welch, barefoot and near naked in animal skins.

There were reasons my interest in the science fiction film had abated. By 1967, the Beatles had given way to the Jefferson Airplane, my life in the suburbs had given way to an apartment in the French Quarter, madras had given way to tie dye, and in essence, a child's imagination had given way to an emerging adult's reality in which decisions had to be made. Should I major in science or drama? Was I the girl who worked as an assistant laboratory technician at the Louisiana State Board of Health? Or was I the hippie manqué who would turn on, tune in, and drop out? Would I become a feminist, flying solo and passionately fighting for equal rights for women? Or would I live out the life my parents had planned for me, letting my father escort me down the aisle at the very same church where I was baptized and where he and my mother had been married?

What does my life, what do these choices have to do with science fiction film, you may ask. Well, just as I imagined the possibilities of my future in the "B" science fiction films of the Fifties, I looked for representations of the course my life could take—indeed, was taking—in the films of the Sixties and Seventies. As I had discovered possibilities in the science fiction films of the Fifties, I looked to that same genre once again to find an extrapolation of reality in which I could situate myself.

One might think that I could have found a suitable virtual reality in 1968, a spectacular, defining year for the science fiction film genre, giving us *2001: A Space Odyssey, Barbarella, Charly,* Robert Altman's *Countdown,* and *Planet of the Apes.* These films were followed by a panoply of science-fiction films such as *Colossus: The Forbin Project, The Illustrated Man,* and *Marooned* in 1969, and *Beneath the Planet of the Apes, The Andromeda Strain, A Clockwork Orange, Escape from the Planet of the Apes, Omega Man,* George Lucas's *THX 1138, Conquest of the Planet of the Apes, Silent Running, Slaughterhouse Five, Invasion of the Bee Girls* (in which I worked as an extra—I played a scientist), *Sleeper,* and *Soylent Green* as we moved into the Seventies. So why did I find the films of this era so disheartening?

Of course I saw *2001: A Space Odyssey*—directed by Stanley Kubrick, written by Stanley Kubrick and Arthur C. Clarke—*2001,* the quintessential science fiction film of all time. The movie won the Academy Award for Special Visual Effects. It was nominated for Best Director and Best Screenplay. It won the BAFTA Film Award for Best Art Direction, Best Cinematography, Best Sound Track, and was nominated for Best Film. It won the Cinema Writers Circle Award in Spain and the David de Donatello Award in Italy for Best Foreign Film. The Directors Guild of America nominated Stanley Kubrick for Outstanding Directorial Achievement. The film was presented the Hugo Award by the World Science Fiction Society for Best Dramatic Presentation, and in 1991 it was selected for preservation and placed in the Library of Congress National Film Registry.

Yes, *2001* was a groundbreaking film. It had cosmic, spectacular visuals and a sound track so compelling that, as Vivian Sobchack writes in the authoritative *Screening Space: The American Science Fiction Film* (1987), "it is really necessary, in order to determine the meaning in a Kubrick SF film, to hear the soundtrack as well as see the visual content of the various images" (213). I so wanted to share the wonder of this film that I took my mother—born in 1909—to see it in Cinerama. She watched it patiently.

After we left the theater, the only comment she had was "I've always loved the Strauss waltzes."

The narrative of *2001: A Space Odyssey* was philosophically and onto-logically sophisticated. I loved the film. I must have seen it seven times, but I never really saw myself in it. What I did see was Keir Dullea as Dr. Dave Bowman and Gary Lockwood as Dr. Frank Poole exercising, eating, watching television transmissions from Earth, playing chess with HAL (and losing), communicating by videophone with their families, lying under a sun lamp, doodling, and performing other ordinary activities (and ultimately even fighting for survival) mundanely, routinely, as if the extraordinary mission they were on was a matter of course. In "Kubrick's *2001* and the Possibility of a Science-Fiction Cinema," Carl Freedman describes Bowman and Poole's characterizations as "conceptually lifeless." This comment is far from derogatory, however, as Freedman considers this "banality" to be an essential component of the film's dynamic (313). Freedman further describes one of the film's themes as "the potential con-flict between men" and then states "(but not women) and machines" (203), and unlike the "B" science fiction films of the Fifties, it is—not about women, that is.

In 1968, I also saw the award winning *Charly*, which earned an Acad-emy Award for Cliff Robertson as Best Actor, the Golden Globe for Best Screenplay, and a Hugo Award for Best Dramatic Presentation. In *Charly*, I saw some options for myself in Alice Kinnian, the film's teacher/psychol-ogist, planning to work on a joint thesis with her fiancé for her doctorate. Not too shabby, Ms. Kinnian was played by actress Claire Bloom, former portrayer of Roxane, Cleopatra, Juliet, Beauty (of *Beauty and the Beast*), Anna Karenina, Cathy of *Wuthering Heights*, and Dorothea Grimm. Ulti-mately, however, her role was not so much about succeeding as a scientist as it was acting the romantic foil for her pupil, played by Robertson, the (and this description is from Wikipedia) "mentally retarded bakery worker who is the subject of an experiment to increase human intelligence."

More important to my disheartenment with this film, however, was one particular scene that upset me when I first saw it and upsets me still when I see it today. As Ms. Kinnian accompanies Charly to his room one night, in a purely professional, yet sympathetic capacity at this point in the film, Charly's suspicious landlady, Mrs. Apple, remarks, "There'll be no hokey-pokey in my house."[3] Later, as Charly has gained intelligence and become more aware of what it means to be a man, he begins to develop romantic feelings for the sympathetic and supportive Ms. Kinnian. He shows up unexpected at her apartment with a gift for her. As she opens the door, we first notice the provocative dress that accentuates her breasts. (She has just returned from a date.) Surprised, cautious at first, she lets Charly in, invites him to sit down. As she begins to open her present (a hand mirror), Charly (as does the camera) cannot help but focus on her shapely legs, accentuated by her fashionable mini-skirt. He confronts her about her date. He tells her he loves her. The more she rebuffs him, the more he focuses on her bare legs until he aggressively, even violently, forces himself on her, throwing her to the floor, pressing his mouth, his hands all over her. Finally managing to extricate herself, she slaps him hard across the face and calls him (unfortunately) a "stupid moron." So much for the hokey pokey.

This exchange between Charly and Ms. Kinnian is a pivotal sequence in the movie, one from which Charly sets out on his own adventures in the world, ultimately to return to Ms. Kinnian's (this time) welcoming arms. What upsets me is that Ms. Kinnian is presented here as bringing this sexual assault upon herself, with the cinematic focus on her breasts and legs, her living in an apartment alone without a man, her having been married before, and her obviously being involved with a new fiancé. In the late Sixties and early Seventies, as the Second Wave of Feminism was percolating, women were allowed to acknowledge our sexuality (a welcome release from the sexually repressive Fifties), yet at the same time, we were almost obligated to be sexual as well as to suffer the consequences we seemed to be bringing on ourselves.

The astonishing opening of Roger Vadim's *Barbarella: Queen of the Galaxy* (1968), which incidentally won nothing, presents an image of the consummate embodiment of woman's sexual liberation. We see an astronaut inside a space vehicle, floating in zero-gravity space, slowly removing first, gloves, revealing graceful, perfectly manicured feminine hands; then one legging, then the other, revealing deliciously creamy thighs. A drum machine, guitar, flutes kick in as the astronaut slowly revolves. The helmet's metallic face plate incrementally, achingly descends, revealing auburn hair, bright eyes. Upbeat vocals rise in the background: "It's a wonder, wonder woman/You're so wild and wonderful." We see a beauty's dreamy expression ... it is Jane Fonda! At her most spectacular! The helmet removed, the hair loosed, soft curls flow as Fonda spins in space. The chorus chimes in with jingle-jangle innocent joy: "Barbarella, Psychedella" (this is the Sixties, after all). The scene ends with Fonda's exuberant delight as she spins into the nakedness of a perfect woman backed by the vocals, "I'm dyin,' girl, to hold ya and make love." Even her feet are perfect.

In *Against Our Will: Men, Women and Rape* (1975), Susan Brown-

Jane Fonda as Barbarella, powerful and sexy, on the DVD cover of *Barbarella* (1968).

miller asserts that "from the humblest beginnings of the social order ... the historic price of woman's protection by man against man was the imposition of chastity and monogamy" (16–17). As women determined to become subjects rather than objects of sexual desire, we were paradoxically made vulnerable to male sexuality at its most unrestrained. Consequently, the empowering representation of woman as Barbarella can unfortunately be partnered with a corresponding increase in filmic images of male violence, perhaps masking the loss of traditional male sexual authority. Take *A Boy and His Dog* (1975), for instance, a film that won a Hugo for Best Dramatic Presentation as well as a Best Actor award for a very young Don Johnson (as pretty as any girl) from the Academy of Science Fiction, Fantasy and Horror Films, USA. As in *Robinson Crusoe*, the hero's co-star is non-human (male this time)—a telepathically talking dog named Blood.

A Boy and His Dog opens onto a post-apocalyptic world (2024) of marauding male "rovers" seeking women to rape. Blood and Vic (Johnson's character) watch as the band of rovers run from their latest attack. We hear a woman's desperate cries and a boy's voice calling out, "Hey, d'ja see her jerk when I cut her?" As Blood and Vic approach the woman's underground refuge, Blood's masculine voice begins comment on the horrific situation:

Young Don Johnson as he appeared in *The Magic Garden of Stanley Sweetheart,* **five years before his starring role in** *A Boy and His Dog* **(1975) (Photofest).**

> **BLOOD**: I wouldn't bother going down in there unless your taste has changed radically. They left an ugly mess. (*Vic ignores him, continuing on.*) I said they left a mess.
>
> **VIC**: I heard you.
>
> **BLOOD**: Ah, pearls before swine. All my directives go completely unregarded. Sometimes you're just as eager as any common rover. One indication of a female and all caution to the wind, the eyes glaze, the glands swell, and the brain freezes. (*Inside, they discover the naked, bloody, spread-eagled victim gutturally gasping what we presume must be her last breaths.*)
>
> **VIC** (*shaking his head sadly*): Ain't that a shame? (*Vic pauses as we wait for*

> *this beautiful man, our presumptive hero, to offer some sort of redemption*
> *for this horror, but he surprises us.*) Hell, they didn't have to cut her. She
> could've been used two or three more times.
>
> **Blood** (*in response to this unexpected comment*): You're so funny when
> you're sexually frustrated.

A Boy and His Dog is touted as "Wildly humorous!" by a reviewer
from the *Austin Sun* on the DVD liner notes. Even though critic Mack. in
Variety's Complete Science Fiction Reviews (1985) panned the film as a
"turkey," he still acknowledged its "redneck humor." The current Internet
Movie Database site classifies *A Boy and His Dog* as a comedy. Am I missing something? Admittedly, *A Boy and His Dog* is somewhat of a cult film,
but its depiction of violence against women is not anomalous to the period.
In 1971, for example, I stood in line to see Stanley Kubrick's *A Clockwork
Orange* on its opening night in Manhattan. I was expecting another transformative, exhilarating, even though bewildering, *2001*-like experience.
What I remember most from the film, however, is my horror at the casual
violence of the rape sequences, one of which, as all who have seen it must
recall, is sickeningly played against the erstwhile charming "Singin' in the
Rain."

In "Professionalism and Femininity in the Giant Insect Films" in
Women Scientists in Fifties Science Fiction Films, I argued that the tension
resulting from an imbalance between expanding roles for women without
a complementary adjustment in roles for men was projected onto giant
insects, which when conquered provided a soothing simulation of order
restored, eliminating any need to explain the particulars of that process.
In the science fiction films of the Sixties and Seventies, there are few
extraordinary symbols onto which a changing interrelation between male
and female can be projected when a woman's gender configuration is so
radically altered, as it was when, as Charles Kaiser writes in *1968 in America: Music, Politics, Chaos, Counterculture, and the Shaping of a Generation* (1988), "Women artists like Aretha Franklin, Janis Joplin, and Grace
Slick as virtual equals of men like Marvin Gaye, Jerry Garcia, and Jimi
Hendrix provided subliminal evidence of sexual equality for teenagers
everywhere" (192). Consequently, in order for a film to succeed, as Melvin
Donalson writes in *Masculinity in the Interracial Buddy Film* (2006), as
"an expressive form that emanates from a society of socialized gender
within a patriarchal power structure" (5), the shift in male hegemony,
unlike in the Fifties films, had to be depicted as well.

Freedman locates *2001* between the science fiction film genre's "two
distinct periods of greatest prominence: the 1950s and the years from the

late 1970s until the mid-to-late 1980s" (301), the most representative films of the latter period being, according to Freedman, the *Star Wars* trilogy (1977–1983), *Close Encounters of the Third Kind* (1977), and *E.T.* (1982). Yes, these are wonderful films: big-budget, auteur-driven, wildly popular, critically acclaimed. Yes, I finally saw myself cinematically represented in 1979 with Sigourney Weaver's portrayal of the remarkably Fifties-like heroine Ripley in Ridley Scott's *Alien*. Nonetheless, I argue that the very films that Freedman overlooks (and that I find disheartening) are ones that can reveal much about fear of change and which are most important to draw on now as American identity configurations—evidenced only in part by the 2012 re-election of Barack Obama (and the determined attempts to obstruct him) as well as a second run at the presidency by Hillary Clinton and challenges from rising Tea Party candidates—continue to shift and re-shift.

In this project I intend to explore the eclectic films of the Sixties and Seventies in order to determine what they tell us not only about the development of the genre, but also about changes involving gender. Chapter 1, "Trajectories of Post-Fifties Science Fiction Films," virtually encyclopedically lists, describes, and classifies sixteen films from 1964 to 1968 as well as significant episodes and characteristics of *The Outer Limits*, as they reflect issues regarding representations of gender and the continuing developments of the genre. As well as analyzing and describing specific episodes from *The Outer Limits*, the chapter covers what I refer to as post–Fifties films such as *Destination Inner Space* and *Around the World Under the Sea*. It also covers early Sixties films such as *Robinson Crusoe on Mars*, *Village of the Giants*, and *Seconds* that illustrate changes the genre was undergoing as it tried to reestablish its grounding in the popular imagination.

Chapter 2, "1968: A Spectacular Science Fictional Year," lists and describes the genre-bending films of that year (*Mission Mars, Countdown, 2001: A Space Odyssey, Charly, Barbarella,* and *Planet of the Apes*), their connection to the dynamic changes of the period, their consequent representations of gender, and their effect on the science-fiction films to follow. Drawing from critical analyses, film reviews, and cultural commentaries on the Sixties and Seventies as well as from close readings of the films themselves, Chapter 3, "Gender and...," examines representations of gender throughout the films of what I refer to as the Middle Period. This chapter covers gender and science in films such as *The Andromeda Strain* and *Colossus: The Forbin Project*, gender and marriage in films such as *Marooned* and *The Stepford Wives*, as well as gender and representations of sex in films such as *A Boy and His Dog* and *Invasion of the Bee Girls*. It also examines gender and race in films such as *The Omega Man* and *Frogs* as well as gender in the dystopian societies that invariably lurk on the periphery of science fiction films such as *Soylent Green* and *Logan's Run*. Finally, the chapter covers representations of advances in artificial intelligence, in particular as portrayed in *Demon Seed*. All of these subjects—science, marriage, sex, race and artificial intelligence—were highlighted in and developed from the films of 1968.

Chapter 4, "The Outliers," examines those films I excluded—why I excluded them as well as why I could have included them in the first place. By elucidating what the science fiction films of the Sixties and Seventies were not, we can see even more clearly what they were and how they represented (and continue to represent) our world. My conclusion, "A Revitalization of the Science Fiction Film Genre," points to the next cosmic shift, as it were, of the genre. *Close Encounters of the Third Kind*, the 1978 remake of *Invasion of the Body Snatchers*, *Superman: The Movie*, *Alien*, *Star Wars*, and *Star Trek: The Motion Picture* set a new trajectory, one that with its representations of space, science, society, and sex not only reflected the changing political and social climate of the late Seventies, but also opened up exciting new possibilities for the science fiction films that followed. The period is exciting enough to write a whole book about...

1

Trajectories of Post-Fifties Science Fiction Films

The 1950s American "B" science fiction film genre began at a finite time, 1950, with *Rocketship X-M* and *Destination Moon* and ended concurrently with our actual explorations of space. Mercury missions included Freedom 7's sub-orbital flight, piloted by Alan Shepard (1961); Liberty Bell 7's sub-orbital flight, piloted by Gus Grissom (1961), and Friendship 7's first manned orbit of Earth, piloted by John Glenn (1962). One wonders, though, what happened to the wildly speculative impulses that allowed astronauts to walk freely about spaceships, that presented advanced civilizations on other planets, that propelled careening rockets into the future, all images we did not see in the televised images of these space flights. One wonders, as well, what happened to the intense speculation on the roles of women in science that these earlier movies explored?

A look at the "B" science fiction genre beginning circa 1964 will show that the sometimes wacky, sometimes progressive impulses that drove the Fifties films proceeded in several trajectories. It is not particularly surprising that remnants of a fading moment in science fiction found one home in television, a relatively new medium hungry for content. In fact, as I argue below, the television series *The Outer Limits* was the true repository of the Fifties genre.

This is not to say that the Fifties science fiction film genre did not crank on in films that faithfully, though often perfunctorily, reproduced the genre's attendant tropes and conventions. *Mutiny in Outer Space, Destination Inner Space*, and *Around the World Under the Sea* reproduced the conventions of the woman scientist and her romantic entanglements that were established in Fifties films like *Them!* and *Tarantula*. Relations between men and women began to take on a more Sixties tone, however, in *The Time Travelers* and *Crack in the World*. Another trajectory the post–Fifties films capitalized on was the era's growing teen market in *Village of the Giants* and *Mars Needs Women*, building on such earlier teen centered films as *Teenagers from Outer Space* and *The Giant Gila Monster*. Attempts at realistic special effects improved dramatically in *Robinson Crusoe on Mars* and *Fantastic Voyage*. A more serious trajectory built on earlier films such as *Invasion U.S.A.*, *Day the World Ended*, *On the Beach*, and *Panic in Year Zero!* that exploited the nation's fear (not unreasonable at the time) of nuclear holocaust in *Dr. Strangelove or: How I Learned to Stop Worrying and Love the Bomb*, *Fail-Safe*, and *The Last Man on Earth*. Films like *Fahrenheit 451* and *Seconds* attempted to create a more literary, artistic trajectory.

As the genre proceeded, the trajectories that followed the Fifties films began to spin out in ever widening directions, struggling (and ultimately failing) to find a successful, coherent new course. Despite their failure to do so, the journey is quite illuminating in the way the science fiction film genre has attempted to follow social trends as well as build a market. The films as well have much to tell us about who we were and who we are. However, I ask that you permit me, in this book about film, just for a moment, to write about television, in particular *The Outer Limits*, where the series' producers, writers, directors, and performers tried their hardest to keep the Fifties film genre alive.

Into The Outer Limits

"There is nothing wrong with your television set..."
—Control Voice, *The Outer Limits*

As the Fifties science fiction film genre waned, its actors, writers, and directors began drifting to television, in particular to the ABC television series *The Outer Limits*, bringing with them the genre's particular tropes and conventions. Immediately, I find this statement challenged. Timm Madden, electrical engineer and senior instrumentation and controls executive for a major corporation, as well as an avid science fiction fan, is vexed and perplexed that I intend to omit *The Twilight Zone* and, more importantly, *Star Trek* as significant repositories of Fifties science film conventions. In response to Madden, as well as other scientists and science fiction film aficionados who may share Madden's concerns, I put forth the following arguments for my decision.

First, both *The Twilight Zone* and *Star Trek* were relatively long-running series that were able to evolve with the times, unlike *The Outer Limits*, which was limited to only two seasons. Madden correctly counters with the fact that the original *Star Trek* series spanned only three years. However, as stated on Wikipedia, "the core of *Star Trek* is its six television series: The Original Series, The Animated Series, The Next Generation, Deep Space Nine, Voyager, and Enterprise. The franchise also includes eleven feature films, dozens of games, hundreds of novels, numerous toy lines and replicas, as well as a themed attraction in Las Vegas." Thus the *Star Trek* series has had much more longevity than did *The Outer Limits*.

Second, while the budgets for *The Twilight Zone* and *Star Trek* were limited, these budgets were in no way as constrained as were those for *The Outer Limits*, not unlike those of so many science fiction films of the Fifties. Madden points out that films such as *The Day the Earth Stood Still, Forbidden Planet, Destination Moon, When Worlds Collide,* and *The War of the Worlds* had substantial budgets, but I would say that these exceptions prove the rule. Most of the Fifties films were made on the cheap.

Star Trek episodes were, of course, in color. Episodes of *The Outer Limits* and *The Twilight Zone* were in black and white, as were likewise many of the films of the Fifties. My primary reason for excluding *The Twilight Zone* from my discussion, however, is one of genre. *The Twilight Zone* episodes, with the exception of a few science fiction titles such as "Third from the Sun" and "The Invaders" can be characterized more often than not as morality plays and stories with O. Henry endings, for example "One for the Angels" and "Execution." Madden points out that *The Twilight Zone* presented more science fiction episodes than I give it credit for, such as "The Silence," "Will the Real Martian Please Stand Up?," "To Serve Man," "The Parallel," and "The Long Morrow." He has a point there, but it is still my opinion that the bulk of the episodes can be classified as fantasy, horror, or sometimes simply drama. Finally, while I must acknowledge that *Star Trek* plots did indeed revolve around travel into space and unnatural creatures, unlike in *The Outer Limits* and the films of the Fifties, main characters from week to week were consistent.

Now on to my discussion of the reasons why *The Outer Limits* best represents the characteristics of the Fifties films. The first similarity between the Fifties films and *The Outer Limits* is that both the films and the series spanned a limited time frame—the films from 1950 until actual space travel began, and *The Outer Limits* from the series' start in September 1963 with "The Galaxy Being" to its final January 1965 episode "The Probe." Thus, both the films and the series are situated within finite periods of a particular paradigmatic shift in science and culture—the films, at the beginning of the post-war age of optimism; and the television episodes, nearing its end.

A second similarity is that just as most of the "B" science fiction films of the Fifties are immediately recognizable from their opening frames, so are the episodes of *The Outer Limits*. Just as the opening monologues of the Fifties films evoke cosmic concepts (such as "man," "the world," "science," and "the unknown") so do the portentous pronouncements by the Control Voice that open *The Outer Limits*. "The Borderland," for example, opens with "The mind of Man has always longed to know what lies beyond the world we live in."[1] "Cry of Silence" opens with "In the not-distant future, the sound of Man will invade those unknown depths of space which as yet we cannot even imagine." "The Production and Decay of Strange Particles" opens with "In recent years, nuclear physicists have discovered a strange world of subatomic particles."

Another obvious similarity between the television series and the films is that approximately 75 percent of the "B" science fiction films of the Fifties were filmed in black and white. I arrived at this approximation by using my Filmography from *Women Scientists in Fifties Science Fiction Films* (2005). I simply divided the number of films in black and white (86) by the total number of films in the Filmography (114). It turns out my crude calculations were not too far off. In *Film: An International History of the Medium* (1993), Robert Sklar states that "in 1950 the number of color films screened in the United States theaters still represented less than 20 percent of all releases" (345). More importantly, filming in black and white imparted the traditional Fifties sense of documentary truth to the scenes of extraordinary phenomena depicted in *The Outer Limits*.

In fact, in their indispensable *The Outer Limits: The Official Companion* (1986), David J. Schow and Jeffrey Frentzen relate the desire of Conrad Hall, a Director of Photography on the series, to make *The Outer Limits* look specifically like a black and white movie. They write,

> Some of *The Outer Limits film noir* aspects were also tested in "Architects" by Conrad Hall. "There were TV technicians telling me things like I *had* to have a two-to-one lighting ratio, or people wouldn't be visible on TV," said Hall. "Well, people don't *have* to be visible all the time. Sometimes their outline is enough. When it's important to see their faces, you put light on them, or have them move into the light. We handled the show as if it was not an electronic medium, with certain technicalities required for reproduction. I made it look as if it was going to be seen on a motion picture screen, and what the 'experts' did not understand was that it was

better! In every instance where they said, 'It won't look good on television,' they were wrong ... because I'd seen it, and it looked great!"

This reasoning made it impossible for Hall to conceive of the program being done in color: "The *Outer Limits* look was very much a product of black-and-white photography," he stated (83–84).

Another similarity between *The Outer Limits* and many of the films of the Fifties is that they both were produced under limited budgets. Schow and Frentzen also relate how *The Outer Limits* team had to scrimp on mimeographing, not to mention special effects, in order to save money (221). They cite James Goldstone, one of the series' directors: "I have a memory of the question of *how* to get that plywood starship to go up into the air at the end of 'The Inheritors.' We couldn't do it optically, and didn't have the time or the money to shoot it any other way, so Ken Pesch and I just dollied the camera back until we were off the stage, then tilted up to the sky" (340). In *Keep Watching the Skies!: American Science Fiction Movies of the Fifties* (2010), another indispensable resource, Bill Warren comments on the special effects in Roger Corman's *Beast with a Million Eyes*. They "are elementary," he writes, "as the budget was extremely low.... There's a model of the spaceship complete with blinking lights, but it's so poorly designed that it looks like a tiny miniature; it's a bit of a surprise to eventually learn it's about six feet tall" (100). Such budget constraints forced viewers of both the series and the films to surrender more completely than usual to the suspension of disbelief particularly required for enjoying works of science fiction.

The plots of both *The Outer Limits* episodes and the films of the Fifties are also quite similar. The Fifties film genre has three basic plot types: travel into space (*Destination Moon, Flight to Mars*), arrival of aliens on Earth (*The Day the Earth Stood Still, The War of the Worlds*), and unnatural creatures (*Attack of the Crab Monsters, Them!*). *The Outer Limits* episodes can be similarly categorized. "Specimen Unknown" and "The Mutant," for example, deal with travel into space. Aliens arrive on Earth in "The Galaxy Being" and "The Chameleon." A "prehistoric amphibian" (69) appears in "Tourist Attraction." "Alien parasites" (186) appear in "The Invisibles." (These brief descriptions and the ones that follow throughout this chapter are taken from Schow and Frantzen. Their descriptions of the creatures in *The Outer Limits* are so accurate and well stated that I saw no reason to try to paraphrase them.)

The science fiction films of the Fifties were further imbued with under-lying themes of metamorphosis (*I Married a Monster from Outer Space,*

Invasion of the Body Snatchers) and science gone mad (*The Hideous Sun Demon, The Fly*), and so it is with *The Outer Limits*. In "ZZZZZ," the "queen of a superintelligent hive" is transformed into a "ravishing girl" (193). In "The Architects of Fear" a scientist is transformed into "a perfect inhabitant of the planet Theta" (78). "The Galaxy Being" and "The Architects of Fear" are only a two of the episodes in which scientists overreach their limits.

Additionally, as did the films of the Fifties, the episodes of *The Outer Limits* fall under a particular definition of science fiction. That is, each episode is grounded in and extrapolates from a perhaps outlandish but at least not known to be impossible scientific premise that develops logically within the episode. Scanning hydrogen static through a transreceiver—not a magic ray—establishes contact with an extraterrestrial being in "The Galaxy Being." A scientist is converted into an alien being by detailed surgical procedures and transplants of extraterrestrial matter—not by drinking a fantastical potion—in "The Architects of Fear." Deceased researchers are re-animated by pacemakers—not enchanted wands—in "It Crawled Out of the Woodwork." A professor's mind expands as a result of his taking consciousness-expanding drugs—not as a result of inhaling fairy dust—in "Expanding Human."

Along with similarities in conventions, there are also similarities in personnel. Just as Fifties "B" science fiction films had a stable of writers and directors such as Bert I. Gordon and George Worthing Yates, so did *The Outer Limits*. Byron Haskin directed six episodes; Gerd Oswald, fourteen, for example. Joseph Stefano wrote nine episodes; Robert C. Dennis, four. In addition, several writers and directors of the Fifties films also wrote or directed episodes of *The Outer Limits*. David Duncan of *The Leech Woman, Monster on the Campus,* and *The Black Scorpion*, for example, wrote "The Human Factor," and Ib Melchior of *The Angry Red Planet* wrote "Premonition." As well as writers and directors, actors from Fifties science fiction films—such as Grant Williams of *The Incredible Shrinking Man,* John Hoyt of *The Attack of the Puppet People,* and Russell Johnson from *It Came from Outer Space*—play important and visible roles in *The Outer Limits* episodes. Admittedly, these actors were ubiquitous in films and television shows of the era. Nonetheless, seeing one of them in an episode of *The Outer Limits* was like running into an old friend, one you met in a special place when you were just a few years younger.

As did the science fiction films of the Fifties, plots in *The Outer Limits* established an iconography of characters. In *Them or Us? Archetypal Interpretations of Alien Invasion Films* (1987), Patrick Luciano identifies two primary types of male icons from the science fiction films of the Fifties: the "romantic visionary hero," exemplified by actors such as Richard Carlson (amateur astronomer John Putnam in *It Came from Outer Space*) and John Agar (Prof. Clete Ferguson in *Revenge of the Creature*); and the "practical 'guts 'n glory' guys," exemplified by Kenneth Tobey (Cmdr. Pete Matthews in *It Came from Beneath the Sea*) and Marshall Thompson (Cmdr. Charles Prescott in *First Man into Space*) (38). *The Outer Limits* male iconography is exemplified by what I refer to as the "self-sacrificing hero" and the "young rebel redeemed." Robert Culp, for instance, like Agar and Thompson in the Fifties films, was a regular on *The Outer Limits* series. As Allen Leighton, the "uncomplaining" "idealist" (82) in "The Architects of Fear," he wants to save the world from itself. As Trent, the solitary "agent of humankind's salvation" (321) in "Demon with a Glass Hand," he is ultimately left "totally alone" (321). As Dr. Paul Cameron in "Corpus Earthling," he is the hero who "loses everything, but survives" (157) to save the world from an alien virus.

The young rebel redeemed icons are exemplified by Henry Silva and Don Gordon. As Chino Rivera in "The Mice," Silva, a brooding, resentful convict, "stamped by society as a misfit" (182), is eventually seen "in a new and honorable light" (182). As Dr. Dave Crowell in "Second Chance," Gordon is a "discontented dreamer" (223) who successfully negotiates a solution between an alien and his "abductees" (223). As Luis Spain in "The Invisibles," he is a "social disaffiliate" (188) who allows himself to be "pushed to the razor's edge of endurance" (188) in order to thwart an alien takeover of the U.S. government.

"I'm a woman, more woman than scientist..."

With the exception of Barbara Rush (John Putnam's fiancée Ellen Fields in *It Came from Outer Space*) in "The Forms of Things Unknown" and Salome Jens (a woman from the future in *Terror from the Year 5000*) in "Corpus Earthling," actresses from Fifties science fiction films, unlike the actors, are not represented in *The Outer Limits*. However, a female iconography can clearly be identified. Complementary to Luciano's focus on male characters, in *Women Scientists in Science Fiction Films* I propose that the Fifties films exhibited two primary types of female icons: the "smart and sexy woman in charge," exemplified by actresses such as Faith Domergue (Prof. Lesley Joyce in *It Came from Beneath the Sea*) and Marguerite Chapman (Martian scientist in *Flight to Mars*); and the "spunky, indefatigable girl next door," exemplified by Beverly Garland (brave wife of a deluded scientist in *It Conquered the World*) and Gloria Talbot (deceived wife of an alien in *I Married a Monster from Outer Space*).

Ann Barton (Geraldine Brooks) with her husband Brig. Gen. Jefferson Barton (William Shatner) in *The Outer Limits* episode "Cold Hands, Warm Heart" (Photofest).

The main categories of female characters in *The Outer Limits*, however, can be described as various types of wives. Geraldine Brooks, for example, plays Yvette, the exemplary good wife of the dedicated but misguided Allen Leighton in "The Architects of Fear" as well as Ann, the loving wife of beleaguered astronaut Brig. Gen. Jefferson Barton in "Cold Hands, Warm Heart." In both episodes, she is attractive, supportive, happily dutiful as a wife, and genuinely loved by her husband. In "Keeper of the Purple Twilight" and "Specimen Unknown," Gail Kobe portrays the type of devoted and fragile wife who can make a courageous and adventurous man feel even stronger.

Jacqueline Scott and Priscilla Morrill are quintessential nagging wives, unsatisfied not so much with the role of traditional wife as they are with their husbands. Scott, as Carol Maxwell, belittles her husband's dreams of glory in "The Galaxy Being." Likewise, Morrill, as Vera Finley, refers to her husband as "a little man, a nobody" in "The Man with the Power." (It is not coincidental that both women are threatened nearly to death by their husbands' scientific discoveries.) Sally Kellerman deliciously plays the spoiled, selfish wife of a daring entrepreneur, appropriately punished at the end of "The Bellero Shield." Constance Towers and Phyllis Love play unhappy wives in "The Duplicate Man" and "A Feasibility Study." Barbara Rush, Vera Miles, and Janet Blair play not wives, but frustrated mistresses in "The Forms of Things Unknown" and "Tourist Attraction." Miriam Hopkins plays an aged spinster, thwarted at the altar yet still wearing her wedding dress in "Don't Open Till Doomsday." June Havoc, Signe Hasso, Catherine McLeod, and Marion Ross play the traditional wives of an older generation in "Cry of Silence," "The Production and Decay of Strange Particles," "Soldier," and "The Special One," respectively. Peggy Ann Garner and Shirley Knight play young wives-to-be in "The Probe" and "The Man Who Was Never Born."

While most of the women in *The Outer Limits* are characterized in reference to their male counterparts, there are several roles for women in science, just as there were in the films of the Fifties. Mathematician Eva Frazer (played by Nina Foch) competently utters expressions such as "Polarity minus five zero degrees" and "Primaries one seven one, stroke, one one, stroke, one seven" while operating complex equipment in "The Borderland." Research scientist Dr. Stephanie Linden (played by Joan Lamden) literally gives her life to her work in a physics research center in "It Crawled Out of the Woodwork." Dr. Alicia Hendrix (played by Jacqueline Scott) is an anthropologist in "Counterweight." Along with Hendrix, the other selected participants in the experiment she is undertaking are a newspaper reporter, a construction engineer, an ecologist, a botanist, and a doctor (all male). Betsy Jones-Moreland plays biochemist Julie Griffith in "The Mutant." Like Hendrix, Griffeth is the only woman in a group of six scientists researching another planet. Lunar scientist Prof. Diana Brice (played by Ruth Roman) does her best to protect intelligent alien beings in "Moonstone." Diana Sands plays medical doctor Julia Harrison in "The Mice." One of the joys of science fiction is seeing a character from a drama transported into a different, more progressive reality. In 1961's *A Raisin in the Sun*, for example, Walter Lee Younger angrily says to his sister Beneatha, also played by Sands, "Who in the hell told you you had to be a doctor? You're so interested in messing around with sick people, go on outta here and be a nurse, like other women, or get married and shut up." What a pleasure it is then in "The Mice" to hear a male colleague say, "Is it true, Dr. Harrison?" and see that Dr. Harrison is being played by Sands, just a little older than she was in *A Raisin in the Sun*.

As I argue in *Women Scientists and Fifties Science Fiction Films*, the

Mathematician Eva Frazer (Nina Foch) at the controls in *The Outer Limits* episode "The Borderland" (Photofest).

films of the Fifties exhibit a sense of equilibrium between a woman's professional power (particularly in the fields of science) and the traditional gender characteristics she is required to enact and embody. Further, the tensions involved in any disruption of this sense of equilibrium (particularly disruptions initiated by a woman's stepping outside of her traditional gender roles) are often displaced onto rampaging oversized creatures—

telepathic crabs, rampaging crickets, a prehistoric praying mantis, spiders, mollusks, a gigantic octopus, ants. The ultimate defeat of these creatures promotes a sense of order restored, but this reassurance provides only an illusion of tensions resolved. Without such a pantheon of spectacular, rampaging creatures to defeat in *The Outer Limits*, tensions over colliding gender roles had to be addressed more directly.

In "The Borderland," for example, mathematician Eva Frazer has made certain compromises with respect to her career. While she is renowned and respected enough to hold the "Rensselaer Chair at the Midland University," she does not do her scientific work independently, but rather works in partnership with her husband. Moreover, when a character says in reference to the couple, "You can appreciate how they're working together, like the Curies did on radium," Frazer immediately defers. "I had very little to do with it," she says. "My husband's a genius." Frasier's relinquishment of total independence, however, is compensated for by the fact that it is she who is the hero who rescues her husband from an experiment gone wrong. "I'm here," she shouts as he reaches out to her from the 4th dimension. Moreover, her relationship with her husband is depicted as not only mutually respectful but also physically affectionate. This ability to negotiate her own borderland is visually embodied in Eva's attire: a white lab coat and ever-present tasteful and distinctly feminine pearl necklace. The absence of a rampaging creature to be conquered allows real-world speculation on how men and women could—respecting current gender proscriptions, that is—live and work together.

"A Feasibility Study" depicts a relationship where a woman who has made a choice to give up her budding career as a photojournalist for marriage now regrets it. In *Women Scientists in Fifties Science Fiction Films*, I describe Marge Blaine, a magazine editor and photojournalist for the Museum of Natural History in Washington, as an "adjunct science professional" (90) in *The Deadly Mantis* (1957). Likewise, I include photojournalist Audrey Aimes of *Beginning of the End* (1957) as well as darkroom technician Vera Hunter of *Kronos* (1957) in my work on women scientists, not only because they all participate in risky scientific adventures. Their work in film photography, as well as benefitting from an artistic eye, requires knowledge of sophisticated equipment, some knowledge of chemistry for film development and printing, and knowledge of optics to select the correct lens. Having established this lineage, as it were, of photojournalism as a para-scientific profession, I here include (lapsed) photojournalist Andrea Holm in my discussion of women in science in *The Outer Limits*.

At the start of the episode, Andrea Holm (played by Phyllis Love) is preparing to leave her stubborn husband of a year and a week. Because she and her husband do love each other, despite their difficulties, they talk:

> **ANDREA**: I can't live with you if life has to be lived according to your restrictions. I can't. No matter how benevolent or secure you'd make it, it's slavery. It's a kind of slavery!
>
> **SIMON**: Andrea, I'm not trying to deprive you of your rights. I just don't want you wandering around the world with your camera and your typewriter worrying about everybody else, when I need you *here*, always at home and some of that crusader instinct working on our marriage. Marriage has become insignificant in this big troubled world or ours. Maybe that's one of the reasons the world is in such big trouble.
>
> **ANDREA**: I thought marrying you would be the greatest adventure I'd ever know, but it isn't. It's a dead end world walled in by curtains that don't even get dirty. Why must that be? Why can't I go on being part of everything? I *want* to worry. I *want* to care about making the world a better place. Why is that wrong now just because I'm married?

This discussion takes on very real constraints under which many women who wished to marry and have a career were conventionally obliged to operate.

Yes, Andrea refers to these constraints as slavery. Lest you think this reference is too exaggerated, you should be aware of the constraints against which women before the Second Wave of Feminism were pressing, as laid out in *The Bride's Reference Book: A Guide for Young Marrieds* (1957). In the chapter entitled "The Most Important Career," the working wife is admonished that "it devolves upon you to prove that a woman's place is in the home first—and secondly in the office. From the day you say 'I do,' your home and your husband come first" (299). Helpfully, working wives are advised "a dull job is seldom a threat to your marriage" (300). Further, a daily schedule is thoughtfully provided for the new bride. Here are some of her duties:

> *Get out of bed—and on time.
> *Get the breakfast under way and set the table.
> *Bathe and dress.
> *Eat breakfast, and if humanly possible, together.
> *Wash dishes.
> *Make the bed.
> *If time allows, do a quick dusting job on top surfaces at least.
> *On leaving, put out contents of waste baskets, any trash or garbage.
> —
> *Upon arriving home [after work], freshen up, change into some more relaxing at-home costume.
> *Get the dinner under way, and while doing this set the table.

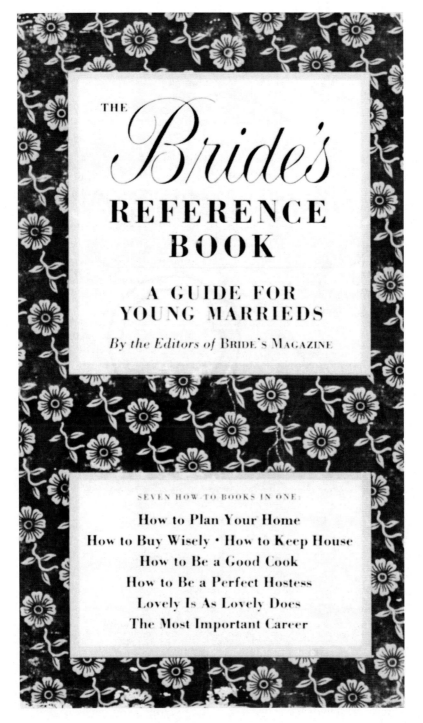

THE

Bride's

REFERENCE
BOOK

A GUIDE FOR
YOUNG MARRIEDS

By the Editors of BRIDE'S MAGAZINE

SEVEN HOW-TO BOOKS IN ONE:

How to Plan Your Home
How to Buy Wisely • How to Keep House
How to Be a Good Cook
How to Be a Perfect Hostess
Lovely Is As Lovely Does
The Most Important Career

Cover of *The Bride's Reference Book: A Guide for Young Marrieds* (1956).

*Run the carpet sweeper if necessary.
*Eat dinner and wash the dishes.
*Relax!
*And before retiring, neaten-up [305–306].

This relentless routine does sound a bit like servitude, no?

Not only does Andrea complain about what she sees as the slavery of a woman's married life, the underlying theme of "A Feasibility Study" is resistance to slavery. As we soon discover, the Holms' neighborhood and all the people in it have been ripped from the earth and transported to the planet Luminos. The Luminoids, described as an unconvincing "bunch of *rocks*" (108), have abducted this particular group of people in order to test their ability, and thus the ability of all the people of Earth, to endure a lifetime of slave labor. The people of the neighborhood, led by Dr. Holm, who finally wins the approval of his wife, mutually sacrifice themselves to the to the Luminoid virus that will kill them, if they do not surrender to slavery. How else could this conflict that explicitly categorized the situation of contemporary married women as slavery be resolved and still leave viewers with a sense of hope without a powerful monster onto which the concomitant anger and tension could be displaced? Whether the resistant woman would have come to her senses or the stubborn husband would have come to his is left open to interpretation, and the episode concludes with all viewers satisfied ... sort of.

An even more polarizing example of how *The Outer Limits* represented women in conflict with their traditional roles is seen in "Counterweight." Like Prof. Eva Frazer and Mrs. Andrea Holm, Dr. Alicia Hendrix made a choice. While Eva and Andrea chose to integrate marriage and career—one successfully, one not—Dr. Hendrix's was a zero sum choice. She chose her career. The monster in the episode, an Antheon being described (disparagingly) as an alien "light ball" that "extracts skeletons from the mental closets" (301) of participants in the simulated space flight this episode dramatizes, is presumably the counterweight to this carefully selected group. The counterweight Dr. Hendrix is carrying is her regret at having chosen science over marriage and family. As the Antheon being invades her sleeping mind, we hear her thoughts: "I'm a woman, more woman than scientist, and try as I will, I can't forget it. I'm getting old. I'm wasting more of the few years left to me on this trip—more of the last few years." Her resolution to these mutually exclusive options is as frightening as it is ridiculous. Dr. Hendrix turns into a vamp—an inappropriate, embarrassing spectacle of festering sexuality, sporting a spit curl and twirling a dangling necklace. "Alicia is for woman. Hendrix is for anthropologist, so

I've decided to become Alicia," she singsongs as she unsuccessfully comes on to one man after another. Even the other characters see her as pitiful.

And so it seems in *The Outer Limits* that women who wanted to work in science had to make gender specific sacrifices. They might bask in the glow of their husbands' successes (or fume at their failures), they might work alongside of their husbands as lesser partners, or they might wind up regretting their lives of barren womanhood. In her Introduction to *When Everything Changed: The Amazing Journey of American Women from 1960 to the Present* (2009), Gail Collins writes, "In 1960...when it came to women, the age-old convictions were still intact. Everything from America's legal system to its television programs reinforced the perception that women were, in almost every way, the weaker sex" (6–7). As depicted in *The Outer Limits*, the post–World War II moment that represented women as having new and exciting aspirations, particularly in the fields of science, had stabilized. Yes, women worked in the field of science. Yes, their presence was not considered abnormal. However, unlike the women scientists in the Fifties films, their sphere of influence and the scope of their lives had become limited.

Post-Fifties Films

"Just sit back and let the electronic skipper
sail you safely through the hazardous
seas of star-studded space..."

In film, as it did in *The Outer Limits*, the "B" science fiction movie machine steadily cranked on, often perfunctorily. Just as veteran space pilot Maj. Towers told the newcomer in *Mutiny in Outer Space* to "sit back and let the electronic skipper sail you safely through the hazardous seas of star-studded space," the creators of the post–Fifties films sat back, echoed the conventions, and employed the stars of their predecessors.

The Fifties films often began with recognizable voice-over monologues and opening screens about man, space, and science. Similarly, *Around the World Under the Sea* begins with a relevant opening screen with a quote by astronaut M. Scott Carpenter: "the sea is a tough adversary—much more hostile an environment than space...." *One Million Years B.C.* begins with a dramatic voiceover: "This is a story of long ago, when the world was just beginning." The opening screen in *Dr. Strangelove* is a (more than likely mandatory) legal disclaimer: "It is the stated position of the U.S. Air Force that their safeguards would prevent the occurrence of such events as are depicted in this film. Furthermore, it should be noted that none of the characters portrayed in this film are meant to represent real persons living or dead." The opening screen of *Fantastic Voyage* has the opposite intent, intensifying the possibility of the science the film depicts: "The makers of this film are indebted to the many doctors, technicians and research scientists whose knowledge and insight helped guide this production." *Mars Needs Women* ends with a closing screen, again not atypical for the Fifties genre. As the Martian spaceship begins its return to space, the following quote by Russian rocket scientist Konstantyn Tsiolkowsky reads, "Earth is the cradle of man, but he cannot live in the cradle forever."

However, the genre began to eschew such simplistic guides to what we were about to see. *Fail-Safe*, for example, begins with an opening screen informing us as to where the action is taking place: "NEW YORK CITY 5:30 AM." In *Fahrenheit 451* the opening film credits are innovatively spoken, which makes sense since the film takes place during a time when reading is forbidden. Otherwise, most of the post–Fifties films open more conventionally, with appropriately dramatic music played over establishing shots and a listing of the credits. Occasionally, the film opens with an extended prologue before the credits begin.

As with the Fifties films, many post–Fifties films were made on the cheap, some (*The Last Man on Earth, Mutiny in Outer Space*) still in black and white. *Dr. Strangelove, Fail-Safe*, and *Seconds* are black and white, however for reasons more artistic than budgetary. Again, as did the Fifties films, post–Fifties films dealt with space travel (*Robinson Crusoe on Mars*), aliens (*They Came from Beyond Space*), unnatural creatures (*Destination Inner Space*), metamorphosis (*Village of the Giants*), and science gone mad (*The Human Duplicators*). There was occasionally the requisite Fifties conflict between the military man and the scientist. Cmdr. Wayne in *Destination Inner Space*, for example, wants to destroy the underwater creature that SeaLab has discovered and thus save the world from its inevitable rampaging. Research scientist Dr. LaSatier, of course, wants to study the creature. "You forget, Commander. We're here to explore the unknown," he says. In *Crack in the World* a military officer excoriates a scientist over a project gone wrong: "I always said we should not have left this in the hands of civilians," he angrily tells him.

More importantly, all of the films fall (albeit tenuously) under the traditional definition of science fiction. Whether a biochemical plague has transformed humans into bloodsucking vampires (*The Last Man on Earth*), a spaceship has picked up an alien fungus that threatens to destroy it

(*Mutiny in Outer Space*), an electronic snafu has opened a portal into the future (*The Time Travelers*), or extensive surgery can be performed to make an old man younger (*Seconds*), all the scenarios in the post–Fifties films are presented as imaginary—sometimes extraordinarily so—but somehow possible.

Additionally, as did *The Outer Limits*, post–Fifties films incorporated personnel from the Fifties films. In 1965, for example, director Hugo Grimaldi and writer Arthur C. Pierce teamed up again after their (evidently) successful collaboration on *Beyond the Time Barrier* (1960) and *The Phantom Planet* (1961) to produce *The Human Duplicators* (color) and the cheaper *Mutiny in Outer Space* (black and white). *Mutiny in Outer Space* features Richard Garland of *Attack of the Crab Monsters* (1957) and Glenn Langan of *The Amazing Colossal Man* (1957). *The Human Duplicators* features George Macready[2] of *The Alligator People* (1959) and Hugh Beaumont of *The Mole People* (1956). Both *The Human Duplicators* and *Mutiny in Outer Space* feature Dolores Faith of *The Phantom Planet*. Pierce was at work again in 1966 with *Destination Inner Space,* a feeble underwater version of *The Thing* (1951). Also in 1966, Marshall Thompson of *Fiend Without a Face* (1958), *It! The Terror from Beyond Space* (1958), and *First Man Into Space* (1959) went *Around the World Under the Sea,* and John Agar, the "B" science fiction film's most ubiquitous actor,[3] visited Pierce's *Women of the Prehistoric Planet.*

Several of these films feature representations of the beautiful woman scientist. However, the tensions that erupt as a result of a woman's working in science as opposed to accepting her more traditional role as wife and mother had not so much stabilized as ossified. In fact, this complex trope from the Fifties films is reduced to an image of a photograph in *The Human Duplicators.* "Here's one I wouldn't mind having under surveillance: Dr. Lin Young. Chemical Research Division, Pacific Laboratories," the film's hero comments as he admires Young's image. The next and only other time we see Dr. Young, she is deceased, already killed by the duplicating aliens. Though *Mutiny in Outer Space* features two animate women in science— Dolores Faith as civilian biochemist Faith Montaine and Pamela Curran as communications officer Lt. Connie Engstrom—the trope is superficial. How either Montaine or Lt. Engstrom wound up in her career is not mentioned. There are no supportive father figures as there were in Fifties films such as *Them!* in which Dr. Patricia "Pat" Medford was introduced into the field of entomology by her father, or *Tarantula* in which biology graduate student Stephanie "Steve" Clayton worked under the auspices of the esteemed Prof. Deemer. Clearly, this autonomy can be viewed as a positive development. A woman's significant presence in either the military or the laboratory is not depicted as anomalous. However, a romantic attachment to a male automatically supersedes her commitment to, even interest in, her career.

The gallant Maj. Towers in *Mutiny in Outer Space*, for example, boasts to a colleague about Fontaine, "In one month, she'll be transferred back to Earth and into the arms of her Prince Charming and happiness ever after." A situation with the potential to disrupt the traditional gender binary is not displaced onto a marauding creature. Neither are its complexities acknowledged, much less explored. Lt. Engstrom, gratuitously referred to as "that great big beautiful blonde with the binary brain" is denied the romantic happiness she desires or even its attendant complexities. It turns out that the primary reason she is stationed on SS X-7 is to capture the heart of the ship's commander, who consistently treats her only as a useful crew member, not as the love interest she would prefer. "I wouldn't take that kind of treatment from a man I wanted unless ... unless he asked me to," she disturbingly tells a sympathetic colleague after the commander again rebuffs her attentions. Whether her future holds a heightened dedication to her career, continued pursuit of the disobliging commander, or pursuit of yet a new male was not considered by the scriptwriters to be significant, even perfunctorily.

Similarly, in *Destination Inner Space*, one woman in science establishes a relationship with a man while another woman is denied. Marine biologist Dr. Renee Peron and military Cmdr. Wayne engage in cheeky banter with each other as they first avoid and then plunge into their inevitable relationship while stationed on the Institute of Marine Science underwater SeaLab. "You might have a few surprises in store for you, *Doctor*. Store that under your microscope and study it awhile," he sportively growls after she rebuffs his advances. Likewise, underwater photographer Sandra Welles snubs her new partner, diver and engineer Hugh Maddox, when he tells her that he has "waited thirty years for you to come along." "Then you won't mind waiting another thirty," she coolly responds. After Maddox courageously confesses to a cowardly act in his past, however, Welles does an immediate about face. "Until a few minutes ago, I couldn't find much in you I really liked. Now I think I could fall in love with you," she suddenly decides. Alas, in an act of atonement, Maddox sacrifices himself as well as this potential romantic relationship in order to dynamite the interstellar probe ship threatening the planet. "Every time I'd look at you, I'd be reminded of the coward in me," he tells her before their first and final kiss. Dr. Peron, on the other hand, turns the tables on the self-satisfied commander after he proves his heroism. "Well, Commander, you still might have a few surprises in store for you," she confidently declares as she thrusts herself into his arms.

While romance supersedes career for the women in *Mutiny in Outer Space*, in *Destination Inner Space*, career and romance appear to coexist with few complications at all. It is clear in both films that women and men will meet and engage in the workplace. In his 1968 book *The Exceptional Executive: A Psychological Conception*, Harry Levinson cited the U.S. Labor Department's 1963 *Handbook on Women Workers*, which stated that "women comprise 34 percent of the American work force" (72). He also observed that "women are increasingly becoming the occupational equals of men, particularly as there is less need for the physiological strength of men" (104). Indeed, the women professionals do not physically grapple with their alien adversaries in *Mutiny in Outer Space* (a moon fungus) and *Destination Inner Space* (a murderous finned creature from outer space). Their work—analyzing complex specimens, operating sophisticated communications equipment, administering necessary medical treatment, providing photographic documentation—is less physiologically demanding but equally valuable as the work done by the men.

What science fiction often does, though, is estrange contemporary realistic situations by propelling them into imaginary (but possible) futuristic possibilities. Thus men and women are not merely working together in these films; they are working together at very nearly equal professional levels and, more importantly, working together in remote, confined spaces (a space station in *Mutiny in Outer Space* and an underwater lab in *Destination Inner Space*). While Fifties films such as *Rocketship X-M* and *The Thing*, for example, chastely explored potential attractions occurring between the sexes (in a rocketship and a remote Arctic research station respectively) *Mutiny in Outer Space* and *Destination Inner Space* allow these attractions to manifest in physical (but not blatantly sexual) contact. What these two films do not do, however, is explore how (or whether) these attractions will continue beyond the workplace forcing potentially difficult choices for either party, or even how the workplace might be affected by their evolving complexities. *Around the World Under the Sea*, however, albeit rather unfairly, begins to address this issue.

Around the World Under the Sea noticeably echoes conventions of the Fifties films with respect to representations of a woman in science. Following in the footsteps of Dr. "Pat" Medford and "Steve" Clayton, Dr. Margaret Elizabeth "Maggie" Hanford is known professionally as Dr. M.E. Hanford, resulting in the misconception that allows another scientist to

Dr. Maggie Hanford (Shirley Eaton) tantalizing the men on the Hydronaut in *Around the World Under the Sea* **(1966) (Photofest).**

recommend her for the intrepid Hydronaut team: "He's done some very impressive work in marine biology." Our first glimpse of her, just like our first glimpse of Dr. Medford, is of her shapely bare legs. (Medford is descending from an airplane; Hanford's legs are protruding from under a desk.) While other females are shrieking, Dr. Hanford, like Steve Clayton before her, confidently handles a lab rat.

Like Fifties heroines Dr. Lesley Joyce of *It Came from Beneath the Sea* and Dr. Iris Ryan of *The Angry Red Planet,* not to mention Dr. Peron from *Destination Inner Space,* Hanford is a biologist (evidently a suitable field for filmic women in science). Like Dr. Pat Blake *of Invaders from Mars* and Dr. Mary Royce of *It! The Terror from Beyond Space,* Dr. Hanford is also a medical doctor. Like research assistant Kay Lawrence of *Creature from the Black Lagoon* she executes a swimming sequence replete with flowing blonde locks and an enticing bathing suit. (While Lawrence's is a one-piece, Hanford's is a revealing bikini.) Unlike Lawrence, however, Dr. Hanford is not innocently tantalizing a helpless creature; she is willfully tantalizing the defenseless men on the Hydronaut. There is no alien fungus. There is no man in a fluorescent rubber monster suit. Dr. Hanford herself is the unnatural creature, a creature which is described by an outraged team member (who eventually becomes one of her targets) as "a woman on this submarine for three or four months!?!"

Dr. Hanford, played by James Bond's former *Goldfinger* girl Shirley Eaton, is accurately described on the Internet Move Database as "stunning," so it is not surprising that the men on the Hydronaut are attracted to her. One of the crew members, for example, is a former lover, still longing for her. "Maggie, bring me a cup of coffee," he commands while he is on watch. She compliantly does so, and then proceeds to so mesmerize him with her feminine beauty that he crashes the Hydronaut. Another team member with whom she is currently involved proposes to her as he holds her in his arms. "Oh, Orrin," she provocatively demurs, "can you imagine spending our honeymoon on a submarine with four other men?" Even the elder team captain confesses, "If I weren't a happily married man with a couple of kids, I might be causing you a little trouble too." The man Dr. Hanford is really after, however, and the one she eventually snares, is the one man who persists in refusing to respond to her.

Eventually, this woman on the submarine must be either reprimanded or instructed, depending on whether one interprets her behavior as narcissistically voracious or innocently clueless. "You're pretty rough on a man's blood pressure," the crew captain tells her. "Where shall I hide myself," Dr. Hanford helplessly responds. "In your work," is the captain's advice, and here Dr. Hanford, like Dr. Alicia Hendrix from *The Outer Limits*, is faced with the zero sum choice between being either a woman or a scientist— one must be sacrificed for the other. A resolution is intimated, however, near the end of the voyage when the initially recalcitrant love interest firmly reassures Hanford, "We've got maybe one month on this submarine and after that, after we've got our work done, we have a whole lifetime, a lifetime to find out what our feelings are for each other." As with Faith Montaine in *Mutiny in Outer Space* or Dr. Renee Peron in *Destination Inner Space*, whether or not this lifetime includes a woman's continued work in science is not acknowledged.

In sum, these derivative films of the mid–Sixties accept the conventions of the Fifties films regarding the post–World War II emergence of women professionals but ignore the complexities such a shift in gender prescriptions engenders. Further, without the successful annihilation of a formidable alien creature onto which a sensation of resolution can be displaced, these films are, unfortunately, neither emotionally nor intellectually rewarding.

Here Come the Sixties

*"The way a girl goes about catching a man
here is to be faster than he is, and we've
got some real athletes..."*

The trajectories of some films, however, while still incorporating aspects of the Fifties films, also began to incorporate and reflect the developing cultural changes of the period, in particular with respect to gender and sexual behavior. In his Introduction to *Making Peace with the Sixties* (1996), David Burner writes, "In the sixties restraints of all sorts shattered." He describes the era: "The bonds of institutional racism broke because its victims no longer would tolerate them. Conventions of decorum crumbled with the lengthening of men's hair and the shortening of women's skirts. Sit-ins, marches, street theater swept into formal space and avenues. Music filled the air and the times" (5). In her memoir titled simply *The Sixties* (2009) Jenny Diski goes beneath women's short skirts, as it were, and writes about the sexual changes of the period: "Sex was written about and acted out in private and public with enthusiasm in the name of the sexual revolution. The idea was to have fun" (52). Indeed the Sixties were an exuberant and naively innocent time.

Released in 1964, and written and directed by Fifties science fiction film auteur, Ib Melchior—of *The Angry Red Planet, Reptilicus*, and *Journey to the Seventh Planet*—*The Time Travelers* (color) began to reflect some of the era's burgeoning sexual exuberance. The film, in which scientific researchers accidentally travel through a time portal, is an amalgam of plot elements from Fifties films *When Worlds Collide, World Without End*, and *Beyond the Time Barrier*. It features Fifties "B" science fiction film actor John Hoyt[4] of *When Worlds Collide* and *Attack of the Puppet People*. The film also features women in science: senior scientist of the future (2071) Gadra (played by Joan Woodbury) and laboratory technician from the present Carol White (played by Merry Anders). Like mathematician Eva Frazer in *The Outer Limits*, White wears a tasteful dress, lab coat, and low-heeled pumps (instead of pearls, though, her dress has a noticeable round white collar). Stationed at a console like the men on the team, she contributes essential comments such as "Cathode's at 67,000 volts" and "All systems go."

The women of the future, however, are more progressively represented. Gender differences are lessened, if not elided. Men and women wear similar clothing (though the women's outfits are much more form-fitting). More importantly, women and men are shown working side-by-side on all sorts of technical tasks, and Gadra sits on the Council as an equal partner. "I would like Dr. Connors to work with Willard and myself on the photon drive," Gadra proposes at a critical meeting. Her proposal is accepted. As in *World Without End*, however, the women of the future are as sexually aggressive as they are equivalent in the workforce. As the determined Reena explains, "The way a girl goes about catching a man here is to be faster than he is, and we've got some real athletes." Eventually, she encourages White to do a little catching of her own. Sure enough, as Reena is seducing one of the men from Earth by dancing tantalizingly in front of a psychedelic, light-flashing "Lumichord," we see White and her handsome colleague Dr. Steve Connors entwined together on a leather chaise longue, kissing full on the mouth. Such an overt (though admittedly brief) image of intimate behavior between a young female scientist and her male colleague is more connected to the percolating Sixties than to the staid sexual mores imposed upon the characters in the Fifties films.

In 1965, Janette Scott and Keiron Moore, once again playing romantic partners and professional colleagues as they did in 1962's *The Day of the Triffids*, are eventually able to stop a *Crack in the World*. Like the more expensive studio films of the Fifties (*Conquest of Space*, *Forbidden Planet*), *Crack in the World* has high production values, supervised by Eugene Lourie, who also worked on *Beast from 20,000 Fathoms* and *The Giant Behemoth*. Indeed, in *Variety's Complete Science Fiction Reviews* (1985), critic Whit. praised the film's "startling special effects."

The film also presents a woman scientist (who unfortunately does not have that much to do as a scientist). Despite her title, Dr. Maggie Sorenson's primary function is to look good.

With her coiffed blond hair and perfectly applied makeup, she is quite beautiful in an array of outfits throughout the film: a cream colored suit, a pale blue negligee, a green dress, a charcoal jacket, and a pink suit and sun hat. We see her offer support and encouragement to her increasingly ill and over-stressed husband, director of a massive drilling project. She even offers to darn a young scientist's socks for him. However, she does provide a thorough overview of her husband's project to a convoy of visiting government officials. She works with a partner to provide figures on residual radioactivity. She assists another scientist in measuring the speed and direction of increasing volcanic activity. She operates a circuit panel. She even wears a white lab coat, albeit one fashionably tailored with a lavender straight skirt and heels. More significantly, however, like Marge Blaine in *The Deadly Mantis* or Vera Hunter in *Kronos*, both released in

1957, she participates in an exciting (though ill fated) scientific adventure every step of the way from beginning to end.

In the Fifties films, the woman scientist was often situated between a supportive father (or father figure) and a dynamic young iconoclast. For example, entomologist Dr. Patricia "Pat" Medford was supported by her father Dr. Harold Medford and romantically pursued by government agent Robert Graham in 1954's *Them!*. Biology student Stephanie "Steve" Clayton was supported by Prof. Gerald Deemer and romantically pursued by Dr. Matt Hastings in 1955's *Tarantula*. A new element in *Crack in the World*, however, is the fact that the older man is not the woman scientist's father, but rather her husband (and former professor), liberating the young woman scientist from direct dependence on patriarchal support. The younger man, as in the Fifties films, ultimately becomes the woman scientist's love interest, thus tacitly acknowledging a woman's right to express marital dissatisfaction.

Of course one could suggest that the trope of the father/daughter relationship has become sexualized in the film, that a father figure is exacting a sexual cost from a female protégée in exchange for integrating her into his career. However, the film does not really support this interpretation. Dr. Stephen Sorenson is played by an attractively distinguished Dana Andrews (who also starred in 1957's *Curse of the Demon*), and we do not see any salacious behavior between him and his wife. In fact, the husband, knowing he is terminally ill and not wanting to risk a pregnancy, regularly rejects his wife's advances. One can certainly note, however, that the student fell in love with her professor, as has often happened (and still does), which in itself evidences a certain patriarchal exploitation.

Zontar, Thing from Venus (1966) was connected to "B" science fiction films by its star, John Agar (yet again) as well as by the way the woman in science is represented. In the Fifties films, as a woman's professional presence in the public sphere became less important, it also became more accepted. Louise, the woman professional in *Zontar*, is a technician at Zone 6, the United States Orbital Rocket Control and Tracking Station. Stationed at a radar screen, like Carol White in *The Time Travelers*, she wears a lab coat and heels and is unspectacularly relied on by her colleagues for the information she can provide. "Be sure and get those reports to Washington tonight by scrambled transmission," Agar's character, the lab supervisor, matter-of-factly directs her, for example.

However, unlike the earlier films, there is a subsequent moment in the film that frankly acknowledges the sexual body of the professional woman. As with Dr. Hanford in *Around the World Under the Sea*, this acknowledgement is especially relevant when men and women are confined together. Because of the trouble Zontar has created, all personnel have been restricted to the lab. In one scene, we are privy to a surreptitious view of Louise in her slip, in three-quarter view, rising from her makeshift cot in the morning, slipping her bare feet into her sensible heels. This tacit acknowledgement of the everyday female body (as opposed to the body in the bathtub being terrorized through a window by a creature from another world or even Dr. Hanford in her tantalizing bikini) is countered by the very real vulnerability of that body when it transgresses traditional boundaries dividing private and public spheres: Louise is soon strangled to death by one of the men, whose minds and wills have been taken over by Zontar, indicating, at least surreptitiously, the fear that women's overt sexuality began to engender in films that eventually follow.

"All of us against the adults..."

Two films epitomizing the trajectory of the science fiction film into the teen market are *Village of the Giants* (1965) and *Mars Needs Women* (1967). *Village of the Giants*, directed and produced by "B" science fiction film auteur Bert I. Gordon, updates the setting of H.G. Wells' 1904 *Food of the Gods* from an experimental farm in mid-nineteenth century England to the small town of Hainesville, CA, in the mid–1960s. Gordon's work on the Fifties films included *King Dinosaur* (1955), *Beginning of the End* (1957), *The Amazing Colossal Man* (1957), *Earth vs. the Spider* (1958), *War of the Colossal Beast* (1958), and *Attack of the Puppet People* (1958), so of course, he relied on standard Fifties conventions, particularly metamorphosis and science gone mad. True to form, he relied on the audience's necessary suspension of disbelief required by such obviously fabricated special effects as a giant roasted duck and a motorcyclist riding through a giant pair of legs.

On the other hand, with its rampaging band of oversized teenaged hedonists opportunistically taking over the town, *Village of the Giants* is grounded in the early Sixties establishment's fear of the countercultural rebellion that reached its apotheosis (and ultimate decline) only a few years later. Even before their transformation into the film's "Giants," the teenagers exhibit raucous behavior. While swingin' Sixties music plays from the radio of their broken down car, they frolic in muddy pools left by a sudden rainstorm. Barefoot, they dance, drink beer, and roll around on top of each other in their halter tops and hip-hugger pants in a scene eerily presaging 1969's Woodstock Music Festival. Once ensconced in the small town they have invaded, they don costumes and play act on stage in the town's unoccupied theater, music playing all the while in the background.

Once enlarged by the film's magical "Goo," the teenagers realize the power they have to flaunt authority. "Just wait till the next guy asks me for my ID card. Oh boy!" one of the boys says excitedly. "Now it won't be easy for *them* to kick us around anymore," another boy responds. "Wait till my old man gets tough with me again!" an angrier boy chimes in with a clenched fist. Like oversized hippies, they storm into town in their bright colored satin clothes made from theater curtains, their love beads, fringe, sashes, and nearly bare chests, demanding food, attention, and subservience. They even kidnap the daughter of prominent man in the town in order to ensure that their demands are met—not unlike the Symbionese Liberation Army that kidnapped Patty Hearst in 1974. "This isn't their world anymore. It's gonna be ours" is their anthem.

Inopportunely, however, the film reflects ambivalent attitudes toward the burgeoning sexual liberation of women in its salacious scenes of nearly naked shimmying gals, and in particular, in the scene where a comparatively tiny Johnny Crawford is lifted into the (obviously papier mache) bosom of one the giant young females. While he squirms uncomfortably, titillated members of the audience can delight in (or recoil from) the prurient image.

As *Village of the Giants* both reacted to and capitalized on the rebellious youth zeitgeist of the Sixties, teen film *Mars Needs Women* both resisted and misread social changes already in force. Though his character is a Martian (named Dop), Tommy Kirk, the film's star, exhibits the typical characteristics of a dutiful All-American boy. Unlike the teens in *Village of the Giants*, Dop and his crew elect to wear conservative navy blue suits, white shirts, and ties in order to fit in with mainstream America. Dop is unfailingly polite, even though he can use the power of hypnosis to get whatever he wants. He takes a girl he is interested in on a date to a planetarium, not to a music club, where he charmingly winds up entertaining a group of grammar school children when the sound system breaks down. In the end, as armed soldiers close in on Dop and his Martian crew, he sacrifices himself by electing to return to Mars, where he will be killed for failing in his mission, rather than let his fellow Martians abduct the girl he has fallen in love with.

Just as Dop embodies resistance to an encroaching hippie rebellion, the film also misreads the era's increasing restlessness with proscriptive sexual mores. The film's attempt to represent sexual liberation is embodied by actress Bubbles Cash, playing a very Fifties-type stripper who mesmerizes one of the film's other male Martians in a club called Athens Strip with

Tommy Kirk as Dop and Yvonne Craig as Dr. Marjorie Bolen in *Mars Needs Women* **(1967) (Photofest).**

her bawdy, borderline vulgar, extended performance—not at all what the candid sexual openness of the Sixties was all about.

In *Prime Green: Remembering the Sixties* (2008) novelist and screenwriter Robert Stone disapprovingly reflects on the films of the era. He writes,

> American films of the middle sixties were among the worst ever made. I put this down to the influence of television and hackery, but most of all to the fact that the older generation of American filmmakers were confused by social change and the expectations of their young audience. They simply had not found the range. They were firing blind, trying to get hip [179].

Stone clearly has a point about the disconnect between older filmmakers and their young audiences. However, as Hunter Thompson writing about the Sixties in *Fear and Loathing in Las Vegas* (1971) remarks, "History is hard to know, because of all the hired bullshit, but even without being sure of 'history' it seems entirely reasonable to think that every now and then the energy of a whole generation comes to a head in a long fine flash, for reasons that nobody really understands at the time—and which never explain, in retrospect, what actually happened" (66–67). Despite their ties to outdated Fifties special effects and sometimes inaccurate attempts to represent impending social changes, both *Village* and *Mars* were indeed tuned into the onset of that "long fine flash."

"I feel a little bit like Columbus—set down in a strange new land, full of new wonders, new discoveries..."

Another trajectory, while retaining many of the conventions of the Fifties films, begins to reflect changes in representations of both science and gender.

Robinson Crusoe on Mars (1964), the first half of it at least, is further differentiated from Fifties "B" science fiction films than the films discussed above. True, it was directed by Byron Haskin. True, Ib Melchior co-wrote the screenplay. True, the plot is centered on travel into space and exploring another planet. However, unlike Fifties films such as *Cat Women of the Moon*, where telepathic women congregate in an underground community, or *Forbidden Planet*, where remnants of an extinct civilization provide access to extraordinary mental powers, this film, surely in reaction to the new wonders and new discoveries of the Mercury space flights, attempts to present a reasonable approximation of what survival on another planet might be like.

Cmdr. Kit Draper, the film's "Columbus," for example, deals with, as he states into his recorder, his "two most difficult problems ... air and water." The film posits that Mars has a low level of oxygen (though much higher than the trace amounts it actually has). Thus, Draper can breathe Martian air for brief periods, but must periodically breathe pure oxygen from his (limited) supplies. This procedure is shown meticulously and repeatedly as Draper stops speaking into to his recorder, turns the dial on his oxygen supply, lowers the face plate on his helmet, breathes good air, turns the dial back off, lifts the face plate, and then resumes recording. Likewise, the process Draper discovers for replenishing his air supply is meticulously worked out and utilized repeatedly: Draper states into his recorder, "These yellow stones that burn like coal.... It must be similar to solid rocket fuel with its own built-in oxygen. Heat and flame release it. And it's breathable." Likewise, although it is unlikely that there are hidden pools of water on Mars, assumptions about polar ice caps, observable weather patterns, and hypothetical canals could certainly have led to that speculation. In *Destination: Mars*, science fiction writer Robert Sawyer acknowledges, "The

Cmdr. Kit Draper (Paul Mantee) and his little monkey Mona (The Woolly Monkey) in _Robinson Crusoe on Mars_ (1964).

Mars in _Robinson Crusoe on Mars_ was pretty accurate for the time it was made."

According to Darko Suvin, as cited in Carl Freedman's _Critical Theory and Science Fiction_ (2000), "The operation of cognition ... enables the science-fictional text to account rationally for its imagined world and for the connections as well as the disconnections of the latter to our own empirical world" (16–17), and I believe that *Robinson Crusoe on Mars* makes a concerted effort to do this. Thus, if there is water, then it is not unlikely that there will be plants, and how convenient (though admittedly improbable) that these plants can be both eaten and woven into clothes.

Another issue the film attempts to deal with realistically is male independence. Where a full crew of space travelers lands on the moon in *Cat Women of the Moon* and on Altair in *Forbidden Planet* (as well as finding other inhabitants to relate to), Draper is alone—except for the space monkey Mona, who has also survived the emergency landing. The complexities of gender issues are thus easily elided for the sake of a more streamlined science fiction story. Monkey Mona does not talk back, she does not distract, and she is cute as, well, a little monkey, squawking and chattering in her tiny orange and yellow spacesuit. More importantly, she does not expect Draper to marry her, and he does not expect her to give up a budding career in science for him. The narrative can thus focus on the hard science fiction of survival and rescue in outer space, as in fact often did reality.

When the alien Friday enters the picture, however, with his oxygen pills and his whole other planetary civilization (from the system of Osatanango—or as Draper translates, the center star in the belt of Orion), the film takes on elements of more typical Fifties science fiction fare. Mind you, I understand that like *The War of the Worlds*, *The Time Machine*, and *Journey to the Center of the Earth*, *Robinson Crusoe on Mars* is based on a literary classic—Daniel Defoe's 1719 *Robinson Crusoe*—and that introducing the character of Friday is essential to the plot. To me, the introduction of the fantastical literary aspect of the story makes the attempt at realism in the first half of the film even more extraordinary.

Robinson Crusoe was a Paramount production with a decent budget, and as such, its effects like those in *Crack in the World* are quite good. A thin reddish-orange glow, for instance, smolders on the horizon between Death Valley mountaintops and a pitch-black, star-lit sky. Aurora Borealis–like curtains of light shimmer under golden moons. Red and silver spaceships dart across the screen, shooting laser beams like video games of the future. The effects in *Fantastic Voyage*, released two years later, are even more fantastic. Produced by Twentieth Century–Fox, the film was adapted by Fifties stalwart David Duncan[5] and as such certainly has elements of the Fifties "B" science fiction film. There is the scientific sounding, but nonetheless farfetched "Combined Miniature Deterrent Forces" organization that shrinks the film's protagonists so they can enter the body of an important diplomat and destroy a clot in his brain. There is a detailed scientific exposition scene explaining just how this process will unfold. There are, of course, as in films like 1957's *The Amazing Colossal Man* and *The Incredible Shrinking Man*, effects that deal with disparities in size. And like so many of the films of the Fifties, the film ends on a triumphant note: a crisis has been averted.

Two aspects of the film, however, are new and different. The first is the primacy of special effects. In a *Variety*, July 27, 1966, review of the film, critic Murf. described the special effects as "brilliant," and now thirty years later, they still are. In *Screening Space: The American Science Fiction Film* (1987), Vivian Sobchack states that "the film's visual conception is remarkably profound" (95). The effects include a lavender, luminescent sterilization corridor through which the crew proceeds. Their miniaturized submarine navigates through iridescent corpuscles, and into a whirlpool in the main branch artery to the brain. (This thrust of the submarine into a whirlpool in the circulatory system that forces the crew to take an alternate, dangerous route is not unlike the convention of the meteor shower of the Fifties films that throws the rocketship off course and into uncharted territories.) The submarine continues along the cellular walls of a capillary in the pleural cavity, through seaweed-like reticular fibers in the lymphatic system, and finally into the sparking electricity of the brain itself.

In "Kubrick's *2001* and the Possibility of a Science fiction Cinema" (1998), Freedman acknowledges that "special effects ... have a special affinity with science fiction cinema" (306). More importantly, he describes those special effects particular to science fiction cinema as those that "are not only radically filmic moments of film, but moments that ... self-consciously *foreground* their own radicality" (307), and this is what *Fantastic Voyage* does, even more than did the films of the Fifties. In fact, one could say that the effects *are* the film; they are the story. Dr. Duval, the renowned brain surgeon charged in the film with destroying the diplomat's clot, remarks at one point in the journey, "We stand in the middle between outer and inner space and there's no limit to either." Indeed, with fantasies of outer space now restricted by televised depictions of actual travel into space, creating fantastic effects that speculate on a new unknown seems a logical step.

The second aspect of the film that is new and different is the introduction of Raquel Welch, the actress who portrays technical assistant Cora Peterson. As did the filmic women in science who preceded her, Cora Peterson wears a lab coat, black dress, and low-heeled pumps, has a modest hairdo, often sits quietly in the background—her womanly allure, almost deliberately it seems, sacrificed to her role as a woman in science. Even as she swims about in a wetsuit, it is often difficult to distinguish her from the rest of the crew. This is not to say that her allure is ignored, however. In fact, as with stripper Bubbles Cash in *Mars Needs Women*, Welch's sexuality is occasionally exploited in a clandestine, degrading sort of way, particularly when the crew must grapple and paw at the vicious antibodies that have attached themselves to her breasts. Nonetheless, Peterson is primarily represented, as was Louise in *Zontar, Thing from Venus* and Carol White in *The Time Travelers*, as a member of a team, albeit an assistant, successful at doing a job.

Reviewing *One Million Years B.C.*, a film released just six months after *Fantastic Voyage*, however, *Variety* critic Rich. ebulliently stated that "at last, the nubile Raquel Welch is on view." Likewise, an excerpt from the *Los Angeles Herald Examiner*, cited on *One Million Years B.C.*'s DVD liner notes, proclaims, "The movie has one delightful asset. A vision of Amazon-like beauty known as Raquel Welch." Indeed, Welch's representations of

Raquel Welch as Cora Peterson being miniaturized along with the rest of the team in *Fantastic Voyage* (1966).

women in the two films are strikingly different. *Variety* critic Murf. wrote of Welch's character in *Fantastic Voyage* simply that she is "included in the group." In *One Million Years B.C*, however, Welch's Loana wears animal skins, is often barefoot, has an untamed flowing hairdo, and emerges from a mountain lake a near-naked golden Venus. She is as perfect a vision of unguarded female sexuality as is Jane Fonda in the opening sequence of *Barbarella*. While her depiction of a woman in science in *Fantastic Voyage* is grounded in reality, her emergent persona in *One Million Years B.C.* is more representative of the hypersexualized images of women to come.

"What does it all mean?"

In a *Variety*, June 3, 1964, review of *Robinson Crusoe on Mars*, critic Tube. described that film as "an enthralling screen experience for people of all ages" as was (and still is) *Fantastic Voyage*. Stanley Kubrick's *Dr. Strangelove or: How I Learned to Stop Worrying and Love the Bomb* and Sidney Lumet's *Fail-Safe*, both released in 1964, as well as François Truffaut's *Fahrenheit 451* and John Frankenheimer's *Seconds*, released in 1966, however, characterize the more serious trajectory the science fiction film would ultimately take. All four films were released by major studios. All were based on previously published literary works. All were helmed by important directors. Three, bucking the trend to color, were filmed in black and white, using frame composition and lighting to emphasize mood, project atmosphere, and create meaning. All deal so uncompromisingly with serious issues as to be as thought provoking as they are entertaining.

Dr. Strangelove exemplifies what Sobchack describes as "*imaginary action* occurring in what seems to be documented *real space*" (140). As a result of precise replications of the interiors of military aircraft, documentary-like back projection footage, and meticulous editing, to cite only a few of the film's realistic features, the doomsday scenario it presents seems frighteningly possible. On the other hand, Kubrick's exaggerated representations of characters such as Gen. Buck Turgidson, President Merkin Muffley, Col. Bat Guano, Maj. King Kong, Gen. Jack D. Ripper, and Dr. Strangelove himself, as well as the surrealistic war room set, contribute to the film's comedic intent, creating a sense that of course this devastating scenario will not happen if mankind just gets a grip his ego— an almost perfect 50/50 tension between the ordinary and the extraordinary. *Fail-Safe* is a speculative drama depicting a scenario similar to *Strangelove*'s, only like *On the Beach*, realistically and consequently heartbreakingly so.

A different type of doomsday scenario was also presented in 1964 with the release of the Italian/American production *The Last Man on Earth* (also black and white), based on science fiction writer Richard Matheson's *I Am Legend* (1954). In this film renowned horror film star Vincent Price plays the film's eponymous hero, battling this time both vampires and the deadly microbe that spawned them. The film reiterates the trope of masculine independence evidenced in *Robinson Crusoe on Mars* and soon to evolve in films to come. *Fahrenheit 451*, likewise set in a dystopian future deals with, as critic Myro. wrote in a *Variety*, September 14, 1966, review of the film, "a serious and even terrifying theme." Indeed, in this film, as well as discomfiting images of book burning (*Don Quixote, Vanity Fair, Madame Bovary, Jane Eyre, Moby Dick, Lolita*) we see the subtle, creeping horrors of an authoritarian state, a society dependent on medication and senseless entertainment, an impersonal medical system, mindless police brutality, suspicion, informing, a woman burning to death in her house with her books, murder.

Seconds, set in a speculative present of the socially and sexually turbulent Sixties, deals with, as Mosk. wrote in a *Variety*, May 25, 1966, review of the film, "the yearning for youth and a chance to live life over again by many men," expressed in the complicated psyche of the film's conflicted hero: a man desperately searching for the meaning of his life. After his transformation, he tries to become a painter (but cannot find a subject), he goes to a bacchanalian stomping of the grapes (but does not fit in), he tries to live a sophisticated life in Malibu (but longs for his old life and family), he meets a beautiful woman (but cannot relate to her). "What does it all mean?" the film's Old Man asks, trying to sell his latest middle-aged prospect on a radical rejuvenation procedure. "It can't mean anything now anymore. There's nothing anymore, is there?"

Representations of gender in *Dr. Strangelove* are appropriately absurd. The men in the film are not conflicted. Rather they are egotistical, stupid and childish, so much so that they eventually bring complete destruction on the world. The one female character in the film, Miss Scott, is depicted as a "floozy," as Tracy Reed, the actress who played Scott, states in "Inside the Making *of Dr. Strangelove or: How I Learned to Stop Worrying and Love the Bomb.* She is even pictured as the *Playboy* playmate that Maj. Kong is studying on the B52. Equitably, this character appears as dim-witted as the men. As conventional as *Dr. Strangelove* is preposterous, *Fail-Safe* portrays men and women in comfortably traditional roles. The film opens, in fact, with a scene of tender marital affection as Gen. Black tells his loving wife, "I don't know what I would do without you." The President of the United

States is played by Henry Fonda, cinematic paragon of masculine American integrity. The First Lady, however, like Dr. Lin Young in *The Human Duplicators*, is reduced to a photograph. As marriage superseded career for cinematic women in science, duty supersedes marriage in *Fail-Safe*. Both the General's wife and the President's wife are ultimately tragically sacrificed by their husbands for the good of the country.

Complicated representations of women in both *Fahrenheit 451* and *Seconds*, though not of women in science, are neither superficial nor demeaning. Furthermore, both films have roles for more than one significant female character. In *Fahrenheit 451*, as Myro. writes, "Julie Christie is standout in her dual roles. As the wife, her long flowing blonde locks emphasize her looks and also her simple-minded acceptance of the official way of life; while the close crop she sports when playing the teacher completely transforms her appearance and character, and makes her thoroughly acceptable as the earnest and rebellious young woman." In the commentary track for *Seconds*, Frankenheimer states that he cast Salome Jens for the part of Nora Marcus because of her "divine figure," her "wonderful quality of strength and vulnerability," "her great, great voice." Unlike Andrea Holm in *The Outer Limits*, Nora has a conversation with the newly rejuvenated Tony Wilson (played by Rock Hudson) that more forcefully reflects nascent feminist dissatisfaction with traditional married life:

> NORA: That was my life. Two boys, ages ten and twelve. Successful and indulgent husband. A beautiful house complete with microwave oven, intercom, station wagon, etcetera, ad infinitum. And...
> WILSON: And?
> NORA: I made myself a cup of coffee, dressed, and left. That was four years ago.
> WILSON: You never went back.
> NORA: I've seen them from time to time, but it's different now. Maybe because I'm different.

On the other hand, Frankenheimer describes filming Francis Reid in her role of the older Emily Hamilton, wife of pre-transformation Tony Wilson, whose husband "feels nothing for her," as "difficult," "personal," and "intense," indicating the depth of emotion women can feel.

Finally, both films have endings more provocatively literary than cinematically optimistic, reflecting the distrustful, rebellious, one could even say thoughtful mood of the Sixties to come.

•••

As science fiction film trajectories progressed, representations of gender became at times more bound to reality than in earlier films and at other times quite fantastic. As we shall see in the next chapter, the science fiction films of 1968—*Mission Mars, Countdown, 2001: A Space Odyssey, Charly, Barbarella,* and *Planet of the Apes*—present females as wives, stewardesses, clerical workers, students, scientists, galaxy queens, and even monkeys. Males, on the other hand, in order to reassert the dominance that was challenged by the burgeoning Second Wave of Feminism, are represented as heroes, savants, scientists, sexual predators, and in an egalitarian gesture, as monkeys just like the females.

2

1968: A Spectacular Science Fictional Year

I left home in 1967. Even though I was barely eighteen, I had already been working for a year as an Assistant Laboratory Technician at the Louisiana State Board of Health. Though I longed to be in San Francisco, I took an apartment in the hippest place I could get to in New Orleans: the French Quarter, half a block off Bourbon Street. The Doors lit my fire. I listened to that last long chord at the end of "A Day in the Life" on the Beatles' *Sgt. Pepper* album (it was an E major) over and over, trying to pinpoint the exact moment it ended. Arrested and beaten African American Newark cab driver John Smith was on the July 21st cover of *Time*. The People's Republic of China exploded a hydrogen bomb. *Divorce American Style*, *Bonnie and Clyde*, and *The Trip* were playing in theaters. Most of the boys I knew were desperately trying to get out of the draft. NASA's Lunar Orbital 4 was circling the moon. It was the Summer of Love, the beginning of the ascent to the peak of the Sixties. I painted my face and went to a Be-In at Audubon Park.

By the summer of 1968, Rev. Martin Luther King, Jr., had been assassinated, Andy Warhol had been shot by a feminist, and Robert F. Kennedy was dead. Surveyor probes 5, 6, and 7 had landed on the moon. Allen, an old boyfriend from junior high school, had lost an eye and an arm in the Vietnam War. A black man was sitting on the U.S. Supreme Court, Lyndon Baines Johnson had signed the Fair Housing Act, and Shirley Chisholm was running for Congress. Otis Redding's "Dock of the Bay" was the song of the times. Ronald Reagan, Governor of California, had appeared on the cover of *Time* as a possible candidate for President. Elvis Presley's *Speedway* and Roman Polanski's *Rosemary's Baby* were in the theaters.[1]

More importantly, for an aficionado such as myself, the science fiction film was back.[2] In 1968, an almost alchemical transformation of the genre occurred. Similar to the way the science fiction films that emerged in the early Fifties (*Destination Moon, Rocketship X-M, The Thing*) represented a rupture from the classic films that preceded them (*La Voyage dans la Lune, Metropolis, Things to Come*), the films that came out in 1968 incorporated both a resistance to and an embracing of the paradigm shift brought about by the Sixties. Of course, the Sixties are not actually defined by the period lasting from 1960 to 1969, but rather are identified by the period that began in 1965 when, as reported by Judith Goldsmith on *A Timeline of the Counterculture*, "Boomers born in 1947 are turning 18 & enter college." The headiness of this era lasted into the early Seventies, ending more or less around the time of the disastrous Altamont concert, Charles Manson's Helter Skelter murders, and the eventual American retreat in Vietnam.

In 1968, however, realistic depictions of space travel, evolving representations of gender, foregrounding of race, predictions of a dystopian future, and examination of artificial intelligence exploded spectacularly in science fiction cinema. The films released in that year, and which exemplify all of these developments, were *Mission Mars, Countdown, 2001: A Space Odyssey, Charly, Barbarella,* and *Planet of the Apes.*

Realistic Representations of Science and Space

The space race between the United States and Russia culminated in success on July 20, 1969, when American astronauts Neil Armstrong and Buzz Aldrin of Apollo 11 landed on the moon. Not surprisingly, depictions of science and space travel in the science fiction film necessarily were becoming significantly more realistic than they had been in the films of the Fifties, reflecting and building on televised images with which the world had been rapidly becoming familiar.

*"M-1 to C-K. We've got booster jettison.
Do you confirm?"*

Mission Mars. *Mission Mars,* the first feature made at the ambitious Studio City Complex in Miami, for example, begins with what appears to be documentary countdown and liftoff footage intercut with scenes of Mission Control. (These images turn out to be a nightmare an astronaut's wife is having.) The ensuing plot concerns a manned flight to and subsequent landing on Mars. Urgency exists because Russian astronauts previously sent there have disappeared. It is expected that the trip to Mars and back will take a year and a half. The first third of the film consists of images of the astronauts inside of the space capsule intercut with point-of-view shots of space through the capsule window. Details of commands and compliance lend authenticity to the fictional aspects of the flight. For example, Mission Control reports to Col. Mike Blaiswick, "M-1 to C-K. We've got booster jettison. Do you confirm?"[3] Facts about Mars given in "rebriefing sessions" lend further authenticity: "Item: Mars is 35,112,500 miles from Earth. At an average speed of 63,000 miles per hour, the trip should last 230 days, 5 hours, and 15 minutes. Item: The circumference of Mars is 13,180 miles at the equator. Item: The temperature range in the Northern hemisphere is from 15 to 40 degrees daylight, dropping to minus 95 at night."

However, as with *Robinson Crusoe on Mars*, the film's initially realistic depiction of contemporary space travel is not sustained. After they reach orbit, just as in the Fifties films, the astronauts take off their helmets, remove their spacesuits, walk around the cabin (when they are not sitting in office chairs), eat scrambled eggs and pastrami sandwiches, shave, cut each other's hair, ride an exercise bike, arm wrestle, play chess, sun tan, and otherwise male bond to jammin' Sixties music. In *Variety's Complete Science Fiction Reviews* (1985), Byro. praised the film's "exciting climax" which, though indeed exciting, is as far-fetched and imaginative as those in any of the Fifties films: Once the astronauts land on Mars, they are forced to do battle with a spherical "Polarite," controlled by beings from another planet.

Countdown. In "The Science Fiction Film as Marvelous Text" in *Science Fiction Film* (2001), J.P. Telotte includes Robert Altman's *Countdown* among those films that "simply extrapolate from the known and abide by the scientific laws that govern the world, particularly works focusing on space exploration" (145). Capturing as realistically as possible the scenarios of space travel in the 1960s, the film opens with what appears to be actual NASA footage of a Saturn rocket and space capsule. The ensuing plot concerns the selection, training, and experiences of a pilot who will blast off as part of the Pilgrim mission, the film's fictional emergency back-up plan to Apollo. (The emergency is that Russians, as in *Mission Mars*, have been discovered to be already on their way to the moon, and the United States wants to beat them, directly connecting both of the films to the contemporary space race.) Once the astronaut lands on the moon, he will remain in a shelter, already stocked with food, oxygen, life support, and communication, until Apollo astronauts pick him up eight months to a year later.

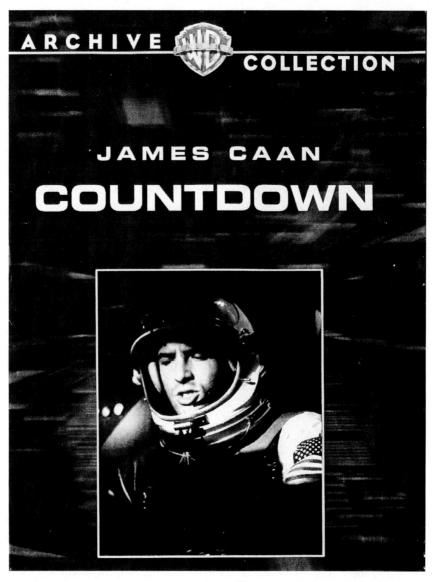

James Caan as Astronaut Lee Stegler on the DVD cover of *Countdown* (1968).

Augmenting the fictional elements of this storyline are realistically grounded scenarios from inside a supposed NASA facility, detailed training procedures, low gravity exercises, and detailed flight simulations inside a Gemini capsule. After the Pilgrim capsule is in space, images of astronaut Lee Stegler are intercut with images from the fictional Space Control Center, in Houston, Texas, and point-of-view shots into space through a window in the capsule. Once the capsule has landed on the moon, the bare set consists of rock formations, stars, and Earth in the background. There are no signs of a destroyed civilization, transmogrifying fungi, women without men, men in need of women, escaped slaves from another galaxy, or hostile pulsing Polarite orbs. What we see is not much different from what we saw (other than the stars, which are in actuality too dim to be seen from the moon) when Apollo 11 actually landed on the moon in 1969.

2001: A Space Odyssey. While *Countdown*, and to a lesser degree *Mission Mars*, imaginatively depicted representations of contemporary space travel, Stanley Kubrick's *2001: A Space Odyssey* extrapolated from those images thirty-three years into the future. The film's depiction of space flight begins with one of the most famous match cuts in film history as an alabaster animal bone thrown upwards into a blue sky is suddenly replaced by the sterile white of a space vehicle, followed by the prescient image of a revolving circular space station, in the star-lit blackness of outer space. The ensuing plot concerns first a routine shuttle trip to the moon and ultimately a one-and-a-half-billion mile trip to Jupiter in response to a signal sent by a mysterious monolith. As in *Mission Mars* and *Countdown*, Russia is again presented as a contender in the race to space.

The middle of the film contains images consistent with what one in 1968 would imagine actual space travel in 2001 to be. Zero gravity, for example, is depicted as a matter of course when the sleeping Dr. Heywood Floyd's arm and pen float in the air as he shuttles to the space station. Zero gravity is likewise depicted humorously as he attempts to decipher posted instructions for using a zero-gravity toilet. "Grip shoes" allow a stewardess to walk down the aisle and retrieve Floyd's pen for him. (Likewise, a rounded head covering attached with a chin strap keeps her hair from floating ridiculously upward.) We are shown the detailed minutiae of a complicated landing process, aided by IBM computer graphics. As in *Countdown*, a realistic lunar landscape set consists of a stark black sky, stars, and silver-lit cliffs. Once on the surface of the moon, the scientists wear space suits and helmets similar to those 1968 audiences had been accustomed to seeing in images of previous NASA flights. In the "Jupiter Mission" section of the film, we see the detailed and precarious process of an astronaut donning a space suit and helmet, entering a pod, exiting, floating through space, and then hanging upside down to replace a (supposedly) malfunctioning Alpha-Echo–35 unit on the exterior of the space vehicle, unlike in, for example *The Phantom Planet*, where the astronauts casually walk through a door and along the perimeter of the spaceship to repair meteor damage. (We do see in both *2001* and *Phantom Planet*, however, as we do in 2000's *Mission to Mars*, the archetypal scene of horror in which an astronaut, untethered, floats off into eternal doom.)

In *Screening Space: The American Science Fiction Film* (1987), Vivian Sobchack, citing contemporary reviewer Penelope Gilliat, states, "Perhaps no film to date ... has visually evoked the reduction of space flight to 'the ultimate in humdrum as has *2001: A Space Odyssey*'" (75). This "ultimate humdrum" conditions audiences to accept scenes of astronauts Dave Bowman and Frank Poole walking about the space vehicle (jogging even), eating pureed space food, and conversing with their computer HAL as believable and possible. Likewise, by the time of the spectacular light show and rebirth section of the film ("Jupiter and Beyond the Infinite"), audiences have been primed to accept the suggestion that perhaps a very strange world exists beyond our own.

Charly. The award-winning *Charly* was not about travel into space; however, the presentation of science in it is analogous to the realistic representations of space travel in *Mission Mars* and *Countdown*. According to the film's Dr. Richard Nemur, Charly Gordon's severe mental deficiency was the result of "a maverick enzyme of the kind which induces defective biochemical reaction and causes brain damage." Nemur explains further,

> Fortunately, while the destruction to the tissue is irreversible, the protein process is not. Many researchers are able to reverse the process through control of chemicals which combine with the defective enzymes and change the molecular shape of the key, as it were. This is also central in our technique. But first we remove the damaged portions of the brain and permit the implanted tissue, which has been chemically revitalized, to produce brain protein at an accelerated rate.

This sophisticated explanation requires much less suspension of disbelief than did Dr. Mark Sinclair's explanation of how "hopelessly mangled accident victims on the point of death" were made "completely whole" (with injections of hydrocortisone) and subsequently devolved into reptiles in *The Alligator People* in 1959, or how Prof. Walgate was able to materialize thought (using the techniques of sibonetics [sic]),[4] which eventually evolved into brain-sucking spinal columns in *Fiend Without a Face* in 1958, or how injections of irradiated coelacanth blood could reverse evolution and turn a man into a prehistoric killer in *Monster on the Campus* also in 1958. (I could go on...)

As science fiction tends to do, however, the film's science gets sketchy, relying on scientific advances not yet accomplished, if even possible, as evidenced in the following exchange between Charly, his intellect now vastly enhanced, and a computer programmer:

CHARLY: One area for investigation is the doctor's hypothesis that the mind can be permanently improved through surgery and enzyme enrichment, thereby utilizing unused portions of the brain. Can you program that?

PROGRAMMER: It's a little vague, Mr. Gordon. Could you give me more detailed specs?

CHARLY: Well, it correlates to what we've already programmed on DNA conversion.

PROGRAMMER: I see. Can we use the same system?

CHARLY: Right. Just change the variables. Is mental improvement temporary because it lacks appropriate DNA conversion? Because of storage limitation, which tends to overload and disable the repaired area? Any combination of those factors?

PROGRAMMER: Run it.

Just change the variables and run it. Despite this facile suggestion, the makers of these 1968 films did seem to take into account their audience's growing familiarity with scientific methods.

Unstable Representations of Gender

In the films of 1968, gender is depicted in several ways. Realistic depictions of space travel and science are partnered with depictions of gender relations conventional to the times. In both *Mission Mars* and *Countdown*, the brave astronauts, as they were in reality, are men. The women in the films play their anxious wives. In *Charly*, the male lead is the film's (temporary) genius; the woman, the student who falls for him. On the other hand, life in a post-apocalyptic future in *Planet of the Apes* includes a progressive representation of a relationship between a male and female scientist. Not surprisingly, the enigmatic *2001* portrays an enigmatic representation of women. Finally, unrealistic depictions of space travel in *Barbarella* are partnered with unrealistic depictions of almost everything.

"I need you and I'll wait for you, but please don't be a hero..."

Mission Mars. After Blaiswick's wife wakes from the frightening dream of a rocket blasting off and exploding that opens *Mission Mars*, her confident husband consoles her: "It's all right, darling. I won't fall, and you'll always have me to hold onto." (This being the Sixties, they then make passionate love on a beach.) Even more dependent, geologist Nick Grant's wife Alice resentfully tries to quell her husband's adventurous spirit:

NICK: Everything'll be all right when I get back.
ALICE: When you get back—you mean *if* you get back.
NICK: I'll get back.
ALICE: Nobody can guarantee that, not even love. There'll always be that one more place where nobody's ever been before till one day you just don't come back.
NICK: This is the last adventure, I promise.
ALICE: I need you and I'll wait for you, but please don't be a hero. Please come home.

Meanwhile, the third astronaut in the film has no female baggage. When Blaiswick asks him if he is packed for the trip into space, he replies, "What's to pack? A bachelor just locks the front door and pays the rent for a year or so." Perhaps metaphorically, the hostile Polarite that the astronauts discover (inside of which a Russian astronaut refers to as being "in utero") has a peculiarly vaginal-appearing, pulsing opening into which Grant (as well as the bachelor), sacrificing himself for the mission, is sucked into and burned to death.

Countdown. In a *Variety*, February 14, 1968, review, Murf. praised *Countdown*'s "strong script emphasizing human conflict." Indeed, there is conflict in the film between the two male astronauts competing to be the first to land on the moon as well as between the astronauts and their respective wives, who fear their going. When it looks as though the tough, older career astronaut Col. Chiz Stewart will be chosen, young, non-military astronaut Stegler, who is eventually selected instead, expresses admiration for Stewart's wife Jean. "She's a tough babe," he tells his wife Mickey. The film further acknowledges the stress under which astronauts' wives must operate when Mickey responds matter-of-factly, "Yeah, we're all tough." Likewise, the film acknowledges the hard choices the men have to make in a later scene as Stegler speaks to Mickey:

There wasn't enough time when I had to weigh the mission on one side with my life with you and Stevie [their son] on the other....It's not fair, but that's the way it's gonna be. I can't go with a choice like that one.... I spent years thinking of myself taking this trip. I always thought I'm the guy that's gonna do it. That's who I am. If I don't make this trip, then who the hell am I? Forgive me. Forgive me.

While the young Steglers are affectionate and communicative with each other, the toll a life in space travel has taken over years is reflected in the relationship between the older Stewarts, Chiz and Jean, who are both bitter—Chiz because he has been passed over for the opportunity he has worked for all his life, and Jean because of Chiz's dedication to his career at the expense of their marriage. Murf., in fact, comments on both Chiz's "immersion in work" and Jean's "increasing dependence on booze." In contrast to married life, a third astronaut, unmarried and not particularly committed to taking a risky, though career-making trip into space, complains to Chiz's wife about a potential girlfriend: "You go over there, and first thing you know, she's got a little niche for your toothbrush."

Charly. As its representation of science became more credible, as with *Mission Mars* and *Countdown*, so did *Charly*'s representation of gender roles become more conventional. Gone is the chemical engineer on her way to the moon from *Rocketship X-M*, the doctor of biology and zoology on her way to Mars from *The Angry Red Planet*, the Venusian scientist Talleah (played by a be-gowned Zsa Zsa Gabor) from *Queen of Outer Space*, the world-renowned marine biologist deferred to by the Navy in *It Came from Beneath the Sea*. Instead, the film includes the characters of two easy-to-accept women in science: the young Alice Kinnian, who is working on a Ph.D. in psychology in conjunction with her fiancé, and the elder, established psychiatrist Dr. Anna Strauss.

Kinnian (alternately addressed as Miss and Mrs.—she is a young widow) is shown at a blackboard teaching ESL to both male and female adults, administering psychological tests to Charly while Drs. Nemur and Strauss observe, and methodically directing Charly's post-surgical program for intellectual development. Both doctors respect Kinnian's opinions when she challenges their approach. Kinnian's attire is professional but, this being the Sixties, also acknowledges her sexual body. In a scene where she is working with Charly in a lab, for example, though her dress has a high collar and long sleeves, it is nonetheless tight, soft, and short (inadvertently stimulating Charly's sexual desire for her). Strauss is a senior member of research team, working at a clinic to improve the brain power of "retardates." She and her colleague Nemur are slated to jointly address a conference held by the Society for Cerebral Research about their work with Charly. She dresses as an older professional would in tasteful dark dresses, sometimes a lab coat, and often stylish jewelry signifying her femininity.

Though certainly inspiring to young women looking for role models in science, these women do not threaten traditional social conventions. From the beginning, Kinnian is compassionate toward Charly, sensitive to his feelings. Patient and respectful, she is interested in him as a human being, not solely a test subject. Likewise, Strauss compassionately gives instructions to Charly as if he were a child. Contrasts in gender roles are especially apparent when Strauss's characterization is contrasted with Nemur's. For example, while Strauss is openly supportive to Charly, Nemur dispassionately observes his reactions. While Strauss casually wears her lab coat open, Nemur's is usually buttoned professionally. While Strauss's specialty is art therapy with children, Nemur's is brain chemistry. While Strauss works with Charly's emotional development, Nemur is concerned with his intellectual progress. Gender roles are contrasted most overtly when the now brilliant Charly remarks to a nervous Nemur at the conference, "Come on, Professor, cheer up. After tomorrow, you're gonna be on the cover of *Time* and *Newsweek*. And you, Dr. Strauss, are gonna be in the centerfold of *Playboy*." Of course, this pronouncement is followed by good-natured laughter. What other accolades Strauss might receive, however, are not mentioned.

All this is not to say that Strauss has no power. First, she speaks with an authoritative German accent. One is immediately reminded of the celebrated child psychologist and member of the Vienna Psychoanalytical Society Anna Freud (who like the women scientists in the Fifties films was introduced into and supported in her profession by her father). When she and Nemur disagree about an important aspect of the conference presentation, Strauss's view prevails. Further, Nemur and Strauss are jointly announced at the conference as follows: "You are all acquainted with their eminent qualifications through their published papers." A young woman watching this film could envision herself, represented in the character of the young Kinnian, having achieved, like Dr. Strauss, a contented, full emotional life with a distinguished career in science.

If one scours the film for details, however, one will notice—be this observation petty or emblematic—that Strauss wears no wedding ring while Nemur does. Of course a successful male scientist would have a wife. Of course a successful female scientist might have had a more difficult time coordinating a demanding career with the duties of traditional married life. No overt mention is made in the film of Strauss's personal life, however, so the young woman proposed above could, at least on first viewing, imagine Strauss's life to be however she desired it to be. How this young woman would go about creating such a life for herself would, of course, be the movie her own life would eventually write.

Unfortunately, the movie does not bear out this potentially positive life-writing. In a *Variety*, July 3, 1968, review, Beau. lamented that a "fascinating sci-fi premise gets lost in welter of corny romance." It seems that

Charly (Academy Award winner Cliff Robertson) and Alice Kinnian (Claire Bloom) canoodling by the lake in *Charly* (1968) (Photofest).

Kinnian gives up everything to be with Charly. We hear no more about her Ph.D. or see her at the clinic working with Nemur and Strauss. What we do see are innumerable images of her canoodling with Charly—under a blanket, in the woods, at an amusement park, in a boat, on a ship (where Charly declares, "As captain of this ship, I now declare us man and wife"), in a convertible, by the water. In fact, when chastised by Nemur for her unexpected, unreported absence (it seems to have been four weeks), she nonchalantly replies, all concern about her career seemingly gone, "I didn't have a dime, I didn't have a stamp, I didn't have the time."

As with the relationship between the scientist and his young wife in *Crack in the World*, there are certain Oedipal aspects to this otherwise idyllically depicted love affair. Consider the fact that Kinnian nurtures Charly, serving as a mother figure, disciplining him through his "terrible twos," then appropriately rejecting his exaggerated adolescent entrance into the genital phase as any mother figure would (or should). Charly's easy replacement of Kinnian's lurking fiancé as the adult male figure in Kinnian's life, however, can (rather creepily) be interpreted as his successfully possessing the mother and removing the father. As with Sophocles' Oedipus, at the end of the film, Charly, again emotionally and mentally regressed, is (fortunately) blind to the significance of his former stages of psychosexual development. Kinnian, somewhat like Jocasta, seems to have committed both romantic and professional suicide.

Charly, attempting to reassure himself before going on stage to impress the world with the development of his intellect remarks, "There's only a few hundred of the world's most eminent scientists out there. No reason to be nervous." Kinnian reassuringly responds, "Never mind about them. You are talking directly to me." Clearly, she is no longer in the running to become one of the world's most eminent scientists, or even a scientist at all. She has made a choice between science and love, as even Dr. Strauss may have had to do.[5] Nonetheless, as in the science fiction films of the Fifties, images of a young woman attempting to reconcile science and love, intellect and emotion, public and private, imprint themselves on the minds of those audience members seeking to do the same.

2001: A Space Odyssey. *Mission Mars, Countdown,* and *Charly,* while presenting contemporary approaches to science and space travel, likewise depict contemporary representations of gender. One would then expect *2001: A Space Odyssey,* a film extrapolating from contemporary approaches to science and space travel decades into the future to likewise project evolving representations of gender. Paradoxically, the film's representations of gender are (on first look, at least) as retrograde as the film's science is futuristic. Superficially, gender roles are reflected in the clothing the actors wear. The men—Dr. Floyd, Mr. Miller of Station Security, Dr. Andre Smyslov, astronauts Bowman and Poole, and an anchor man and a reporter—all wear masculine dark brown, gray or blue, indicating their seriousness of purpose.

Moreover, the entire crew of Discovery One (and thus in the entire final two-thirds of the film) are male, including HAL, the crew's putative sixth member. The characters of Bowman and Poole exaggerate representations of men, as did Cmdr. Kit Draper in *Robinson Crusoe on Mars*, as brave, confident, and self-sufficient—advancing the trope of masculine independence that later science fiction films began to develop. Though Bowman and Poole certainly do work together as a team, there is little need for them to communicate incidental feelings and thoughts. In fact, it is a full twenty-five minutes after we first see them together that they actually speak to each other: "Oh Frank, I'm having a bit of trouble with my transmitter in C-pod. Would you come down and take a look at it with me?"

In contrast, the women in the film, most of whom play characters who are supportive of the film's more significant male characters, are dressed in lighter more feminine tones. The stewardesses who fetch Dr. Floyd's pen and serve food to the passengers and pilots, for example, are dressed in white; the receptionists (only one of whom has a name: Miss Turner), in pink; and the Voice Print Identification clerk (seen only on a monitor), in yellow. Moreover, all of them wear cute, matching, color-coordinated caps, indicating their very feminine availability for service. Further supporting their service capacity is their deferent dialogue: "Here you are, sir. Main level please" (the first words spoken in the film, by the way); "Good morning, sir. Did you have a pleasant flight, sir?" "May I call him for you?" Another female character in the film is Dr. Floyd's daughter, with whom he speaks on a Bell Picturephone. She is being taken care of by Rachel, the babysitter, because "Mommy" is out shopping and says she wants a "bush baby" for her birthday—all traditionally sociable feminine signifiers. Poole's mother, who speaks to him via computer transmission, is a second-grade school teacher (another traditionally feminine signifier). Poole's father, by the way, who is also seen in the computer transmission, is dressed in dark gray. When Poole sees this transmission from half a billion miles away—on his birthday no less—his behavior is stoically emotionless, impassive, solitary.

On closer look, however, all the film's representations of gender are not so traditionally coded. It is a minor scene, but when Dr. Floyd congratulates a convocation of eleven important people on the moon about "your discovery which may prove to be among the most significant in the history of science," two of those convocants are women. They seem to be the same middle age as the men and are dressed as the men are in dark colors. Secondly, there is a scene on the Space Station where Drs. Floyd and Smyslov collegially confer with a group of Russian women scientists (all dressed in dark colors) returning from Tchalenko: Dr. Kalinan, Dr. Stretyneva, and Elena (we are not given her last name, but she is clearly a scientist, the elder of the three and spokesperson for the group). Reference is also made to Elena's husband, indicating that at least one of these scientists, unlike *Charly*'s Dr. Strauss, has managed to achieve both a successful marriage and a significant career in science. How both she and her husband managed to merge success in both public and private spheres, as in the science fiction films of the Fifties, is elided.[6]

Now, as well as when I first saw these films of the Fifties, Sixties, and Seventies, I scour them for images of successful, self-realized women in non-traditional roles that can hearten a young woman's development as a fully realized person. In the case of the very male-oriented *2001*, sometimes I feel as if with these perceptions of female empowerment, I am manufacturing reasons for the fact that I like and have liked this film so much over all these years. At the 2004 Popular Culture Convention in San Antonio, however, I was on a Science Fiction and Fantasy Panel for which Barry Keith Grant delivered a paper entitled "*2001:A Space Odyssey*, Feminism, and Science Fiction."[7] Grant's thesis in this paper—which referenced critics such as Laura Mulvey, Vivian Sobchack, and Evelyn Fox Keller as well as other Kubrick films such as *Dr. Strangelove, A Clockwork Orange*, and *The Shining*—was that the "sensibility of masculine mastery, as conveyed in popular culture's representations of space travel, is purposefully undermined by *2001*." "That is to say," he continued, "Kubrick's space epic explores a discursive space as much as physical space in that it seeks for a stylistic alternative to science fiction film's conventional depiction of space exploration as an act of phallic masculinity, of penetration and possession."

One of these alternatives, Grant stated, is the film's "motif of spiralling imagery" which "refuses to orient spectators with fixed reference points," and thus deliberately subverts the camera's traditional patriarchal gaze. In fact, except for the early images of stewardesses and hostesses, there is—as Mulvey states in "Visual Pleasure and Narrative Cinema" (1975)— no "image of woman as (passive) material for the (active) gaze of man" (846–847) on which viewers could orient themselves on at all. Another point Grant made in support of his thesis was that the image of Bowman's eye as he travels through the Stargate "changes to the same hues that color the Stargate images," signifying a "merging with nature rather than conquering its secrets." Perhaps scouring films as I do in search of evidence to support a very personal felt-sense just below the level of consciousness, Grant noted that "in the film's final shots, the star child's gender is indeterminate." "The first glimpse of it," he corroborated with detail, "is a quick long shot which shows no visible genitalia, while subsequent shots do not show it below the chest." "The star child," he concluded, "has transcended the patriarchy's characteristic binary thinking about gender." He even suggested that the mysterious monolith (a floating signifier if ever there was one) is representative of the phallic masculinity the film, in his reading, is undermining.

My relief in hearing Grant's analysis was that the "identification" of my "ego with the object on the screen through the spectator's fascination with and recognition of his like" (Mulvey again, 841) was neither negating my professed woman-centeredness nor anomalous to the position of the film's implied narrator. In "The Spectator-in-the-Text: The Rhetoric of *Stagecoach* (1975), Nick Browne writes, "We can identify with a character and share her 'point of view' even if the logic of the framing and selection of shots of the sequence deny that she has a view or a place within the society that the mise-en-scène depicts" (127). As a result of my scrutiny and Grant's analysis, I can correlate Browne's statement with one of my own: A woman can identify with a film even if the apparent logic of casting, costuming, and script seems to deny that she has a view or a significant place within the society that the mise-en-scène depicts. Browne further writes, "Reading, as distinct from interpretation, might be characterized as a guided and prompted performance that ... recreates the point of view enacted in a scene" (132). Incorporating Mulvey's position—a position both broader and more focused than Browne's—I feel I can state that even if the implied narrator's point of view is not one the spectator/reader embraces, she can still create (or perform) a meaning that inspires her, as I have done and am doing here.

Planet of the Apes. In *Planet of the Apes as American Myth: Race and Politics in the Films and Television Series* (2006), Eric Greene asserts that the original film, as estranged as it is from conventional reality, remains conventional with respect to the issue of gender. He notes that the film has only three significant female characters: Zira, a scientist chimp; Stewart, a white astronaut; and Nova, a mute white human. He notes that Stewart is dead when the film begins. He further notes that Nova is not only mute, she is "hyper-sexualized" and thus an undemanding and accommodating companion for Charlton Heston's characterization of Taylor as a self-sufficient manly man of the 20th century. Greene approvingly describes Zira not only as "a character of great courage and conviction," but also as one who "competes with male apes as a career 'woman.'" He conversely contends that her "stolen kisses with her fiancé

Cornelius are more humorous than passionate," that she is "stronger and more assertive" than the "timid" Cornelius, and that she is "'ugly' by traditional standards"—all to reinforce his point that filmic females can be beautiful (like Nova) or smart (like Zira), but not both (like the deceased Stewart) (37–38).

However, like *2001*, *Planet of the Apes* can be read as more complex below the surface with respect to representations of gender. When one considers the trajectory of women scientists from the Fifties films, such as Dr. Lisa Van Horne of *Rocketship X-M*, Dr. "Pat" Medford of *Them!*, and Dr. Lesley Joyce of *It Came from Beneath the Sea*, the fact that a woman scientist's successful relationship is a central part of her characterization (Dr. Zira is an animal psychologist) is a significant step in the possibility of a woman's (and a man's) ability to integrate public and private spheres in an equitable manner. For example, Zira's fiancé, archeologist Dr. Cornelius, matter-of-factly tells her, "We have fine futures—marriage, stimulating careers." That Cornelius is the gentler of the two characters indicates a dissolution of strict gender proscriptions on behavior. The fact that Zira is an ape allows for a representation more progressive than traditional. Moreover, within the context of the film, as in *The Twilight Zone* episode "Eye of the Beholder," Zira is not the ugly one; the conventionally beautiful human Nova is.

Barbarella. *Barbarella* may, or may not, be considered a science fiction film. It certainly has the trappings of advanced technology that characterize the genre. A destructive "positronic ray" "deminimalizes" persons and objects in its path in order to place them irretrievably in the 4th dimension. The President of Earth bestows on Barbarella a "portable brain wave detector" that will allow her to identify the evil Durand Durand when she eventually encounters him. Necessary equipment is sent to her through an atom transmitter. She wears a "tongue box" in order to be able to decode alien languages. A lake of energy (the Matmoss) feeds on the psychic vibrations of evil because it is magnetic and therefore negatively charged. Certainly, devices in earlier films have existed in order to perform these types of futuristic or extraterrestrial acts. (Think *Earth vs. the Flying Saucers*, *The Fly*, *The Magnetic Monster*, or any of those films that easily explain away, for instance, why beings on Mars or Venus or a Phantom Planet can immediately converse with each other.)

Likewise, *Barbarella* concerns space travel. Barbarella is referred to by the President of Earth as a "five-star double-rated astronavigatrix," and he assigns to her an important interplanetary mission. Her spaceship, the Alpha–7, is composed (in part) of "hypodontical molecules" and accelerates into "temporal space." (Think of *Star Trek*'s "warp speed" device.) Equipment consists of "magnetic screens," a "xylo-compass," and even a gaily chatting computer named Alfie. As does *2001*, the film acknowledges the effects of zero gravity in space. Barbarella wears a realistic-looking spacesuit and helmet. In the opening images of the films, we even see into the interior of Alpha–7 through a rectangular window, not at all unlike what we see in *2001* as the transport ship carrying Dr. Floyd docks at the space station on his way to Clavius. Also as in *2001*, psychedelic light shows exemplify the spectacle of interplanetary travel.

However, unlike in the most illogical of the Fifties films, no attempt is made to extrapolate from a reasonable, if even far-fetched, premise to explain the film's futuristic devices and processes. The spaceship itself is foolishly shaped and fluorescently colored. Moreover, once we actually enter Alpha–7, we see that the entire interior is covered in fur (or shag carpet—it is hard to tell). Instead of the futuristic office chairs, streamlined consoles, and buzzing electrical panels we see in so many earlier films, Barbarella's ship is adorned with flamboyant objets-d'art. And as it turns out, the zero-gravity effects and meticulous spacesuit are only in the film as vehicles for Barbarella's defiantly delicious striptease. She then dons a sheer leotard with gold lame accessories (necklace, bikini bra and panties, boots, and cape) that she wears while exploring Tao City's ice plains, as well as while she is traveling through space, having sex across the galaxies.

Nonetheless, the film is included in *Variety's Complete Science Fiction Reviews*. In his October 9, 1968, review, critic Murf. described the film as a "flat sci-fi comedy." In her October 12, 1968, *New York Times* review entitled "Science + Sex = 'Barbarella,'" Renata Adler concedes that the film has "all the gadgetry of science fiction" but then admits that it is "not really science fiction, since it has no poetry or logic." She ultimately, rather mercifully, refers to the film as "an uninspired omnispoof." In her November 2, 1968, *New Yorker* review, esteemed critic Pauline Kael, rather affectionately, in fact, classifies the film as "pornographic comedy." So why include *Barbarella*—which I could say is neither pseudo-science nor even pseudo-science fiction—in a treatise on science fiction films? Well, 1968 was a spectacular year, *Barbarella* is a spectacular film (and I mean this in the context of *spectacle*), and Jane Fonda's portrayal of a futuristic space heroine embodies so much of what was so right and so wrong about sexual liberation for women in the Sixties. As Andrea Dworkin wrote in *Woman Hating* in 1974, "Just as the pill was supposed to liberate women by liberating us sexually, i.e., we could fuck as freely as men, fucking is supposed to liberate women and men too. But the pill served to reinforce our essential bondage—it made us more accessible, more open to exploitation. It did not change our basic condition because it did nothing to challenge the sexist structure of society, not to mention conventional sexual relationships and couplings. Neither does promiscuity per se" (81–82). In sum, she exposed the "patently untrue notion that a woman who fucks freely [as does Barbarella] is free" (84).

Nonetheless, as well as being a beauty, Barbarella holds an important position, answering directly to the President. And eschewing violence as she does, she does not try to emulate stereotypical male values in order to succeed in that powerful position. She openly enjoys sex—and isn't that what women have (if only secretly) always wanted? Moreover, her uninhibited enjoyment of sex is not looked upon as scandalous or shameful. The men she has sex with not only enjoy her as she enjoys them, they also respect her. Even one of the women finds her appealing. Just as the film is a science fiction enigma, so is its beguiling protagonist's representation of feminism.

Representations of Race

Admittedly, the "B" science fiction film genre of the Fifties is a very white one. As Marleen S. Barr writes in *Afro-Future Females: Black Writers Chart Science Fiction's Newest New-Wave Trajectory* (2008), "Science fiction, as we all know, reflects reality. How, before the mid–1960s, could blacks see themselves as starship captains if reality denied them the opportunity to pilot airplanes? Why would blacks recast themselves as extraterrestrial aliens if they were alienated from everyday American life?" Indeed, the situation of black actors in early science fiction movies is quite similar to the situations Barr puts forth. However, if one scrutinizes the science films of the Fifties, one will be rewarded with several representations of African Americans, not as starship captains or aliens, but as representatives of life more or less as they lived it.

In *The Day the Earth Stood Still*, for example, if you look closely and pause your DVD player, you will notice two unique extras in the large crowd assembled at the landing of Klaatu's spaceship on the Mall in Washington, D.C.: two African American women, nicely dressed, one with a hat; both attractive, one strikingly so. You will see four deliberate one-second reaction shots, mid-level close ups, indicating that while African Americans may not have been largely represented in film or in government, their presence at least could not be ignored. In *Them!*, if you look very closely, you will notice an African American shoeshine man—again, an extra. He has a conservative close-cut hair style. He is youngish, wearing khaki pants, sweater, and a collared shirt, polishing a white man's shoes while another white man waits in the next chair. They are downtown listening to announcements warning of "lethal monsters" (the giant ants). His face is in three-quarter profile, but you can tell he is handsome. He turns from the other men and walks toward the street with great moment, helping us believe the seriousness of this threat, a full six seconds.

In his 2011 *New Yorker* review of Lynn Nottage's *By the Way, Meet Vera Stark*, drama critic Hilton Als lays out that play's primary dynamic between a white "B" movie actress named Gloria and her black maid, Vera. He writes,

> These two women depend on each other: Gloria because she needs someone to take control of her life, her excessive drinking, and her galling self-regard; Vera because she wants to be an actress, too, and hopes that Gloria can help her get ahead. In the meantime, she runs lines with Gloria, who is up for a role as a tragic antebellum chick. Surely the movie will need some maids, Vera thinks. She is filled with dreams that she wants to make real. She has more talent in her little finger than Gloria has in her whole inebriated body; and, besides, she's more beautiful and charismatic. But what does that matter if because of your race you can play only a maid or a chauffeur or a dithering idiot? [86].

But what do you do, if your destiny is to act, despite all the obstacles in your way? I think you would act, despite the indignities, and bestow your work with every bit of your talent, your charisma, your beauty, and your drive.

"This is a trouble house..."

The Alligator People (1960) is set in deep South Louisiana bayou country. Consequently, there are three (uncredited) speaking roles for African Americans actors. The first is Dudley Dickerson as a train porter. "Isn't he an expert, Paul?" Beverly Garland's character says after Dickerson ceremoniously pops the cork and pours champagne for her and her new husband in their Pullman car. After Paul tips him, Dickerson, dressed in a short white double-breasted waiter's jacket, responds, "Thank you, sir. Thank you. Good night, sir." During this time, he makes four genial, deferential bows. He comes back in to the car a second time to bring telegrams and says to Garland, "Here you are, Miss. You folks certainly must be popular, especially with the telegraph company." He adds this final comment as he chuckles his way out of the car, making the most of his scene. Dickerson's Wikipedia entry states that "he appeared in nearly 160 films." A search of the Internet Movie Database reveals that the types of roles he played (mostly uncredited) were chauffeur, safari member, janitor, butler, shoeshine man, bathroom attendant, red cap, laundryman, elevator operator, valet, waiter, doorman, orderly, cook, bellboy, and prisoner. The Wikipedia entry also notes, "It is to his credit that he took pride in each and every role," and in *The Alligator People*, he did.

Also in *The Alligator People*, the uncredited part of Toby, the black butler at The Cypresses, a plantation-type home, is played by Vince Townsend, Jr. Older, dressed in a dark suit, white shirt, and bow tie, Townsend plays Toby with a resigned almost sad expression. His soft voice gives dignity to remarks like "Yes, Miss," "But ma'am...," and "I'll try, ma'am," especially when played against the harsh commands of the mistress of the house, Mrs. Hawthorne. The dignity and patience of Toby's character are exemplified in a scene where he confronts Manon, another servant (Cajun), played by Lon Chaney, Jr. (credited) who is drunk and raving in the swamp. Still dressed in his black suit, Toby firmly speaks: "Now, Mr. Manon, you better stop it! Mrs. Hawthorne say stop. She don't want you shooting at gators around here." As if he understands a loss they both must live with daily, Toby puts his hand on Manon's shoulder and leads him away. It is a great scene in which an uncredited actor competently holds his own against a scenery-chewing celebrity.

The part of LouAnn (uncredited), the Cypresses's black maid, is played by Ruby Goodwin, a working actress of the time. Older, wearing a black dress, white apron, her graying hair pulled back in a bun, Goodwin's expressive face reacts with veiled worry in every scene she is in. At great risk to herself, she cautions the film's erstwhile daring heroine: "This is a trouble house, real deep big trouble. Like the old country woman in Big Bayoe say—Miss Hawthorne, she deal with evil ones. She got big sorrow. Like you get if you stay here. Go chile. Please go. This is a trouble house. Real deep big trouble." In order to facilitate the suspension of disbelief that science fiction films require, these actors had to play their scenes very realistically. Consequently, they were allowed to act with dignity, not with the stereotypical monkeyshines many black actors were forced to adopt.

Pauline Myers (credited) plays Millie, a frightened maid in *How to Make a Monster* (1958). Her realistic emotive intensity contributes greatly to our suspension of disbelief as she legitimizes our fear of the film's low-budget monster, when she reports to the police captain, "It looked like he walked right off the screen. Big, huge man with ... one eye out of his socket.

Oh, it sure was a nightmare. He hit me and knocked me down. Must of had something in his hand, the blow was that heavy." *The Leech Woman* (1960) credits two African American actresses. Old Mala, a 140-year-old African woman, is played by 73-year-old Estelle Hemsley, Golden Globe nominee for supporting actress in *Take a Giant Step* (1959). Kim Newman plays Young Mala, rejuvenated to youth, beauty, and sexual vivacity by a combination of the exotic Nipe plant and fluid extracted from a living male's pineal gland. Along with roles for these two African Americans, the film provided roles for scores of non-speaking (but chanting and dancing) extras, costumed elaborately in skins, feathers, bones, beads, masks, and curly black wigs, as members of the African Nando tribe.

In 1959's *The World, the Flesh, and the Devil*, popular personality and Civil Rights icon Harry Bellafonte plays Ralph Burton, lone survivor of an atomic catastrophe—until he encounters Sarah Crandall, a young white woman, played by Inger Stevens. They develop a friendship, and why not? They are the only two people left on Earth. Yet Burton cannot bring himself to grant Crandall the affection she desires from him. "You want to kiss me? Make love to me? Then go ahead. Kiss me. Make love. Make me feel. Make me forget everything. Harder!" Crandall begs in futility. Fortunately, a suitable white man arrives on the scene, and a crisis of miscegenation is averted.

And that is about it for representations of race in the science fiction films of the Fifties.

"There isn't anybody in there..."

One would think, then, that when 1968's alchemical transformation of the science fiction film genre occurred, representations of African Americans would likewise evolve. Not quite so. There are no African Americans in *Mission Mars*, *2001: A Space Odyssey*, or *Barbarella*. Worse, in *Barbarella*, the concept of blackness is represented as evil personified by the Black Guards who guard the insatiable Black Queen (though the character is Caucasian). The angel Pygar explains why the Guards disintegrate after dying. "There isn't anybody in there," he says. "The black guards are leathermen; they are without fleshy substance." Further emphasizing the non-person-ness of blackness, The Black Queen's throne is an ebony sculpture of a nude female body. There is one black man in *Countdown*, however. He is a technician (uncredited), wearing a headset, sitting at a panel of consoles at a Mission Control training center with four white men. His is a small speaking part, which includes a direct command regarding an anti-gravity training device: "Release the Peter Pan." While not offering much of an opportunity for a black actor, the role does represent an African American as other than an affable train porter or a butler on a Southern plantation.

Similarly, careful scrutiny of *Charly* reveals a multitude of non-menial roles (uncredited) for black actors. We see a black female student on a college campus discussing Goethe and Faust with other white male and female students; an African American baker; a black man in scrubs in the operating room; a black man dressed in a suit and tie at an outdoor market; a black man in an audience of doctors at a symposium; and two black men in suits and a black woman in a green dress walking down a busy street with other pedestrians. More importantly, the computer programmer (uncredited) with whom Charly has his ultra-intellectual discussion regarding DNA conversion is a black male.

The one black character in *Planet of the Apes* is a male astronaut/scientist named Dodge, who unfortunately is killed 34 minutes into the film. The apes are played by white actors in simian makeup. Even the humans of the 40th century into which the astronauts have found themselves are all Caucasian. Nonetheless, as Greene states, "the five *Planet of the Apes* films allegorized racial conflict during the late sixties and early seventies" (ix). In support of his argument, Greene points out that "historically discourses about apes and monkeys and discourses about race and 'people of color' have been continually intertwined" (5). Further, he delineates the way in which "the film also presents visual correspondences to the racial conflicts of the times" (36). In Greene's reading, the casting of Charlton Heston as the film's protagonist brilliantly capitalized on Heston's persona as "a film icon of white heroic strength and Western indomitability" (41) allowing the film to personify a "white fear of racial apocalypse" (24) at the same time that it allowed a celebration of racial reversal by the racially disenfranchised. Subsequent to 1968, representations of African Americans became more central as opposed to metaphorical, advancing filmic representations of race in the science fiction film at the same time that they intertwined ideological concepts of race and gender.

Representations of Dystopia

So many science fiction films of the Fifties ended with crises averted that one could say this plot structure was a convention of the genre. A giant, raging cephalopod, for example, is defeated in *It Came from Beneath the Sea*. Towns are spared total destruction by the diverting of salt water in *The Monolith Monsters*. *Tarantula*'s killer spider is wiped out by a squadron of B-52 bombers. Rampaging locusts are led into the water and drown, forestalling the *Beginning of the End*. Moreover, even in the face of apocalyptic devastation, a sense of hope prevails. Despite the devastation of 20th century civilization in *World Without End*, for example, a new society with wholesome Western values arises. A spaceship filled with virtuous people is able to start a new Earth after our own Earth is destroyed by a rogue comet in *When Worlds Collide*. Even *The Incredible Shrinking Man* willingly acquiesces to becoming one with his god as he continues to grow infinitesimally smaller. "With God there is no zero," he reassures himself (and us).

"Brave new dreams, brave new hates, brave new wars..."

Such unbridled optimism is not a characteristic of the films of 1968. Not surprisingly, *Mission Mars* and *Countdown*, films that present a realistic view of space travel, end realistically as well, evidencing both hope and loss. In *Mission Mars*, despite the unfortunate loss of crewmen, space exploration will continue, and the fallen are honored as heroes. In *Countdown*, after a precarious flight and landing, the film's protagonist—low on oxygen, disoriented, and wandering on the surface of the moon—fortuitously spots the shelter that will house and support him until the second ship arrives. The music swells. Audience members hope for his survival. We know, however, as we did in reality, that this survival is not guaranteed.

As expected, the conclusion of the enigmatic *2001* can be interpreted in more than one way. The soaring notes of "Also Sprach Zarathustra," the unexpected Space Child with its promise of new creation, the expectation that our hero's unwavering struggle somehow signifies triumph—we feel great hope for humanity amidst our uncertainty of just what these images and sensations mean. Grant is sure that "*2001* seeks to restore to us a sense of wonder that modern man has forgotten in embracing a masculine quest for scientific mastery." Indeed, as a young feminist leaving the theater in 1968, I felt a profound sense of mystical exhilaration. However, in his commentary on *2001* in *101 Sci-Fi Movies You Must See Before You Die* (2009), Peter Hutchings attributes a more negative significance to the film's conclusion. "For Kubrick," he writes, "human evolution is inextricably linked to violence, with the initial fights between the ape men eventually becoming the Cold War tensions and secrecies that permeate the latter part of the film." The Star Child, he argues, "is a considerably more disturbing figure than has sometimes been supposed. It might well be a source of hope for humankind, but seeing the film in terms of Kubrick's pessimism offers another possibility, namely that its appearance is just a sign that things are going to get worse" (138).

Clearly, the dreadful revelation at the end of *Planet of the Apes* indicated the despair in the air in 1968. By 1968, CORE had adopted Black Power concepts; half a million troops were putting their lives on the line fighting an unwinnable war in Vietnam; the National Guard had been called out to cover uprisings in more than one hundred cities; and hippies who had congregated in San Francisco for a Summer of Love were succumbing to drugs, unemployment, homelessness, and venereal disease. However, the ending of *Planet of the Apes*, in which Taylor and Nova ride off together into a destroyed world, does provide a brief glimmer of hope—hope that perhaps, with luck and hard work, the human race will in the end prevail. *Charly*, on the other hand, as well as ending unhappily on a personal level, forthrightly portends hopelessness for the future. With his biologically enhanced super intelligence and eyes that as he says see "things as they are," Charly prophesies a future of "rampant technology; conscience by computer; brave new weapons; joyless, guideless youth; preachment by popularity polls; test tube conception; laboratory birth, TV education; brave new dreams; brave new hates; brave new wars; a beautifully purposeless process of society suicide."

In "Don't Look Where We're Going: Visions of the Future in Science Fiction Films. 1970–82" (1983), H. Bruce Franklin writes, "By the end of the 1960s, it seemed that we were experiencing the most profound crisis in human history. Although our species now possessed the science and technology potentially allowing us to shape the future of the planet according to human needs and desires, we faced these forces as alien powers ... slipping out of our control and threatening to wipe us off the planet" (19). Indeed, only two years subsequent to Charly Gordon's dystopian pronouncements, John Lennon and Yoko Ono had been arrested for possession, Jim Morrison was arrested in Florida for showing his penis, and Jimi Hendrix and Janis Joplin had overdosed and died. Richard Nixon, finally ensconced in the White House, secretly began bombing Cambodia. The Ohio National Guard fired into a crowd at a Kent State University anti-war demonstration, killing four students. Charles Manson was arrested and charged for the senseless and gruesome Sharon Tate murders. A young black man was stabbed to death by Hell's Angels at a Rolling Stones concert in Altamont. Gay people had had enough and rioted on Christopher Street, abortion was legalized, and four men had walked on the moon.

Barbarella, despite its images of cruelty and degradation, ends happily ever after. It is only fitting, though, that the blind angel Pygar, who flies Barbarella and the Great Tyrant off into the sunset, "has no memory." Illusions of optimism seem to have been forgotten.

Representations of Computers

In 1970, George A. Nikolaieff wrote in his Preface to *Computers and Society*, "As recently as the early 1950s the computer was still an intellectual toy, something for academicians to play with and science fiction writers to speculate about" (4). And indeed, computers played significant roles in two particular science fiction films of the Fifties: *Kronos* and *The Invisible Boy*. (Here I am dealing specifically with representations of computers, as opposed to traditional science-fictional robots, such as those depicted in Fifties films such as *Tobor the Great*, *Forbidden Planet*, and *Colossus of New York*.)

In his April 10, 1957, *Variety* review of *Kronos*, Whit. commented that the film "boasts quality special effects," yet he makes no mention of S.U.S.I.E., the film's futuristic (and female) computer. Likewise, he minimizes the contribution of Barbara Lawrence, the film's female lead, stating that her role is "strictly for distaff interest," despite her character's support of the film's hero—both professionally (she competently develops his film for him) and personally (she is also his accommodating fiancée).[8] In his 1969 article "Machines Are Talking Back," Dr. Richard H. Bolt described a computer as a device that "can serve man as a close partner, helping him while he works in creative, intellectual pursuits." "This partnership, as it evolves," he continued, "will expand the range of tasks man can undertake and will enable him to solve problems that are much too complex for him to solve alone" (54). Both the female S.U.S.I.E. and *Kronos*'s distaff character function in this supportive (and often under recognized) capacity.

When the computer is represented as male, however, it is much more powerful, and in *The Invisible Boy*, even deadly. *The Invisible Boy*'s computer has no name. It is referred to throughout the film as "the computer" or "it." Nonetheless, it has a male voice and all the trappings of traditional male power. In his October 16, 1957, *Variety* review, for example, Whit. noted that the "super computer is in constant use by the Pentagon for solution of complex scientific problems." Moreover, its power is so strong that it must be located nine levels below ground. Even in 1970, Nikolaieff acknowledged "the suspicion that the quickly developing machines may learn to think—and then what?" (5). That suspicion culminates in terror as *The Invisible Boy*'s computer—referred to by Bill Warren in *Keep Watching the Skies! American Science Fiction Movies of the Fifties* (2010) as a "villainous machine" (437)—murders, threatens torture, and mentally dominates all those (even a child) with whom it comes in contact. In his climactic moment of realization, the computer's creator bemoans, "It's achieved true thought, true personality. It lives. It never sleeps or lies idle. It's never at conflict with itself over such human considerations as honor or love and pity. It's motivated by an instinct for survival. In obeying this basic urge, it can tolerate no interference on the part of the human race. Earth will be its slave."

"Open the pod bay doors, HAL..."

While *Kronos* and *The Invisible Boy* represented computers on opposing ends of a gender table—one a helpful female, the other a dominating male—two films of 1968 represented computers on opposing poles of what Carl Freedman refers to in *Critical Theory and Science Fiction* (2000) as cognition and estrangement (16). In his pamphlet "Introducing the Computer" (excerpted in *Computers and Society* in 1970), Fred C. Gielow, Jr., senior associate engineer in IBM's Systems Development Division, matter-of-factly described the way a computer works: "The computer cannot think, any more than the washing machine can think. What it can do is extend man's problem–solving capabilities by performing many arithmetic, logic, branching and input-output instructions with lightning speed" (75). Such is the functioning of the computer in *Charly*. What we see is a mundane (Freedman's word) representation of what an admittedly advanced computer could potentially be programmed to do. In *2001*'s HAL, on the other hand, we see an advanced computer represented in a way that legitimately interrogates not only our nagging suspicions about computers but the very essence of artificial intelligence itself.

When he senses trouble, HAL quietly and effortlessly murders the mission's hibernating scientists—easy enough, because they have allowed him complete control of all of their life functions. When he senses that his intentions have been discovered, he has the sense to eavesdrop by lip reading the conversation between the two astronauts he presumes are colluding against him (which they are)—again, easy enough. His intelligence and adaptability have been, disastrously for the two astronauts, seriously underestimated. When his back is against the wall, he locks the one surviving astronaut out of the space vehicle—easy enough because, in order to be involved with higher order pursuits, humans have ceded mundane mechanical operations to his capacious computer mind. Even when he is being dismantled, he has the innate sense to know that a human could respond to an emotional plea. He promises Dave that he will do better. "I feel much better now. I really do," he tells him. He uses reverse psychology: "Look Dave, I can see you're really upset about this." "I want to help you," he lies. He appeals to Dave's sympathy: "I'm afraid, Dave." Even his pathetic childlike singing of "Daisy" could be a manipulation.

Both HAL and the computer in *The Invisible Boy* are destroyed in the end by man, victorious. The potential for mankind's subservience to a disembodied emotionless intellect has been forestalled. We can rest easy. Or can we?

•••

In her Introduction to *Alien Zone: Cultural Theory and Contemporary Science Fiction Cinema* (1990), Annette Kuhn writes that "studies of individual film genres" initially proceeded "via descriptions of shared surface conventions of plot and iconography across groupings of film texts defined in advance as belonging to a particular genre" (3). This is the methodology I used when classifying the science fiction films of the Fifties. I characterized these films according to plots, themes, characters, iconographies and tropes initiated by the early films of the period: *Destination Moon*, *Rocketship X-M*, and *The Thing (from Another World)*. These categories included travel into space, aliens on Earth, science gone mad, unnatural creatures, and of course, the woman scientist. (I admit that this reasoning was somewhat circular, in that I first selected the films that I thought were science fictional and then used those very films to articulate the characteristics that defined the genre. Nonetheless, I tried to be as inclusive and thorough as possible in the films I investigated.)

Likewise, in this project, I am arguing that the science fiction films of 1968 set a new trajectory for the genre, a trajectory I refer to as the Middle Period. Kuhn further states that "theoretical arguments concerning the ways in which cinema, film genres and film texts express, enact and produce ideologies ... raise questions about the relations between cultural practices and the 'real world,' between films or films genres and society" (8). Again, regarding the science fiction films of the Fifties, I connected the characteristics of those films with post–World War II changes in society, in particular with regard to the role of women in science. In the 1968 films and the science fiction films that followed, narrative and culture intersected in ways that reflected social changes brought about by the Sixties revolutions.

Films such as *Marooned* (1969) reflected the realistic progress of space travel, as initiated in *Mission Mars* and *Countdown*. *Barbarella* mainstreamed a sexual way of looking at women. Films such as *Soylent Green* (1973) reflected post–Sixties fears of social collapse, as articulated by Charly Gordon in *Charly*. Unlike HAL in *2001* and the villainous computer in *The Invisible Boy*, Colossus, the super computer in *Colossus: The Forbin Project* (1970), could not be destroyed and succeeded (one hopes only until its creator could figure out a way to disable it) in taking over the world. Racial issues continued to be explored allegorically in the *Apes* franchise and began to be reflected more directly in films such as *The Omega Man* (1971) and *Frogs* (1972). All of these issues—realism in depictions of science and space travel, projections of dystopia, the power of the computer, race—intersected with and affected representations of gender for both men and women in specifically science-fictional ways as the Middle Period progressed.

3

Gender and...

In the Middle Period films, gender roles continue to be depicted in ways that reflect both science and society. Men and women participate in exciting scientific adventures in films such as *The Andromeda Strain* and *Colossus: The Forbin Project*. Marriages are depicted as supportive and good in *Marooned*, as well as dangerous to women in *The Stepford Wives*. Images of sex take a hard turn in films such as *Invasion of the Bee Girls* and *A Boy and His Dog*, in which sexual relations are depicted as lethal, reflecting (one could say even threatening) the vulnerability of post–Sixties liberated women. More African American characters begin to take center stage in films such as *The Omega Man* and *Frogs*, reflecting contemporary ideologies of both race and gender. Representations of dystopian societies in films such as *Soylent Green* and *Logan's Run* reflect the fears of a society fractured by the turbulence of the Sixties. In particular, they portend horrors for any woman who dares to feel she has been liberated. The computer develops malevolently in a frighteningly gender-specific manner in the astounding and terrifying *Demon Seed*. Read on, and I will share with you Middle Period representations of gender and science, gender and marriage, gender and sex, gender and race, gender and dystopia, and gender and computers. Caution: While much of what you will peruse is as thrilling as the science fiction film can be, a lot of it is not very pretty.

Science

In "Computers in Science Fiction: Anxiety and Anticipation," his essay in *Computing and Society: Essays on Interlinked Domains* (2011), Chris Pak writes, "Science fiction, as a very rational genre, is often about the beauty of science and its accomplishments" (39). Indeed, even if the rationality is a bit of a stretch, a big part of the pleasure of watching science fiction films is seeing science pushed to (or beyond) its limits. In the films of the Fifties, for example, paleontologist Dr. Nedrick (Ned) Jackson identifies and helps destroy a giant prehistoric monster inadvertently freed by an explosion from a polar ice cap in *The Deadly Mantis*. Nuclear physicists Drs. Cal Meacham and Ruth Adams work to discover a new energy source to help save a dying planet in *This Island Earth*. Astrophysicist Dr. Leslie Gaskell tracks a dangerous rogue asteroid and determines an ingenious way to neutralize what it morphs into in *Kronos*. Drs. Harold and Patricia "Pat" Medford use their knowledge and training in entomology to discover the vulnerabilities inherent in hordes of giant, rampaging ants in *Them!*

In the films of the Middle Period, adventures in science are just as exciting. In *The Andromeda Strain*, elite team of scientists Drs. Jeremy Stone, Mark Hall, Charles Dutton, and Ruth Leavitt are sequestered deep in an underground bunker in order to determine the cellular makeup of an alien organism that, when inhaled, promptly turns blood into powder. In *Colossus: The Forbin Project*, charismatic scientist Dr. Charles Forbin is the inventor of a super computer that is designed to both monitor and control all Allied defense systems. Well-meaning Dr. Alex Harris creates a computer that swiftly discovers a cure for leukemia in *Demon Seed*. On the other hand, poor deluded Dr. Paul Holliston valiantly conducts an experiment with a human fetus that goes terribly wrong in *Embryo*.

As well as the excitement of feeling as if we are participating cinematically in the wonders of science while engrossed in the science fiction film, we can also feel as we are sharing in the thrills and excitement of space exploration—both speculative and conventional. In the Fifties films, Dr. Iris Ryan and Col. Tom O'Bannion travel to Mars in *The Angry Red Planet*. On a routine flight, Maj. Bill Allison accidentally speeds *Beyond the Time Barrier* to a post-apocalyptic Earth of the future. Lt. Dan Prescott returns from a risky test flight as a desperate blood-sucking monster in *First Man into Space*. Capt. Neil Patterson and his crew travel to Venus and find a very strange world in *Queen of Outer Space*.

Space travel in the Middle Period films continues the trajectory set in the 1968 films, with lead characters working (more or less) realistically in the space program. Reflecting as well the reality of the period, the astronauts in these films are primarily male. Col. Glenn Ross and civilian John Kane are elected to attempt an uncertain and politically sensitive space flight in *Journey to the Far Side of the Sun*. Jim Pruett and his crew must figure out how best to conserve their resources while shipwrecked in space and waiting for rescue in *Marooned*. Working a bit less realistically were futuristic space travelers such as Capt. William H. Kemp, who makes regular flights to Mars and Venus in *Moon Zero Two*, and idealistic botanist Freeman Lowell, who uncompromisingly attempts to preserve a greenhouse in space in *Silent Running*.

As we saw in *The Outer Limits*, representation of women in science in the Middle Period films is neither as generous nor as superficially uncomplicated as it was in the Fifties films—realistically extrapolating, as it had to, from the circumstances of the era. In *Women in Science: Portraits from a World in Transition* (1983), Vivian Gornick relates the experience of an established physicist who decided to investigate her lab's "system of employment and advance" after "the women's movement began making trouble." She reported to Gornick that two classes existed. "One class," she said, "was that of Senior Technical Assistant—straight technician, a decent enough job from which there was no place to go, but one in which you could remain for the rest of your life if you wanted to. The other class—the Graduate Studies Program—was a job in which people could go on for an M.S., and then take a place somewhere on the ladder leading to Senior Scientist. When we looked closely," she disclosed, "we saw that the first class was all women, the second class all men" (70).

This class is cinematically represented by head science librarian Julie Zorn in *Invasion of the Bee Girls* and medical technician Karen Anson in *The Andromeda Strain*. Following the trajectory set by Carol White in *The Time Travelers* (1964) and Cora Peterson in *Fantastic Voyage* (1966), these women are content (or not) to operate as reliable, indispensable technicians. While perhaps not as advanced as the work these women could have performed, the exacting scientific work that we do see them accomplish is valued by those in their field and more than likely interesting and rewarding to perform.

One must note as well the conditions for women who desired to work beyond a technical capacity. In her study, Gornick relates what one student of science had to endure. "A twenty-two-year old woman who graduated from Harvard in the summer of 1980 with a BS in psychology had entered the university as a chemistry major but dropped out at the end of the year," she relates, because she had been so discouraged, intimidated, even humiliated by her famous freshman chemistry professor (74). Indeed, most of the women in the cinematic science of the Middle Period, like Gornick's student, are accomplished in psychology or psychiatry, fields traditionally considered more acceptable for women. Even Gornick does not look at clinical psychology as a hard science. "I narrowed my definition of a scientist down to those who did basic research, and accepted as my subjects biologists, chemists, physicists, physiologists, and experimental psychologists," she writes in her Introduction (14).

Of course, even if not hierarchically coded as hard science, psychology is a rigorous and valuable field of study. Dr. Janet Ross is a dedicated psychiatrist who attempts to chart a traumatized Harry Benson's post-surgical neural responses to a multitude of stimuli in *The Terminal Man*. Dr. Fancher is qualified to prescribe medication as well as therapy to a fearful Joanna Eberhart in *The Stepford Wives*. (Unfortunately and not unexpectedly, she interprets Joanna's account of her bizarre situation as evidence of a treatable neurosis.) Dr. Susan Harris is a child psychologist in *Demon Seed*, who compassionately and persistently encourages an angry girl to acknowledge the source of her emotional pain. Of course animal psychologist Dr. Zira returns in 1970's *Beneath the Planet of the Apes* and is protected and defended by animal behaviorist Dr. Stephanie Branton in 1971's *Escape from the Planet of the Apes*. And in a remarkable intersection of science fiction and what Annette Kuhn refers to as the "real world," celebrity psychologist Dr. Joyce Brothers makes a brief appearance as psychologist Dr. Joyce Brothers in *Embryo*.

There are two cinematic roles for women in science, however, that are in fact coded as hard science. They are Dr. Cleo Markham (played by Susan Clark) in *Colossus: The Forbin Project* and Dr. Ruth Leavitt (played by Kate Reid) in *The Andromeda Strain,* Each of these roles extrapolates in a very science-fictional way from the quotidian, exhibiting what could be permitted for a woman in science (as well as what could not).

"She knows the machine as well as I do..."

Computer scientist Markham is the character most aligned with contemporary reality. The selections in *Computers and Society*, published in 1970, the same year that *Colossus: The Forbin Project* was released, referred to the incipient computer industry as nothing less than transformative. In his Preface, George A. Nikolaieff referred to it as an "extraordinary turning point in the civilization we know" (3). *Fortune* Magazine editor Gilbert H. Burck related that "Paul Armer, of RAND Corporation, estimates that it will create a million new jobs in the next five years" (36). In "Computer Business Races On," *New York Times* reporter William D. Smith concurred: "The computer business is the world's fastest growing major industry," he predicted (39). In "The Search for Meaning Amid Change," professor of government Zbigniew Brzezinski foresaw "a society that is shaped culturally, psychologically, socially and economically by the impact of technology and electronics, particularly computers and communications" (190). Here was a moment analogous to the World War II moment that opened up unprecedented opportunities for women in the work force.

Not unexpectedly, considering the gender conventions of the time period, *Computers and Society* is primarily about computers and men. There are seven direct references to women and computers in the entire collection—a ward nurse who can be told by computer what medications to give (45), a secretary who "performed an input function" when she handed her boss the office pay records (89), a floor nurse whose efficiency can be improved by "substituting a data terminal for multiple paper forms" (92–93), a wife whose husband lost his job due to computer automation (142), two little sisters who play computer games their older brother programmed for them (157–158), a secretary who can "simply type a brief code that directs the computer to produce the full paragraphs" the doctor she works for has checked off (160), and a typist who "can become a 'competent' operator within a couple of days" (161).

Of course there is an exception. An excerpt from technical writer Shirley Thomas's 1965 book, *Computers: Their History, Present Applications and Future*, is included in the collection.[1] The excerpt consists of a historical account of the origin of Electronic Numerical Integrator and Computer (ENIAC) in 1945 and subsequent developments including "the invention of the stored program," "magnetic core memory," "real-time operation," and finally the transistor—"a device with boundless applications"—in 1952. In the course of the excerpt, Thomas mentions a "lady programmer, Mrs. Ruth Horgan [who] once kicked a computer" that was giving her trouble. The excerpt concludes with the optimistic statement, "We have reached the point where the present is a bridge across the growing edge of progress leading us from the past to the future" (125–139).

Indeed, opportunities for women like this "lady programmer" of 1952 did in fact progress. Gornick reports female employment in the field of computer science in 1981 as 21 percent (72). Dr. Cleo Markham cinematically represents a woman who has progressed even beyond these opportunities. In fact, Markham is second in command to Forbin himself. As Forbin states, "She knows the machine as well as I do."[2] When the crisis with Colossus begins, it is Markham that Forbin turns to for information, referring to his staff in the programming office as "Dr. Markham and the rest of you." When Forbin has left the country to confer with Russian scientists out of Colossus's awareness, it is Markham who is called to answer in his stead when the machine demands, "I want Forbin."

And Markham acts in this high-ranking capacity in a relatable way. In *Variety's Complete Science Fiction Reviews* (1985), critic Rick. favorably commented on the actress: "Miss Clarke [sic]," he wrote, "has an attractive look of intelligence that is right for the role, and carries off the right under-played note of quiet professional competence." Internet columnist Brian Wright concurs. He writes of Clark's presence in the control center, "She'd be a good reason for any red-blooded American man of science to hang out there. But consistent with early feminist sensibilities, Dr. Cleo is por-trayed as a genuine contributor in her own right. It's even refreshing: in Clark, Cleo does not have the perfect bodacious figure of a Playboy cen-terfold."

But here is where the science-fictional aspect of the film comes into play. Unlike the women in *The Time Travelers*, for example, who flirted with sex in the workplace, Cleo Markham, despite her lack of *Playboy* dis-tinctiveness, actually does have sex in the workplace, and with her boss

Dr. Cleo Markham (Susan Clark) and Dr. Charles Forbin (Eric Braeden) naked in bed together discussing computer hardware, wiring diagrams, and data coor-dination in *Colossus: The Forbin Project* (1970) (Photofest).

at that. As Colossus, the film's eponymous computer, is in the process of gaining power, he constantly monitors Forbin, his creator, in order to prevent him from sabotaging the system. Forbin concocts a story about his need for privacy the four times a week he requires a woman. The woman he convinces Colossus he requires is Dr. Markham. Suspicious, Colossus demands that they strip before entering Forbin's bedroom. Though Forbin pretended to require Markham because of her sexual attractiveness, he really requires her intellect and powers of scientific observation. Together in bed they discuss computer hardware, wiring diagrams, and data coordination. After a few nights, however, they make love. And why not? They are both consenting adults, attractive, single ... and naked. Ultimately there are no negative ramifications of potential sexual harassment, hurt feelings, or even pregnancy. After all, by the end of the film, the murderous Colossus has taken over the world. What could be worse than that?

"It's just my eyes are tired..."

Microbiologist Dr. Ruth Leavitt provides yet another representation of a woman in science. Markham's character is female in the 1966 novel *Colossus* from which *Colossus: The Forbin Project* was adapted. In the novel from which *The Andromeda Strain* was adapted, however, Dr. Leavitt is Dr. Peter Leavitt.[4] In *The Andromeda Strain: Making the Film* (2001), director Robert Wise tells how screenwriter Nelson Gidding suggested making one of the characters into a woman, in particular a woman doctor. Gidding knew this suggestion was controversial. "At that time there weren't so many women scientists," Gidding surmised. "There were some great ones but it wasn't accepted," he admits. Wise, nervously envisioning "Raquel Welch in a submarine again," says he "called two or three scientists" who assured him that having a woman as a scientist would be fine. "We have many fine women scientists; that would not violate the film at all," Wise says they told him. The idea that even the thought of a woman in science would potentially "violate" a project is indicative of the resistance smart, determined women in the scientific workplace must have had to face.

However, despite the challenges she may have had to face, Leavitt is superficially treated in the same manner as are the male scientists. They are all equally qualified—though Dr. Jeremy Stone is the team leader. They are all middle aged—though, as the youngest, Dr. Mark Hall serves as the film's putative sex symbol. (We are treated to a shot of Hall's bare bottom and of his stretched out nude body—appropriate parts shielded by props—as he undergoes decontamination procedures.) Save for a separate dressing room for Leavitt, all team members undergo the same grueling decontamination and immunization procedures. They each perform equally valuable work.

Nonetheless, in creating Leavitt as a woman, Gidding endowed her with particular characteristics that can be read as analogous to the circumstances of the woman scientist. Unlike Markham and Forbin who are completely attuned to each other, Leavitt and Stone think differently in a particularly gender coded way. Leavitt is intuitive. Sensing that the organism she and Stone are searching for is inside the space capsule, she suggests they immediately search for it there. Stone is methodical, reliant on tradition. "Stick to established procedure, Ruth," he admonishes her. When they discover green splotches (which are indeed inside the capsule), Leavitt quickly senses that they have found the organism (which they in fact have). Stone will not bend. "The best hope of cracking it is to be grudgingly thorough," he dogmatically insists. Unfortunately, Stone's insistence on following established procedures pushes Leavitt to exhaustion and self-doubt. When Leavitt sees the organism mutate (the most important development in the film), she believes she has imagined it. "You okay?" Stone asks. "It's just my eyes are tired. We've been at it five hours straight," she replies. When they both see the organism mutate, Stone assumes Leavitt may have acted impulsively. "You didn't change the lighting?" he questions. Imagine how hard it must be (male or female) to persevere under such unyielding rigor.

Another aspect of Leavitt's character that coordinates with the circumstances of women in science is the fact that she has an obvious handicap, the only member of the team so burdened. She wears glasses, definitely a hardship for a scientist entrusted with detailed microscopic observation. This handicap can be read as symbolic of the built-in discriminations and prejudices against which women scientists had to struggle. Furthermore, unlike Drs. Stone and Dutton, Ruth Leavitt is provided no loving and supportive spouse (as is Peter Leavitt in the book). She is often depicted rubbing her eyes, tired, as single professional women in the workplace must have been—not because they were women, but rather because they were doing double duty managing their homes as well as their professional lives.

More importantly, Leavitt suffers from epilepsy, a condition she keeps secret. This condition can be read in two ways. First, though Leavitt is beyond childbearing age in the film, her situation is analogous to the situation of women scientists who were forced hide their pregnancies in order to continue working. Gornick relates the experience of physical chemist Annie Morris (first in her class at CalTech), who was told after she finally obtained a position (as a technician), "If you become pregnant you'll get fired." Married, Morris did get pregnant and (like Leavitt) was able to successfully hide her condition as long as possible (101–102). The second way to code Leavitt's condition is to read her as a lesbian. In 1971, being a lesbian was not an easy identity to claim openly. Even Betty Friedan, pioneer of the Second Wave of Feminism, railed against "man-haters" whose goal as she saw it was to "proselytize lesbianism" in her 1973 Epilogue to 1963's *The Feminine Mystique* (526).

The film does not explicitly represent Leavitt as lesbian, however— any more than it intimates that she may be pregnant. (However, she is depicted as having a caring, protective female lab assistant.) She smokes cigarettes (unlike Peter Leavitt in the book)—definitely a progressive act for a woman in the early Seventies.[5] And she can certainly be classified as supportive of the counterculture. "Establishment gonna fall down and go boom," she tells Stone after he admonishes her. I present these readings to show how women in science, bucking established parameters, were forced to conceal inherent aspects of themselves and their lives, as Levitt hid her epilepsy. When Leavitt's epilepsy is outed, as it were, Hall is exasperated. "Why in the hell didn't she tell us about it," he asks Stone. Stone, immediately sympathetic, replies, "Probably no top lab would have her if they knew. Insurance, prejudice, all that crap," to which Hall, now understanding, indignantly replies, "From the Middle Ages," indicating in my reading of Leavitt's circumstances progress in the acceptance of women in science.

◆◆◆

In 1983, Gornick optimistically wrote, "While the profession is still without anything that resembles parity—innumerable women in science are where they belong, in possession of grants, professorships, and laboratories, and thousands of young women think it perfectly natural that they should become scientists" (16). Yes, Dr. Markham had sex with her boss. Yet the extenuating circumstances (as well as the willingness of both participants) somewhat pardon that behavior. Yes, Dr. Leavitt wound up missing important data as a result of an epileptic fugue state. Yet the sympathetic treatment she receives in the film (unlike Peter's treatment in the book) somewhat absolves her error. *Colossus: The Forbin Project* and *The Andromeda Strain* could only have reassured young women who saw these films in the early Seventies that they too could beat the odds.

Marriage

There are several happy marriages depicted in the films of the Fifties—Dr. John Rollason and his wife Helen in *The Abominable Snowman of the Himalayas*, Dr. Russell Marvin and his wife Carol Hanley Marvin in *Earth vs. the Flying Saucers*, Dr. Tom Merrinoe and his wife Mary in *The Invisible Boy*, Drs. Eric and Mary Royce in *It! The Terror from Beyond Space*, and Jeffrey and Connie Stewart in *The Magnetic Monster*, for example. Many of the marriages in the Fifties films, however, are beset by monsters—monsters arising from within the marriages themselves. In *Attack of the 50 Foot Woman*, Nancy Archer's already troubled marriage to Harry implodes when she grows monstrous in size. In *Colossus of New York*, Anne Spensser's marriage takes a strange turn when the brain of her husband, renowned Dr. Jeremy Spensser, is implanted into a robot. Helene Delambre is traumatized when her loving husband Andre mutates into *The Fly*. It turns out that Marge Farrell has married an alien, not her fiancé Bill, in *I Married a Monster from Outer Space*. Louise Carey's marriage is destroyed when her husband Scott dwindles into nothingness in *The Incredible Shrinking Man*. David Maclean's erstwhile normal parents are taken over by alien devices in *Invaders from Mars*. Dr. Paul Nelson murders his wife Joan when she succumbs to alien devices in *It Conquered the World*.

The marriages in the films of the Middle Period are not so metaphorically beset. In his 1972 Introduction to *Family, Marriage, and the Struggle of the Sexes*, Hans Peter Dreitzel reported that "the structure of the nuclear family is shaken by its own inherent problems" (5).

Dreitzel's chapters concern issues such as the division of labor, changing sex roles, child-rearing practices, and of course, the effects of the Women's Liberation Movement. And many of the cinematic Middle Period marriages are indeed shaken, some more than others. Allison Stone and Clara Dutton, wives of Dr. Jeremy Stone and Dr. Charles Dutton respectively, are disturbed by the abrupt manner in which their husbands have been called away in *The Andromeda Strain*. Nonetheless, they are depicted as loyal, caring, and appropriately matched spouses. Helen Holliston, Dr. Paul Holliston's pregnant young daughter-in-law in *Embryo*, assertively proclaims to her husband that "God is a liberated female and she is on my side," but only in a playful attempt to cajole him into having sex with her. Jenny, however, is the spoiled, dissatisfied wife of a feckless Clint Crockett in *Frogs*. "You're out drinking in that speedboat all day and all night. Well, I hate it," she complains. "Just shut your mouth," he angrily responds. The marriage of esteemed astronaut Col. Glenn Ross and his promiscuous wife Sharon is in serious trouble in *Journey to the Far Side of the Sun*. She accuses him of being sterile: "The brutal truth of the matter is that you went up there a man, but you came back less than a man." After he discovers her "femina" brand oral contraceptives, however, he smacks her hard across the face. Finally, even though he knows she took him for a ride in their divorce, Peter Martin still misses his wife (and kids) in *Westworld*.

One wishes there were more of the positive images, even a couple enacting the progressive gender representations of Drs. Zira and Cornelius in *Planet of the Apes*, who worked together, cooked together, and planned to be married without either one having to give up a meaningful career in science. Alas, representations of marriage emblematic of the Middle Period films can be found in *Marooned* and *The Stepford Wives*. One film valorizes the traditional conventions of gender and marriage; the other threatens those who would resist those conventions, particularly those advancing the Second

Dr. Jeremy Stone (Arthur Hill) pushing Dr. Ruth Leavitt (Kate Reid) to exhaustion in *The Andromeda Strain* (1971) (Photofest).

Wave of Feminism, a movement that argued sometimes reasonably, sometimes angrily for equal treatment in the social as well as the legal sphere.

"Here I am..."

   Marooned follows the trajectory established by *Countdown* and *Mission Mars*. *Mission Mars* pairs realistic depictions of space travel with the
realistically depicted marital relationships of Nick and Alice Grant and
Mike and Edith Blaiswick. Likewise, *Countdown* pairs realistic depictions
of space travel with the realistically depicted marriages of Chiz and Jean
Stewart and Lee and Mickey Stegler. *Marooned*, a movie about astronauts
stranded in orbit, depicts space travel so realistically that its plot became
reality six months after the film's release with the crisis of Apollo 13,
wherein astronauts James Lovell, Jr., John L. Swigert, Jr., and Fred W. Haise,
Jr., were stranded temporarily in space while the whole world watched on
our TV screens.[5] As Eric Shirey writes in his Yahoo! commentary, "When
Apollo 13 astronaut Jim Lovell took his wife to see the 1969 science fiction
drama 'Marooned,' little did he know it was foreshadowing events that
would hit a little closer to home than I'm sure he expected.... Talk about
real life mimicking the movies."
   Dreitzel acknowledged the "narrowing differences in life-style and
identification between the sexes" as well as their "general depolarization"
in 1972, citing in particular the "trend toward unisex" in fashion and
behavior (13–14). However, these differences are not apparent in
Marooned. The film's representations of gender are as polarized as its
depictions of space travel are realistic. The husbands in the film—Capt.
Jim Pruett (played by Richard Crenna), Dr. Clayton Stone (James Franciscus), and pilot Buzz Lloyd (Gene Hackman)—are exemplars of what real
men should, and should not be. Pruett, aging, regretting the passing of a
life without the big successes he once dreamed of, exemplifies the self-
sacrificing hero. Stone, rational and scientific to the end, cautiously risks
his own well-being to care for a fellow team member. The film's erstwhile
father figures—Charles Keith (played by Gregory Peck) and senior astronaut Ted Dougherty (David Janssen)—are resolute, brave, and take risks
as well as responsibility for the men in their charge.
   On the other hand, Lloyd—unmanly, hysterical, and the film's only
unsympathetic character—cowardly and selfishly jeopardizes the success
of the entire rescue mission. An example of what a man should not be is
seen in the sequence where the astronauts have been instructed to take
sleeping pills in order to conserve oxygen. Lloyd has not taken his. CAPCOM

checks to see if the astronauts are awake: "Say, you guys still asleep?" "No, we're having a wild party," Pruitt jokes in reply. "You're sure you're taking your quiet pills?" CAPCAM responds. "We are, but the girls aren't," Pruitt replies, at which point, Lloyd looks chagrined. Not only has he not taken his pills; he has been accused of behaving like a girl.

Representations of the distaff side of marriage are likewise resistant to the social changes advanced during the Second Wave of Feminism. In *When Everything Changed: The Amazing Journey of American Women from 1960 to the Present* (2009), Gail Collins writes, "By late 1969, what was up with women had become a huge national story. NOW was racking up legal and political victories, while the younger, more colorful feminists fascinated, thrilled, and appalled the nation" (194). *Marooned*'s actresses— Lee Grant, Nancy Kovack, and Mariette Hartley—give stellar performances. However, their characters—Celia Pruett, Teresa Stone, and Betty Lloyd, respectively—seem to have no idea of what, as Collins says, was up with women. Like the wives in *Mission Mars* and *Countdown*, they are indeed "tough babes," but in *Marooned*, they have no existence beyond the (admittedly pressing) needs of their daring husbands. In an emotional eight-minute sequence, the wives—unwavering, fixed on Earth—communicate with their husbands—circling, lost in space—encouraging, reassuring, and supporting them. "It's important to show them how confident you are," the women are told. "Here I am," Celia calmly says to her husband. In this sequence, both the women and their husbands become cinematic embodiments of "A Valediction: Forbidding Mourning," John Donne's exquisite 17th century love poem:

> If they be two, they are two so
>   As stiff twin compasses are two;
> Thy soul, the fixed foot, makes no show
>   To move, but doth, if the other do.
> And though it in the center sit,
>   Yet when the other far doth roam,
> It leans and hearkens after it,
>   And grows erect, as that comes home.
> Such wilt thou be to me, who must,
>   Like th' other foot, obliquely run;
> Thy firmness makes my circle just,
>   And makes me end where I begun.

What happens, though, when the fixed foot chooses—on its own— to move away from center—even just a little? As we see in *The Stepford Wives*, what happens is quite unsettling.

"Every man dreams of having the perfect wife..."

The protagonists in *The Stepford Wives* are Joanna Eberhart, played by Katherine Ross—best known to contemporary audiences for her portrayals of winsome girlfriends in *The Graduate* and *Butch Cassidy and the Sundance Kid*—and Bobbie Markowe, played by Paula Prentiss—introduced to audiences in 1960 as a cute, spunky comedienne in *Where the Boys Are*. A contemporary radio spot for the film lured listeners in with an innocuous sounding maxim "Every man dreams of having the perfect wife," and these two actresses could certainly have represented fulfillment of that desire. The next proclamation intimated that even characters portrayed by these two appealing actresses would be insufficient: "The men of Stepford have done something about it—something that changes women into Stepford wives." In the background, we heard a plaintive voice (which turned out to be Joanna's) saying uncomprehendingly, "There'll be somebody with my name, but she won't be me."

The Wikipedia entry for *The Stepford Wives* describes the film as a "science fiction-thriller." Yet, like *Barbarella*, *The Stepford Wives* does not quite fit the definition of science fiction. Rather, it can more accurately be described as speculative fiction, along the lines of *The Handmaid's Tale* or *1984*, perhaps even Kafka's "The Metamorphosis" or Hawthorne's "The Birthmark." The film's ending—with requisite drenching rain, flashing lightning, crashing thunder, gothic castle with shadowy hallways—can even situate *The Stepford Wives* within the horror genre. In fact, in a December 31, 1974, review found on Variety.com, *The Stepford Wives* is described as "a quietly freaky suspense-horror story." The film is not included in *Variety's Complete Science Fiction Reviews*.

When fun-loving, exuberant Bobbie and aspiring photographer (as well as loving mother) Joanna are ultimately transformed into docile wives, the process is not depicted as scientifically rational but almost supernaturally. We never know what actually happens to their bodies—or to the bodies of any of the other women in the town—or how their replacement bodies have been programmed (or reprogrammed) to perform so realistically. "We found a way of doing it, and it's perfect" is the only explanation the film's male mastermind provides. However, as *Barbarella* contains the element of space travel, *The Stepford Wives* concerns robotics, and several critics have responded to that science-fictional element. In *Science Fiction Film* (2001), for example, J.P. Telotte draws on the work of Mary Ann Doane and Donna Harraway in his discussion of technoculture and feminism in *The Stepford Wives*. More importantly, however, like *Barbarella*,

The Stepford Wives extrapolated from a pivotal cultural moment, and just as *Barbarella* exaggerated the ease of woman's sexual liberation, *The Stepford Wives* likewise misjudged women's intensifying rage.

In *The Stepford Life*, director Bryan Forbes and actor Peter Masterson reveal the production machinations behind the film. They relate how screenwriter William Goldman interviewed Betty Friedan and "all the feminists of the time" in order to create a "feminist diatribe." Forbes, who ultimately softened Goldman's script, was mystified by the angry reaction he received from feminists at the film's premiere. "One really manic libber hit me over the head with an umbrella at the New York press show," he says. In defense of the film, he insists that "far from being anti-woman, it was really anti-men." Masterson concurs: The film used "anti-feminist attitudes by the men to make a feminist point." This point, however, was not a point of which women were unaware.

Many feminists were already subscribing to the radicalism of Andrea Dworkin, who urged women to acknowledge "how our bodies are violated by oppressive grooming imperatives ... how the nuclear family and ritualized sexual behavior imprison us in roles and forms which are degrading to us" (20) in *Woman Hating* the year before *The Stepford Wives* was released. Women were already hearing accusations that "man's love for woman, his sexual adoration of her, his human definition of her, his delight and pleasure in her, require her negation: physical crippling and psychological lobotomy," as Dworkin continued (112).

Thus, even if we were moderates in the movement, we were not surprised by the Stepford men's physical and psychological annihilation of their wives. Many radical feminists even agreed with Dworkin's proclamation that "intercourse with men as we know them ... requires an aborting of creativity and strength, a refusal of responsibility and freedom; a bitter personal death" (184). Even women like Joanna and Bobbie, who loved their husbands and families and only "messed a little bit in women's lib in New York," as Joanna apologetically admitted in the film's early moments, did not rise up enlightened and empowered by the living deaths of our courageous protagonists.

After all, we had already experienced Edna Pontellier walking into the Gulf of Mexico to drown in Kate Chopin's *The Awakening*, Lily Bart swallowing sleeping pills and lying down on her bed to die in Edith Wharton's *The House of Mirth*, Maggie Johnson pondering death at the edge of a dark river in Stephen Crane's *Maggie: A Girl of the Streets*, Emma swallowing arsenic in Gustave Flaubert's *Madame Bovary*. We had already experienced Cleopatra holding an asp to her breast, Antigone hanging herself in a cave.

Victimizing women to illustrate the victimization of women was nothing new. What was new in *The Stepford Wives* was the removal of the literary trope of suicide that clouded the violence perpetrated against women who dared to step out of traditionally prescribed spheres of conduct.

The Stepford Wives is a disturbing film to say the least, but it is made even more disturbing by the fact that Joanna did not have to die. When she realizes that her transformation process is indeed underway, she bashes her complicit husband on the head with a fireplace poker, demanding to know what he has done with her children. He directs her to The Association—the nest of the beast, the very place where the final step in the transformation takes place. Of course she goes there. Filmmakers were quite prescient in representing a woman's propensity to see "a world comprised of relationships rather than of people standing alone" (29), "the contrast between a self defined through separation and a self delineated through connection" (35), as Carol Gilligan observed a few years later in *In a Different Voice: Psychological Theory and Women's Development* (1982). When Joanna confronts the mastermind who has lured her into his lair by playing a tape recording of her children's voices, he talks soothingly to her. "What have you got there? No, no, you're not going to need that at all," he says, noticing the poker. She stands meekly before him as he talks. Then without any resistance at all, she lets him take the poker from her hand. Only after she has let herself become vulnerable, helpless, does she scream and begin to fight. Finally cornered, she is not overpowered by the man, but by the nearly nude, silicon-breasted, blank-eyed robotic version of herself that approaches to garrote her.

The goal of the Women's Liberation Movement, Dworkin rather reasonably wrote was "to destroy sexism, that is, polar role definitions of male and female, man and woman" (153). Feminists did not want to destroy men. Neither did we want to see ourselves, yet again, complicit in our own oppression. We just wanted an alternative to the rigidly patriarchal dynamic of the traditional family. We wanted a little leeway. *Marooned* is an inspiring film that valorizes the bravery of the world's first astronauts and the women who supported them. If its intent was to validate the structure of the traditional family, it succeeded. If *The Stepford Wives* was intended to reinforce the ideals of the feminist movement, it failed.

Sex

Aside from a few make-out sessions on the couch or in the car, the science fiction films of the Fifties displayed little overt sexual behavior.

Teenage couples, like Steve Andrews and Jane Martin in *The Blob* or Stan Kenyon and Susan Rogers in *The Eye Creatures*, were innocently affectionate. The behavior of engaged couples, such as John Putnam and Ellen Fields in *It Came from Outer Space* or Dave Miller and Cathy Barrett in *The Monolith Monsters*, was already moving toward the appearance of chastity that characterized marriage in these films. Of course there were a few exceptions. The alien inhabiting Steve Marsh's body in *The Brain from Planet Arous* causes Marsh to kiss his fiancée so intensely that he makes her "toes tingle." He even rips her blouse before the family dog intervenes. A facially scarred model bumps and grinds in her underwear to sleazy stripper music as a knot of men ogle and photograph her in the foul *The Brain That Wouldn't Die.*

"Of all the social uprisings of the late 1960s and early 1970s, none was more popular than the sexual revolution," Collins writes. Surprisingly, though, the watershed films of 1968 were not much different from the films of the Fifties in the importance they attached to depicting sexual relations. Cmdr. Mike Blaiswick and his wife do make love on the beach in *Mission Mars* before he goes off into space (as a result of which she becomes happily pregnant). However, the married couples in *Countdown* are more at odds with each other than they are sexually amorous. Except for his initial misguided grab at her, Alice Kinnian and Charly canoodle romantically, but there are no overt intimations of sex between them. Cornelius and Zira's kisses in *Planet of the Apes* are affectionate and charming. There is no sex at all in *2001*. But then there was *Barbarella*.

As far as taking an ideological stance or assuming a particular point of view, *Barbarella* is essentially incoherent. Barbarella and the Earth of her time abhor weaponry, yet it is the use of weaponry that protects Barbarella from the Black Guards and others who would attack her. Barbarella is innocent and good and the Black Queen is evil, yet Pygar, the blind angel, rescues them both at the end of the film. Barbarella is surprised by how much she enjoys traditional sex, but the liberated sex that she and the people of Earth have come to enjoy is depicted as fantastic. (It literally curls her hair.) What *Barbarella* actually amounts to is a series of sex scenes taking place in a succession of visually astonishing locations.[6] And the theatrical trailer for the film does not pretend to offer anything other than that. Like a carny barker on a traveling circuit, the male voiceover entices us:

> See Barbarella do her thing with a nice angel, with a warm and friendly ice man, with a cold, evil Black Queen, with a charming hand-to-hand Romeo. See Barbarella do her thing in the wild Excessive Machine, in the Biting

Bird Cage, in the Chamber of Dreams, in the Labyrinth of Love, in the Deadly Doll House, in the Palace of Pleasure. (Suggested for mature audiences.)

In seizing the sexual zeitgeist of the Sixties so immediately and so enthusiastically, *Barbarella* introduced the act of sex as a plausible theme for the science fiction film.

Collins writes, "The big thought of the 1960s was that sex should become a perfectly natural part of everyday life, not much more dramatic and profound than a handshake" (175), as is Barbarella's attitude toward sex. After the virile Catchman rescues her from the Deadly Doll House, for example, Barbarella thanks him. "I'm so grateful for what you've done," she says. "I'm positive I could get you some sort of recompense from my government. If there's anything you need or I can do, please tell me." Obviously attracted to Barbarella's stunning physical beauty, the Catchman replies, "Well, you could let me make love to you." "Well, all right," Barbarella casually replies. They both enjoy the sex and then, without guilt or the pressure of commitment (or the possibility of pregnancy), continue on their way.

Collins further notes, "The older generation blamed the birth control pill for what they saw as a frightening upsurge in premarital sex." "Women weren't afraid they were going to get pregnant anymore, so why not?" she quotes a member of that older generation as saying (159). Indeed, sex on Barbarella's Earth of the future relies on "exaltation transference pellets," also referred to in the film as "The Pill." Not only casual, sex has evolved into an uncomplicated, emotionless quest for carnal pleasure. It has become untethered from love, meaning, morality. In attempting to dissuade the Catchman from having sex with her the old-fashioned way, Barbarella explains to him, "It was pointless to continue it when other substitutes for ego support and self-esteem were made available."

Many of the films in the Middle Period follow this approach of representing sex as a casual act. However, they do so in a way that disavows the innocent pleasure that *Barbarella* portrayed. Moreover, the consequences that the Pill alleviated for women are metaphorically transferred onto their relationships with the men who have sex with them. Of course Mary-Lou is going to have sex with enigmatic and charming Thomas Jerome Newton in *The Man Who Fell to Earth* soon after she meets him, but she recoils when he suddenly ejaculates through the palm of his hand. It does not take his more experienced friend very long to convince Peter Martin to have sex with a robotic prostitute (a Stepford Whore, if you will) in *Westworld*, and he likes it very much—despite the sudden electronic deadening of her eyes that the audience sees as Martin lies spent on top of her. Naturally Dr. Paul Holliston, a sad widower, is eventually going to have sex with the devoted and sensuous Victoria in *Embryo*— despite the fact that he created her from embryonic tissue in his lab and does not yet realize that she is going to metamorphose into a rapidly aging killer.

As well as instances of casual sex, there are two noteworthy incidents of rape in *Barbarella*: one is a metaphorical gang rape, the other an attempt at a non-metaphorical one. In true incomprehensible Barbarella fashion, Barbarella reacts with trust and naiveté toward both. In the beginning of her travels, Barbarella encounters two wicked children who lead her to the Deadly Doll House, where a score of vicious dolls with pointed, bloody, razor-sharp teeth chomp at her inner thighs and in between her legs. Tied up, she throws her head back, writhes, and moans—all in a manner that, despite the wounds on her legs, suggests sexual ecstasy. Though shaken, she is not traumatized. It is this event from which the Catchman rescues her and immediately after which she nonchalantly removes her bloody garments and has sex with him. When Barbarella arrives in Sogo, "a city dedicated to evil in every form," the audience sees three cave-men like brutes ogling Barbarella from above. The next image we see is of a nearly nude woman—unconscious, sliced bloody, legs splayed open—lying right next to her. Then we see two of the brutes come downstairs, grab Barbarella, and throw her to the ground. Frightened, she asks, "What do you want of me?" Leering and drooling, the two men look knowingly at each other. "Oh," Barbarella says, bemusedly. Fortunately, she is saved yet again.

Unfortunately, this trope of sexualized violence against women was seized on by several of the films of the Middle Period. *Barbarella* is a fantasy. Our heroine's hyperbolic innocence and trust protect her from all of the evil she encounters. The scenes of sexualized violence in the Middle Period films, however, are not fantastic. The victims are not rescued. Their ordeals are depicted as stark reality. *A Boy and His Dog*, for example, opens with the aggravated rape of a young woman by a horde of marauding rovers in the devastated post-atomic Earth of 2024. After his experimental brain surgery malfunctions, Harry Benson in *The Terminal Man* stabs his girlfriend to death after he has had intercourse with her. As he thrusts his knife into her again and again and again, she writhes and tosses her head from side to side, her expression not at all unlike Barbarella's as she is being devoured by the razor-toothed dolls. The most egregious examples of this trope, however, are seen in the award-winning, critically acclaimed *A Clockwork Orange*.

Barbarella (Jane Fonda) being rescued by the virile Catchman (Ugo Tognazzi) in *Barbarella* (1968).

Approximately one minute into *A Clockwork Orange* the audience is treated to sculptures of nude women with splayed-open legs and high-lighted pubic areas being used as footstools by Alex and his droogs in the Korova Milk Bar. Four minutes later, we see an attempted gang rape of a woman who struggles and screams as she is stripped and wrestled onto a discarded mattress. As Alex, our charismatic narrator, casually informs us, "it was around by the derelict casino that we came across Billy-Boy and his four droogs. They were getting ready to perform a little of the old in-out, in-out on a weepy young devotchka they had there." A few minutes later, the notorious "Singin' in the Rain" rape sequence begins. Here we see Alex gleefully humiliate, slap, gag, and strip a woman whose house he and his gang have invaded. We see the actual rape through the helpless, horrified eyes of her beaten and ultimately paralyzed husband. As the droogs manhandle her in preparation for the rape, she tosses her head from side to side, but her expression cannot in any way be interpreted as pleasure. Welcome to a "sore and sick community," as one character describes it, of ultraviolent young males, untethered from the civilizing influences of traditional social structures.

There are so many images of sexual violence toward women in this film, that they almost define it. A bar patron drinks a night-cap that spurts from the nipple of a sculpture of a nude woman, for example. A charcoal drawing of a woman lying on her back, legs splayed open, is seen on the wall of Alex's bedroom. Alec's pet snake roosts on a perch between her

Droogs preparing to rape Mrs. Alexander (Adrienne Corri) in the infamous "Singin' in the Rain" sequence in *A Clockwork Orange* (1972).

legs nuzzling her vagina. Two young women in a shopping emporium slurp popsicles shaped like penises. We are first introduced to a woman that Alex and his droogs want to rob by a close-up image of her vagina, her legs splayed open in a yoga pose. Alex rams a giant ceramic sculpture of a penis and testicles into her face, killing her.

In "The Myth of the Heroic Rapist," a section in her groundbreaking 1975 study *Against Our Will: Men, Women and Rape*, Susan Brownmiller cited one of "the ecstatic reviews" of *A Clockwork Orange*, a film in which, as she claimed, "Kubrick glamorized sadistic little Alex to extravagant proportions." The (male) reviewer described the film as "a statement of what it is to be truly human." "Alex appeals to something dark and primal in all of us," he explained. "He acts out our desire for instant sexual gratification, for the release of our angers and repressed instincts for revenge, our need for adventure and excitement." Brownmiller responded that Alex does not act out the desires of women, who "had no role in the picture other than as victim of assault" (302). Having seen the film in 1972 and again now as I am writing about it, I can say most assuredly that I know how Brownmiller felt.

Responding to the charge that the market determines the product, Brownmiller argued, "Movie producers, who are male, give the public *their own* concept of what the world is about" (306). Indeed, *Barbarella* was produced from a male perspective and for the male gaze, but the filmmakers (especially Roger Vadim, the film's director and Jane Fonda's husband) loved Barbarella. They celebrated women's sexual power, as did so many men of the era. Collins writes that "as the '60s rolled along, it seemed clear that quite a few respectable middle-class young women had ditched the double standard completely. And the respectable middle-class young men responded enthusiastically" (157–158), as do the men in *Barbarella*.

While Dildano's hair literally stands on end after he has sex with Barbarella, Pygar is rejuvenated. "I've regained the will to fly!" he shouts as he soars through the air after a most satisfying encounter with our heroine. As the two of them, embracing, fly on to Sogo, Barbarella uses her phallic "mini-missile projector" to fight off attacks by the evil Black Guards. "A little to the right," she directs the blind Pygar as she aims and then shoots bright bursts of light. "Up, Pygar. Up! Oooooooohhhh, Pygar!" she cries out until her "energy box" is finally exhausted. In this metaphorical sex scene, the male is quite willing to follow the woman's directions in order to afford satisfaction for them both.

Two Middle Period films exemplify the parameters filmmakers placed around women's burgeoning sexual freedom as well as male terror of it: the repellant *A Boy and His Dog* and the quasi-pornographic *Invasion of the Bee Girls*. Collins writes, "The sexual revolution was about more than whether women should be able to feel as free as men to have sex before marriage. It was also about whether women—single or married—had as much right to *enjoy* sex (167). Reaction to this rather obvious petition, however, incorporated further information about just would this *enjoyment* would require.

In *Sexual Politics*, Kate Millett cites W. H. Masters and Virginia Johnson, who shared results of their studies in "Orgasms, Anatomy of the Female"[7] as follows:

> If a female who is capable of having regular orgasms is properly stimulated within a short period after her first climax, she will, in most instances, be capable of having a second, third, fourth, and even a fifth and sixth orgasm before she is fully satiated. As contrasted with the male's usual inability to have more than one orgasm in a short period, many females, especially when clitorally stimulated, can regularly have five or six full orgasms within a matter of minutes [117].

As Millett paraphrases, "while the male's sexual potential is limited, the female's appears to be biologically nearly inexhaustible, and apart from psychological considerations, may continue until physical exhaustion interposes" (117–118).

We see a demonstration of this inexhaustibility in *Barbarella*. The evil Concierge installs Barbarella into what he refers to as an Excessive Machine. As he plays "Sonata for Executioner and Various Young Women" on the machine's keyboard, he informs Barbarella, "When we reach the crescendo, you will die of pleasure." Barbarella, however, does not die of pleasure. As a matter of fact, she quite enjoys herself. She writhes, moans, and wails in at first curiosity ("What is this thing?"), then pleasure ("It's sort of nice, isn't it?"), and finally ecstasy (Aaahhhh!). "The energy cables are shrinking! You've turned them into fagots!" the Concierge shrieks in dismay as the machine begins to smolder. "You've exhausted its power. It couldn't keep up with you!" he cries. In the end, Barbarella—victorious—lies back in dreamy satisfaction as flames circle the ruined machine.

Of course the Concierge intends *fagot* to mean, as defined on dictionary.com, "a bundle of sticks, twigs, or branches bound together and used as fuel," but the allusion, of course, is to *faggot*, the more common (and disparaging) term, for a homosexual man. And what stridently heterosexual man would care to have his sexuality so questioned due to the fact that his "cables" shrink when he tries to satisfy the insatiable new woman? Such is the circumstance of our hero in *A Boy and His Dog*.

"You mean you want me to knock up your broads?"

In *A Boy and His Dog*, Vic (played by a tumescent young Don Johnson) is virtually defined by his heterosexual virility. "It's been six weeks since I've been laid," he complains to his faithful dog Blood. "How am I gonna nail her in there?" he asks when he finds a woman hiding in an underground bunker. "You make one move, I'll shoot your leg right out from under you, and you'll still get it except you'll be without a leg," he orders a woman he is preparing to rape.

Tricked by the woman, he soon finds himself in a bizarre post-apocalyptic underground realm, where he is informed, "Our women can't get pregnant. Every once in a while we need new blood. We need a new man. A special kind of man." One of the Elders explains that "metabolic changes have resulted from lengthy subterranean living" (as was often characteristic of post-apocalyptic futures in Fifties films such as *World Without End* and *Beyond the Time Barrier*). "You mean you want me to knock up your broads?" Vic exclaims. He is at first flattered, then jubilant. "You talked me into it. Line 'em up!" he shouts as he begins to take off his clothes.

The next image we have of him, he is lying on his back, hands cuffed, hooked up to another version of the Excessive Machine, his semen dripping continuously into a test tube. His mouth is taped. His lower body is covered by a surgical drape (under which we assume is a pump). He breathes heavily, arching his back, pleading with his eyes, as couple after couple are joined in holy matrimony before him. Eventually, the woman he tried to rape and who lured him into this situation in the first place, decides to rescue him for herself. "I didn't bring you down here so *they* could use you. I brought you down her so *I* could use you," she says. Vic lets her lead him back to the surface, after which, his virility under siege, he kills her, roasts her, and feeds her to his faithful dog. (Sorry for the spoiler, but you should know.)

Admittedly, the woman had her flaws (she was not nice to the dog, for one), but I believe Vic was horrified at what was expected of him as a male. (His sperm was to impregnate thirty-five women and then he was to be killed after his usefulness expired.) It would be much easier for him to relate to a non-human companion (like Cmdr. Kit Draper and his monkey Mona) and occasionally rape someone (like Alex and his droogs) than to be with someone (like Barbarella) who embodied the potential to emasculate him.

"We balled, and we balled, and we balled..."

Invasion of the Bee Girls opens with a prominent scientist (married) found dead from extreme exhaustion in a motel room. Julie Zorn, a research librarian who worked closely with him, is accused by the film's protagonist, government agent Neil Agar and Zorn's eventual love interest, of being involved in his death. "We balled, and we balled, and we balled ...'til he dropped dead," she sarcastically counters. Her statement is prescient, however, as one man after another is soon found dead in the small town of Peckham. Cause of death is "over-exhaustion in the act of sexual intercourse," according to the county sheriff. (One man, a closeted homosexual, escapes this type of death. He is deliberately run over by a car—driven by a spurned Bee Girl—instead.)

Dying from too much sex does not particularly concern the film's heterosexual males, however, as one of them jocularly remarks to his colleagues, "Just think about it, boys. Coming and going at the same time!" No, what the film implicitly cautions against is not just the potential for women to experience multiple orgasms, but also the reality of the clitoral orgasm (and consequent myth of the vaginal one). In "Humiliating Fantasies and the Pursuit of Unpleasure" (1997), Arnold H. Modell explicates Freud's *Three Essays on the Theory of Sexuality* (1905):

> Freud believed that girls at puberty have the difficult task of transferring the zone of sexual arousal from the clitoris—an analogue of the penis—to the vagina. At puberty girls must give up the active masculine mode in order to become passive and feminine. Consequently, vaginal orgasm is the hallmark of mature femininity, where clitoral orgasm is an immature vestige of masculinity [67–68].

Even Modell in his own essay admits that this concept of "female sexual physiology" is "mistaken" (67).

Thus, if the locus of female pleasure does not specifically require penile penetration,[8] then one can conclude that, at least as far as the basics of sex, men could be considered expendable—hence, the looming threat of lesbianism to the heterosexual dyad—lesbianism, the line that even our sexually flexible Barbarella would not cross. Wooed by the Great Tyrant, played by striking Rolling Stone paramour Anita Pallenberg—"You're very pretty, pretty, pretty," she coos—Barbarella's rebuff is swift and certain: "My name isn't pretty pretty. It's Barbarella."

In "What Has Never Been: An Overview of Lesbian Feminist Literary Criticism" (1997), Bonnie Zimmerman rather optimistically asserts, "As lesbians in a heterosexist academy, we have continued to explore the impact of 'otherness,' suggesting dimensions previously ignored and yet necessary to understand fully the female condition and the creative work born from it" (76). In *Invasion of the Bee Girls*, however, lesbianism is not portrayed as something that one can, like Barbarella, simply refuse. Rather we see it as a sinister prelude to the literal death of men. Because the Bee Girls (being bees) can mate only once, as explained in the film's requisite exposition scene, the widows of the dead men are recruited, encased in a pupa-like substance, and subjected to an erotic lesbian ritual (replete with nudity, kissing, fondling, lip licking, and ravenous glances), after which they emerge ready to kill in order to recruit more women.

When Zorn is surreptitiously recruited (she has figured out the scientific process by which the women are being mutated), she is stripped, her long hair is released from its maiden-like bun, and her glasses are removed. Before she is fully converted, however, she is rescued by Agar, who destroys the Bee Girls by shooting out their electronic equipment with his gun thus incinerating both them and their lair (not unlike the fates of the ants in *Them!* or the man-hating Queen Yllana in *Queen of Outer Space*).

In the final scene, Agar leads Zorn into the bedroom (hers) as he indulgently listens to her expound on her latest ideas, then gently lets her hair down, tosses her playfully onto the bed, and pounces on top of her. He kisses her, long and lovingly. "What were you saying?" he asks. "Oh shut up," she responds, and they begin to make love (him on top). *Bee Girls* is a truly cheap and tawdry film. It is not listed in *Variety's Complete Science Fiction Reviews*. Telotte does not mention it. Neither does Vivian Sobchack in *Screening Space: The American Science Fiction Film* (1987). In fact, a Trivia comment on the film's Internet Movie Database site states, "a horrified Hollywood newcomer Nicholas Meyer tried to have his name removed from the screen credits but was talked out of it by his manager." Nonetheless, at the unfortunate expense of the lesbian Other, but in contrast to the misogyny of so many films of the period, a bit of joy has been restored to the contemporary sex act in the end.

This is science fiction. Vagaries and complications of the sex act can be elided when sex becomes estranged in a speculative imagination of the future. Sex can be forbidden as it is in the sterile *THX 1138* ("This is City Probe Scanner. We've run across some illegal sexual activity"). Or it can be made commonplace, even more so than it is in *Barbarella*, as it is with

Sleeper's whimsical Orgasmatron. One of the funniest lines in the film (of any film, in fact) is the heroine's comment to her handsome partner (male) after their brief (but satisfying) dalliance in the machine: "Oh, that was wonderful! I feel so refreshed. I think we should have had sex, but there weren't enough people." Can sex really be that uncomplicated? (Of course not.)

Race

In the films of the Middle Period, African American characters in ordinary occupations are more fully integrated into the periphery than they were in the films of the Fifties. Considering the burgeoning computer industry, many black extras are seen as computer operators (primarily male).[9] Following the trajectory established in the 1968 films *Countdown* and *Charly*, some of these extras engage in (usually uncredited) dialogue. A senior computer analyst in *Westworld* explains to a colleague, for example, "It's only a theoretical concept. There are many ways to order that data." An analyst in *Demon Seed* observes, "The systems are all out-checking themselves."

In *Colossus: The Forbin Project* black actor Georg Sanford Brown has a featured role as Dr. John Fisher, Programming Unit Director. To a suggestion made by his boss Dr. Cleo Markham he responds, "Good. That's well within specification limits." As the film progresses, Dr. Markham clearly enacts a female role, having sex as she does with the film's protagonist. There is no reference, however, to Fisher's race in the film. He participates equitably in the action, even proposing to Dr. Charles Forbin, the film's senior scientist, a way to defeat Colossus, the power hungry computer, in its attempt at taking over the world. "Why don't we try for an overload, giving the system too many tasks?" he suggests. Unfortunately, following the genre's trajectory of a black character's being one of the first to be killed, as seen in Fifties films such as *Attack of the Killer Shrews* and even 1998's *Sphere*, Fisher is executed on Colossus's orders for his insolent attempt to defeat it. Again, on Colossus's orders, Fisher's dead body must remain exposed outdoors on the spot where he was killed (not unlike Polyneices, whose exposure to the elements so antagonizes Antigone) for 24 hours.

As well as workers in the field of computing, African American actors (again, primarily male) appear as athletes and sports auxiliary personnel,[10] news reporters and photographers,[11] policemen,[12] and military men.[13] In *Colossus*, a black man is even depicted as Secretary of Defense. Such representation of African Americans in military positions is consistent with Department of Defense Directive 5120.36, issued in 1963: "It is the policy of the Department of Defense to conduct all of its activities in a manner which is free from racial discrimination, and which provides equal opportunity for all uniformed members and all civilian employees irrespective of their color." There is a brief televised image of a black man (very light skinned) as a high-level corporate executive in *Rollerball*. Black actor Lincoln Kilpatrick plays the featured part of Paul, a disillusioned priest, in *Soylent Green*. Unfortunately, like Fisher, he is killed (by a villainous white man) well before the end of the picture.

African American men and women appear together as party guests,[14] audience members[15] tourists,[16] church congregation members,[17] and more significantly, as would be expected in a genre concerned with developments in science, in groups of doctors and medical personnel.[18] On their own, however, African American women are not so generously represented. Only two African American women are depicted as computer operators—one in *Rollerball* and another in *Demon Seed*. A black actress (uncredited) is a hair salon manager in *Conquest of the Planet of the Apes* ("No, Zelda! Home, Zelda! I'm so sorry, Mrs. Riley. I'll have someone to comb you out in just a minute," she shouts, upset with one of her ape hairdressers). Another is briefly seen in a maid's uniform serving hors d'oeuvres at a party in *Embryo*.

More frequently African American women are depicted gratuitously, as exotics. In its overplayed attempt at Sixties hipness, *Moon Zero Two* begins with a title song sung by the GoJos (a girl group) who jubilantly declare, "We love the world we land on, and love is what we'll be makin.'" Soon we are introduced to an exceptionally beautiful, nearly nude black woman with a dramatic Afro, reclining on a velvet-like couch. She is the mistress of a space lord. It takes a minute before we see the silver handcuffs and chain that restrain her. THX 1138 (a white man) stares at a nude black woman, bald, undulating to rhythmic music on the hologram screen in front of his futuristic masturbation apparatus. In *The Terminal Man*, a nearly nude black stripper performs with a white man (dressed in a suit), who rips off her panties, gratuitously exposing her bare backside to an audience of patrons (including ourselves, who are watching the movie).

In *Black Space: Imagining Race in Science Fiction Film* (2008), Adilifu Nama points out how "past constructions of the black body as primitive, a repository of unbridled sexuality, and a phallic danger ... return camouflaged in science fiction film" (71). Such less than progressive representations apply to the men in the films of the Middle Period as well as to the women discussed above. In *Beneath the Planet of the Apes*, set in 3955 AD, black actor Don Pedro Colley (listed in the film's credits as Negro) is the largest and most vicious member of a council of mutated humans. He is ultimately killed by the film's two white protagonists, his body gruesomely impaled on the protruding spikes of a metal gate. Colley also appears in *THX 1138* as the imposing hologram SRT, his blackness exaggerated by the stark whiteness of the film's mise-en-scène. SRT rescues the film's white protagonist ("That's the way out," he tells him), who ultimately abandons him to a gruesome death by car crash at the film's end.

Colley's is not the only representation of a black man as a loyal aide to a white man. In *Rollerball*, for example, Cletus (played by black actor Moses Gunn) is the trainer and former coach of the film's white protagonist, an athlete. "Shoulder forward left. You're standing on your left skate. You do that in Tokyo, they'll take your arm home for lunch," he advises him as they spar. Further, when the protagonist realizes he might be in trouble, he asks Cletus to help him. "I talked to everybody I could. There is something going on. You're right about that," Cletus reports back. In *Conquest of the Planet of the Apes*, MacDonald (played by black actor Hari Rhodes) is referred to as the white governor's "number one assistant." Sympathetic to the subjugated apes—which one must read as black, especially in this particular entry in the franchise—MacDonald attempts to stop the anxious governor from exacerbating the apes' growing unrest. "Mr. Governor, on investigation many of the reported offenses have been proved minor," he exhorts. In a reversal of the trope, it is the white governor, not his African American ally, who faces death at the end of the film. (However, the filmmakers did not allow the apes to actually kill the villainous white governor; in the end, the ape leaders relent and allow him to live.) In a more progressive perspective on the trope, MacDonald's brother, also referred to as MacDonald (played by Austin Stoker; Rhodes was unavailable), is top aide and confidante to Caesar, King of Ape City. His efforts, however, do not lead to ape supremacy, but rather to an eventual reconciliation between apes and humans.

It should be noted, however, that all the humans in Ape City as represented twelve years after the 1991 ape conquest are white. It is not until 2670 AD that a black human other than MacDonald, a young black girl in pigtails (uncredited), has a presence, uttering the film's penultimate line: "Lawgiver, who knows about the future?" Such token representation of black characters is curious. Did the filmmakers suddenly realize that their future world was devoid of African Americans and attempt finally to address that omission? Did they perhaps introduce a black character as a sop to the box office? One can be grateful for at least the token, however, for there are no black people at all in 2293 AD as depicted in *Zardoz* or in the 23rd century as depicted in *Logan's Run*. Could this omission have been an unintentional oversight?

There are no black people in *The Stepford Wives'* ominous little town—until the final scene, that is. As the white Stepford wives docilely promenade down supermarket aisles, we see in the periphery a black couple. The woman is clearly not a Stepford wife, based on her casual, comfortable clothing, as opposed to the stylized outfits worn by the Stepford wives, and by the animated way she is talking to the man with her. How can this sudden appearance of race be interpreted? Again, did the filmmakers suddenly realize their omission? Or perhaps the filmmakers intended to intimate "You're next," marginally including black women in the struggle for women's liberation. Or perhaps the black woman is exempt, too strong to submit to such patriarchal contrivances. When interpretations are left open (advertently or inadvertently), I like to read the film as I wish.

My often hopeful readings of science fiction films are occasionally supported by the films themselves. In *The Andromeda Strain*, for example, black actress Paula Kelly has a featured role as a woman in science: Karen Anson, a nurse in Wildfire, a government sponsored secure underground laboratory. "Medcom's got one of the best minds here. It's a medical data analyzer that can diagnose as well as prescribe. It's hooked up to the main computer on Level 1. Every console and instrument in Wildfire is plugged into the main computer on a time-sharing basis," she authoritatively explains to the film's (white, male) physician. Like Cora Peterson in *Fantastic Voyage*, she wears a professional outfit: a white pants suit with long sleeves and a high scooped collar. Her hair is styled in a short, straight bob. During the film, she instructs the film's doctor on how to use Medcom, draws blood, and assists him with physical exams and treatments of isolated, infected survivors of a biological catastrophe. She even acts the heroine when everyone in the compound believes that one of the film's protagonists has been infected. Anson understands that the woman is having an epileptic seizure and rushes to help her. Would there were more representations like hers.

Despite the science fiction film's tendency, as Nama argues, to camouflage racist stereotypes, there are also occasions where it can be provocative, confrontational. In *The Man Who Fell to Earth*, for example, former football player Bernie Casey plays the featured role of Peters, a somewhat shady, high-level government operative, whose job it is to sabotage the fantastically successful enterprise the film's alien has established. "The problem with this corporation," he informs his superior, "is that it is technologically overstimulated and the economic trouble stems from that fact." Irrelevant to this character's purpose is a prurient nude scene between him and a white woman (who we only later discover is his wife and mother of his child). In his *DVD Verdict* review, Bill Gibron precisely describes this scene and its effect:

> One of the most amazing moments comes toward the end of the film, when government "fixer" Bernie Casey, a huge, athletic black man, takes a nude swim with his naked blond Caucasian wife. As he rises from the water, glistening and muscled, the couple caresses in a slow-motion embrace meant to make the blood boil in any bigot buying a ticket. Casey's casual glance toward the camera ... creates a kind of middle finger to anyone still debating such "should be settled" issues as race and place.

The speculative nature of science fiction film does allow for such challenging representations.

"Up against the wall, you mother!"

When black actors play more central roles, heightened ideological readings of race cannot be avoided. In *The Omega Man*, set in post-apocalyptic future, paragon of white maleness, Charlton Heston, as in *Planet of the Apes*, plays the film's hero—Robert Neville. In a DVD Special Feature, *The Omega Man* co-screenwriter Joyce Corrington comments on the casting of Heston's co-star, black actress Rosalind Cash, as Lisa, the film's heroine: "It was my idea to make her black. I was teaching in a black university at the time," she says, "and this is the 70s and black power was very big, so we were thinking you have the last man on earth meet the last woman on earth, what's the conflict? I thought, let's make her black and then we'll get a little racial pizzazz in there," and they do. The love scene between Heston and Cash is groundbreaking and beautiful.

> LISA (touching his cheek): Now what's this stuff about me being the only girl in the world?
> (*The two of them engage in a lingering kiss. They fall to the floor in an embrace.*)
> NEVILLE: Do you know it's been a long long time? I'm not sure I remember how this goes.
> (*The music swells as they begin to make love.*)

As hopeful as this scene appears, it is impossible not to notice the overall racial configurations that then result.

Nama astutely reads the film as a coded response to contemporary racial tensions, meticulously citing, as does Eric Greene in *Planet of the Apes as American Myth*, pertinent comparisons between the film's non-human creatures and the circumstances of black Americans (48). "With its visual coding of blackness," Nama writes, "*The Omega Man* was a thinly veiled attack again the black nationalist state of the black freedom movement" (51). There is a moment in the film, however, where the comparison is more direct. One of the film's mutated humans is black—though all of them, as Nama writes, have "acquired an extreme form of albinism, marked by a peculiar grayish white face paint" (47). Zachary (another role for black actor Lincoln Kilpatrick), following the trope of the black side-kick, is second in command to the white leader Matthias. Staring up at Neville's penthouse refuge, they engage in the following exchange:

> MATTHIAS: One creature, caught. Caught in a place he cannot stir from in the dark. Alone. Outnumbered, hundreds to one. Nothing to live for but his memories. Nothing to live with but his gadgets, his cars, his guns, gimmicks. And yet the whole Family can't bring him down out of that ...
> ZACHARY: ... that *honky* paradise, brother?
> MATTHIAS: Forget the old ways, brother. All your hatreds, all your pains. Forget. And remember, the Family is one.

In 1969, historian C. Vann Woodward wrote in *Black Studies: Myths & Realities*, "Denied a past of his own, the Negro was given to understand that whatever history and culture he possessed was supplied by his association with the dominant race in the New World and its European background" (20). Despite the alliance between *The Omega Man*'s black and white antagonists, the idea that once again a black man would be given to understand that his history would be denied, even in this film's post-apocalyptic vision of the future, illustrates the way that ideological readings can arise when blackness is introduced into the plot.

Nama argues that *The Omega Man* is "prominent because of how clearly it imagines and associates race mixing with dire post-apocalyptic consequences" (47), and of course he is right, but a gendered reading of the film indicates as well the precarious position of the African American woman. Once she aligns herself with the white male, according to *The Omega Man*, the black male must be eliminated. In a dramatic scene in which Lisa stands between them, Neville kills Zachary, who falls from Neville's penthouse balcony, his body impaled on metal fence posts. It is only after Zachary's gruesome death that Lisa and Neville make love.

Some time ago, I was able to have lunch with Corrington. (The black university where she had taught, by the way, was Xavier University, where

Lisa (Rosalind Cash) keeps Neville (Charlton Heston) under control in *The Omega Man* (1971) (Photofest).

I currently teach.) She told me that she had written Cash's character as an engineer, familiar as she was with African American women's interest in science. (Corrington was in the Chemistry Department.) This facet of Cash's character was deleted, however. A new character was introduced— a young white medical student (male), who took over the duties that Cash's character would have performed. I asked Corrington why she thought that change was made to her script. She shrugged and said, "That's just the way the movie business works. It was probably too much."

Near the end of the film, Lisa embraces Neville jubilantly exclaiming, "We made it, baby. We really did." Unfortunately for Neville, Lisa ultimately "goes over," reverts to the dark side as it were, succumbs to the inevitable blackness already embodied within her. Nonetheless, just as we can still envision strong women in science from the Fifties films despite the uncertainty of their professional futures, fierce images of an African American woman who was just as apt to shoot a white man ("Up against the wall, you mother!" she commands when she first encounters him) as to make love to him have been indelibly imprinted in our collective consciousness.

"You know, my name's Maybelle too..."

New Yorker writer Tad Friend describes The Bechdel Test, established in 1985 by Alison Bechdel and Liz Wallace as a way of examining movies for gender bias. He writes, "The test poses three questions: Does a movie contain two or more female characters who have names? Do those characters talk to each other? And if so, do they discuss something other than a man?" (52). This test can be extrapolated as well into one that examines a movie for racial bias. Does a movie contain two or more African American characters who have names? Do those characters talk to each other? And if so, do they discuss something other than white people?

Frogs, portent of ecological apocalypse, passes this racial test. Moreover, it passes the gender test as well in a particular scene between two African American women. Bella Garrington is an accomplished African American model and fashion designer (played by Judy Pace, according to the Internet Movie Database often referred to as "The Black Barbie"). She is a confident, outspoken guest of the Old Southern Crockett family at a yearly event at their stereotypical grand plantation. Her personality is established by such confrontational comments as "I didn't *make* this dress. I *designed* it" and "Nobody controls *me*, Mr. Crockett." In contrast, Maybelle, the family's faithful maid (played by actress/blues singer/producer Mae Mercer)[19] makes more subservient comments such as "Another year gone by, Mr. Crockett. Another happy day for errybody [sic]."

For a moment, however, Bella and Maybelle get to connect—as women and as African Americans (as I imagine Maggie and Wangero Lee-wanika Kemanjo, nee Dee, could one day break through

Actress Judy Pace of *Frogs* (1972), also known as The Black Barbie (Photofest).

to each other in a follow-up to Alice Walker's "Everyday Use"). Maybelle, dressed in her gray maid's uniform, is setting the dinner table, not for herself, but for the white family she serves as well as for Bella, their African American guest. Bella, wearing a low-cut sparkling-white gown with dangling black jewelry, offers Maybelle a glass of wine.

BELLA: Maybelle?
MAYBELLE: Oh, I couldn't. Not now.
BELLA: Oh, come on. Live a little bit.
MAYBELLE: Oh well, why not. Don't tell anybody.
BELLA: Hey, a toast to Crockett-land! (Pause) You know, my name's Maybelle too.
MAYBELLE: I thought so!
BELLA: Born and raised in Jackson, Mississippi.
MAYBELLE (as Bella is leaving): Oh, Bella.
BELLA: Yes?
MAYBELLE: There's always hot coffee and a friendly conversation in the kitchen if you ever need it.
BELLA: Thanks, Maybelle. Cause I think I might be needing it.

When I was a student at LSU, I attended a Martin Luther King Day convocation at which critic and intellectual Cornell West invoked an image of the snakes of slavery slithering up the legs of the table on which the Constitution was written. And indeed, this potentially disruptive alliance between two black women on differing paths is not without cost, as we soon see a venomous snake hanging from the chandelier as if to threaten them: "Don't." As Corrington could have said, two strong African American women openly discussing their own lives "was probably too much." By the way, Bella, Maybelle, and the Crockett family's black butler (played by Lance Taylor, Sr.) do not survive the film's catastrophic amphibian assault. The only survivors are the white protagonist, a white woman, and her white children.

◆◆◆

Science fiction films push limits, impressing upon audiences possibilities beyond contemporary mores. However, a science fiction film, extrapolating as it must from reality in order to be science fiction, can only push limits so far without becoming fantasy (or worse, commercially unviable). Science fiction films can show us both what we aspire to and what we must yet struggle for (or against). Applying ideological readings of gender and race can only enhance our appreciation of these films.

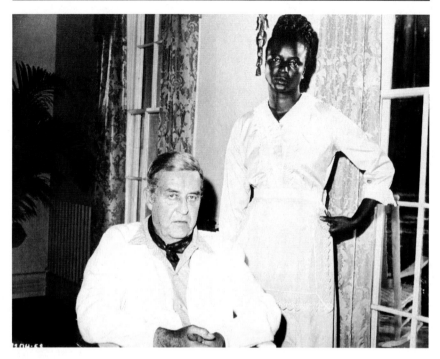

Maybelle (Mae Mercer) tending to Crockett family patriarch (Ray Milland) in *Frogs* (1972) (Photofest).

Dystopia

The science fiction films of the Fifties were characterized more by alien invasions and marauding creatures than by dystopian communities. There were two Earth societies of the future in the Fifties films, however, that suffered particular problems. In the 26th century post-apocalyptic Earth of *World Without End*, the men (not the women) became weak as a result of living underground (in order to protect themselves from the violent, irradiated mutants of the surface), resulting in low birth rates. Moreover, the few babies being born were described as "puny little things." Underground inhabitants of 2024 in *Beyond the Time Barrier* were even more afflicted: The men were sterile. In *World Without End*, Earth's devastation was caused by nuclear war. In *Beyond the Time Barrier*, it was not nuclear war that ruined the Earth, but instead (rather presciently) radiation resulting from the destruction of the ozone layer. In the films of the Middle Period, as a sense of doom began to permeate American society, dystopian futures resulted from more varied causes.

As the Seventies progressed, in addition to the continuing struggles for civil rights and protests against the interminable Vietnam War, America was inundated with clarion calls for precipitous action. The Environmental Protection Agency and Greenpeace were founded, and the first Earth Day was held. Zero population growth was encouraged. Housewives boycotted meat in protest of rising prices. The President instituted wage and price controls. The dollar was devalued. Arab nations instituted an oil embargo. Faith in government waned. The voting age was lowered to eighteen, expanding the influence of America's young people. The country was still reeling in alarm over the Hong Kong Flu pandemic.[20]

True to the genre, science fiction films of the Middle Period capitalized on the nation's anxieties. In *The Omega Man*, humanity has been destroyed by a biochemical plague and one survivor must fight mutated creatures of night that want to kill him. In *Soylent Green*, overpopulation and pollution have resulted in a desperate scarcity of food supplies. A murder has been committed, and a stoic detective must fight increasingly ominous conditions in order to solve it. In *Silent Running*, plant life on Earth has become extinct, and a fanatic astronaut is determined to save it. In *Rollerball*, corporations have taken over the function of government and plot to crush the independent image of a popular sports figure. In *Logan's Run*, no one is allowed to live beyond the age of thirty.

"On the bed now..."

Soylent Green, set in the year 2022, opens with images of massive overpopulation, air and water pollution, homeless people crammed in filthy heaps on stairwells, two men living in an apartment where one has to pedal a stationary bicycle to keep the lights on with only "tasteless, odorless crud" for food. As it turns out though, women—some women, that is—can escape this crumbling of civilization by attaching themselves not to a man, but rather to a building. The nicer the place a man can afford, the fancier is his "furniture." Shirl (played by a youthful Leigh Taylor-Young) comes with the apartment rented by a high level executive. In the face of extreme shortages he is able to treat her to fresh lettuce, a ripe tomato, beef, hot water in the bathroom, and even a new video game. These fancier pieces of furniture—all races are represented equally; youth and beauty, not ethnicity, are the determining criteria—are supervised by building managers (aka pimps) who feel free to slap them around if they step out of line. "I'll teach you to break my rules," Shirl's pimp angrily shouts.

A woman attached to a cheaper building, such as the one occupied by a functionary bodyguard, is not afforded such luxuries. Martha (played by a luminous Paula Kelly) is able at least to scrimp some white rice and a bit of strawberry jam. It is likewise acceptable to knock her around, as does the film's protagonist, Detective Thorn (Charlton Heston). (Thorn does not hit the fancier pieces of furniture; he simply expects one to have sex with him. "On the bed now," he orders.) Comes the apocalypse, the film implicitly warns, women will not be men's equals.

When I was a young adult, I fought the rigidity of stereotypes and insistence on female inequality. For example, I thought it would be fun to be a house painter (as well as its being better paying than being a receptionist). I was told that, as a female, painting houses was something I could not do. So I got a job as a house painter. As Gail Caldwell, Pulitzer Prize winner for criticism, writes in her memoir *A Strong West Wind* (2007), "The earliest effect of feminism was a widening of spirit, which meant simply that you burst through the margins of a preordained life" (103).

Shirl (Leigh Taylor-Young) and Thorn (Charlton Heston) preparing to have sex in *Soylent Green* (1973).

Climbing scaffolds and ladders, slinging paint, cursing with the guys was a great adventure for me with my strong young body. I was cute, too—well, as cute as someone who is not naturally beautiful can be. I sang in an (unintentionally non-profit) all-girl rock and roll band. My concerned mother constantly reminded me that I should be saving and planning for my retirement. Retirement? I was only in my twenties! By the time I reached thirty, however, I was not so strong. I was not so cute. Being a house painter had become not so much a daring jaunt as it had become a tedious occupation for which I—a small woman, with a talent for language as opposed to physical labor—was unsuited. I gave up the deceptive illusions of my exuberant youth. I applied for a student loan. I went back to school. I chose a career. I decided that becoming an adult might not be so bad. Such is the metaphor on which the plot of *Logan's Run* is based.

"Beloved wife..."

When you reach thirty, *Logan's Run* posits, your life is over. You must die. The film opens with an epigram stating, "Here, in an ecologically balanced world, mankind lives only for pleasure." Indeed, Logan's futuristic world embodies all the paraphernalia and pleasures of the Seventies: miniskirts, men with long coiffed hair, flashy colored clothing, casual near-nudity, thoroughly equipped work-out centers with soothing whirlpool baths, mind-altering drugs whenever you want them, non-monogamous sex on request, little need for demanding employment, and everyone beautiful, healthy, and fit. Even Farrah Fawcett-Majors' ultimately ubiquitous shag haircut (I had one) makes its debut.

Additionally, true to the science fiction genre, this world of the future hypothesizes technological advances. There is no longer any need to worry about food. In fact, when Jessica, the film's heroine, encounters abandoned underground "breeding pens," Logan explains to her that "people used to breed animals, fish, anything. To eat, you know?" "Must have been a savage world," she replies in disgust. For nourishment, it seems, everyone sips rose-colored liquid from delicate champagne flutes. There is no need to drive. Rapid transport vehicles are powered by unseen forces. If you get "sick of your face," "New You" emporiums can provide plastic surgery as easily as you can get new eyeglasses. Temperature is regulated for comfort. Logan's entire world, as a matter of fact, is covered by a hermetically sealed, translucent dome, protecting it from post-apocalyptic ravages outside.

More important than the technological presumptions, a critical aspect of this new society is sexual freedom. Logan casually dials up a sex partner from "the circuit," for example, who is delivered right to his living quarters by a transporter-like device. By mistake, he is sent a male. He is unruffled. He simply sends the man back. When Jessica, the woman he is sent, initially resists his advances, Logan suspects another mistake and calmly says, "Oh, do you prefer women?" In this future world, homosexuality does not appear to be a scourge. Perhaps one of the reasons for this acceptance is that the sex act itself has become disconnected from pregnancy, birth, and parenting. There is a nursery with babies, but where they come from is not made really clear. Reference is made to "seed mothers" and apparently outmoded "human mothering," but it is clear that children are raised without even their ostensible parents knowing who they are. Females do not endure the pain of giving birth; neither the male nor the female is responsible for long, even short-term parenting. Further, though the inhabitants of this society are freely engaging in sexual activity, there is no mention of or apparent need for birth control. Sex is represented as easily available, uncomplicated, polymorphous, and consequence free. Discotheques of the Seventies are now portrayed as literal orgy parlors complete with strobe lights, neon, and mind-altering drugs piped in like smoke.

Telotte refers to *Logan's Run* as "an *ironic* utopia" (133). Of course Logan's world of eternal youth is not a utopia at all. Though its inhabitants believe they will be "renewed" on "Carrousel," this renewal never occurs. Carrousel is really a death machine.[21] Telotte reports that ideological critics read *Logan's Run* as "a dystopian story of rebellion against a futuristic, technologically sustained city-state, [one] superficially indicting the military-industrial complex of modern America." Further, he notes, they read the film as ultimately enacting "a fundamentally conservative turn, affirming rather than subverting the individualistic status quo that undergirds American culture, while linking technology to all that might threaten the status quo" (41–42). Yes, Logan and Jessica ultimately escape this ironic utopia in the film's ostensibly optimistic conclusion, but it is not just technology and conformity that they leave behind. What they leave behind more directly, in my reading of the film, is the ideology of radical feminism.

Here is what radical feminist Shulamith Firestone wrote in 1970 in her exhaustive critique of Freudian and Marxist thought, *The Dialectic of Sex: The Case for Feminist Revolution*, stridently described on a Bantam reprint cover as "a slashing attack on male supremacy that charts the end of the sexual class system":

> The end goal of feminist revolution must be, unlike that of the first femi-
> nist movement, not just the elimination of male *privilege*, but of the sex
> *distinction* itself: genital distinctions of human beings would no longer
> matter culturally. (A reversion to an unobstructed *pansexuality*—Freud's
> "polymorphous perversity"—would probably supersede hetero/homo/bi-
> sexuality.) The reproduction of the species by one sex for the benefit of
> both would be replaced by (at least the option of) artificial reproduction:
> children would be born to both sexes equally, or independently of either,
> however one chooses to look at it; the dependence of the child on the
> mother (and vice versa) would give way to a greatly shortened dependence
> on a small group of others in general..... The division of labor would be
> ended by the elimination of labor altogether (through cybernetics). The
> tyranny of the biological family would be broken [11].

Does not this passage quite succinctly describe Logan's world? It is almost
as if the screenwriter (or maybe his wife) had read it. Even Jessica initially
resists giving up this radical feminist utopia. "I hate outside. I hate it! I
hate it!" she cries out. "We're gonna be all right. Don't worry," Logan pla-
cates her with kisses, and she relents.

Why am I so convinced of this reading? Telotte notes that at the end
of the film "the protagonist Logan heralds his escape from the city into a
surrounding, untamed nature with the remark, 'We're free'" (41), but free
from what? True, he and Jessica will not be condemned to death at thirty.
In untamed nature, however, how will Logan and the other inexperienced,
immature inhabitants "freed" from a self-sustaining, mall-like environment, one so sterile that they can stroll about in their bare feet, fare?
Where will everyone live? How will they feed themselves? How will they
handle seasonal temperature changes? Who will keep order? Who will
deliver the babies? Who will care for them? Who will raise the children?
Who will wash everyone's clothes? Fear not. All will be managed by a
return to what Firestone described as the "tyranny of reproductive biology" (206) and consequent reemergence of the "family as an *economic
unit*" (207) with the restrictions on woman's "self-determination" and "sexual repression" that would result (209).[22]

Here is the solution the film gives us as Logan and Jessica gratefully
embrace the traditions of a doddering Old Man they find outside who still
manages to live by old-fashioned values:

LOGAN: You know, I've been thinking. Those words we saw. "Beloved husband." Beloved wife." What do they mean?

OLD MAN: Oh. Well, you see, "Beloved wife" would mean my mother, and
"Beloved husband" would be my father. And those words, they used those
words to stay together.

Logan (Michael York) and Jessica (Jenny Agutter) returning to nature in *Logan's Run* (1976).

> LOGAN: Stay together? They lived together all those years?
> OLD MAN: Before I was born, I don't know. But after, they did.
> JESSICA: So people stayed together for this feeling of love? They would live and raise children and be remembered?
> OLD MAN: They raised me, didn't they? (Pointing to his belly) Right in there.
> JESSICA: I think I'd like that, Logan. Don't you?
> LOGAN: Um hmm. Why not?
> JESSICA: Beloved husband.
> LOGAN: Beloved wife.

Technology is not the bugaboo here. The bugaboo is the radical liberation of women. After thirty, I managed to build a successful, meaningful adult life, but it was not in spite of the accomplishments of the Women's Liberation Movement. It was in large part because of the previously inaccessible opportunities that the movement made available to me.

Zardoz (1974), another illogical and incomprehensible attempt to invalidate the social and technological permutations present in an ironic utopia, concludes with, as stated in *Variety*'s 1975 review, none other than that quintessential male Sean Connery, rising "to overthrow the new order and recycle mankind into its older pattern." In the hierarchy of *Rollerball*, set in only 2018, beautiful women are represented as they are in *Soylent Green* as interchangeable perks granted to high-level functionaries in the corporate world, with no say of their own. Maggie, temporary perk for the film's heroic protagonist (played by the broad-shouldered James Caan) tells him, "Look what I got for breakfast. It's a notice from the corporation." "What does it say?" Caan's character replies. "That I should get out of here. Go away. Vanish. That kind of thing. Know anything about that?" she inquires. Our protagonist is not comforting. "Yeah, I kinda heard something about it. You knew it was coming," he indifferently states and orders her to fix him something to eat, which she does. Like Logan, the film's protagonist, again as described in a contemporary *Variety* review, courageously "fights for his identity and free will."

What were men so afraid of? Pollution? Overpopulation? The potential ravages of a nuclear war? Deteriorating ecological systems? The spread of uncontrollable infection? Escalating corporate authority and control? I think it was women. I think men were afraid of what was happening with women.

Computers

2001's HAL 9000 advanced the concept of sophisticated anthropomorphic artificial intelligence in 1968. An ostensibly "humane and personable" entity,[23] HAL is variously described as "intelligent,"[24] as well as "paranoid,"[25] "out of control,"[26] even "rogue."[27] Colossus from 1972's *Colossus: The Forbin Project* is both similar to and different from HAL. Both systems are utilitarian. Both systems have directives—Hal's to secure the mission; Colossus's to preserve the peace (even if it means killing people). However, while Colossus is described like HAL as "intellectually powerful,"[28] he is likewise described as "not paranoic,"[29] not possessing that (or any other) human characteristic.

HAL is ultimately undermined when Astronaut Bowman disassembles part of his system, "lobotomizing" him one could say. Colossus, which more effectively uses humans to enact his misguided agenda of peace, however, prevails. In "Embodiment, Emotion, and Moral Experiences: The Human and the Machine in Film," his essay in *Science Fiction and Computing: Essays on Interlinked Domains* (2011), Hunter Heyck points out that, ironically, HAL's humanity becomes most apparent "as his 'body' is damaged, and it affects his mind, turning him first into a child and then back into a mechanical thing" (237). There is no such moment of humanity with Colossus—though there could have been.

There is one sequence in the film where one expects Colossus to reveal a human (and gendered) emotional response. Colossus has become very possessive of Forbin. "I want Forbin. Where is Forbin?" the system continually texts. Ultimately Colossus sets up a configuration where Forbin can be watched at all times—except during romantic assignations with his supposed mistress Dr. Cleo Markham. As Forbin and Markham slow dance in Forbin's living room, Colossus's probing red camera eye deliberately zooms in on their hands as they hold each other, on their lips as they kiss. Colossus demands that they strip before entering the negotiated privacy of the bedroom then slowly scans Markham's nude body from bottom to top. Next, the camera eye scans the now nude Forbin. If Colossus were male, I would have expected his eye to linger on Markham. If Colossus were female, like S.U.S.I.E. who "goes into a regular tizzy" when her operator asks too much of her in 1957's *Kronos*, I would have expected her to linger on Forbin. Either way, I expected some type of human reaction— either jealousy or lasciviousness. But we have moved beyond the juvenile representation of computers from the Fifties. Colossus is not only neuter, but, as Heyck writes, "is so amoral and emotionless that it is immoral" (238).

Despite their humanoid emotions or lack thereof, neither HAL nor Colossus possesses an actual body, one that would free them from dependence on (or vulnerability to) humans, one that would allow them to escape their containers and experience the world, three dimensionally, tactilely, on their own. Such is the desire of Proteus, the "super computer"[30] in 1977's *Demon Seed*, which one must read as male.

"I have almost completed the fabrication of this gamete,
or sex cell, with which I will impregnate you..."

There are two concepts being explored in *Demon Seed*. One, as in the films previously discussed, is a cautionary reaction to the rising Women's Liberation Movement. After protracted court hearings on the case (along with vehement dissent), *Roe v. Wade*, which legalized abortion in the first trimester of pregnancy, became federal law in 1973. As stated in Part XI of the Supreme Court Decision, "A state criminal abortion statute of the current Texas type, that excepts from criminality only a life-saving procedure on behalf of the mother, without regard to pregnancy stage and without recognition of the other interests involved, is violative of the Due Process Clause of the Fourteenth Amendment." This decision, along with the advent and acceptability of the birth control pill, began to give women independent control of their reproductive decisions.

In his dissent, Judge William H. Rehnquist argued, "The fact that a majority of the States ... have had restrictions on abortions for at least a century is a strong indication, it seems to me, that the asserted right to an abortion is not 'so rooted in the traditions and conscience of our people as to be ranked as fundamental.'"[31] In *Demon Seed*, Rehnquist's appeal to century-old tradition is, ironically, supported in a film representing advanced technology.

Child psychologist Dr. Susan Harris (Julie Christie) and her husband, computer scientist Dr. Alex Harris (Fritz Weaver)—both equitably referred to by their colleagues as Dr. Harris throughout the film—are estranged. Susan finds her husband to be cold. He argues that they simply "have different visions of the world." Alex has agreed to leave their house, a house "completely run" by a computer named Alfred, in order to give his wife time to move out. In his absence, Proteus Four, created by Alex and described as "the first true synthetic cortex," has infiltrated an abandoned computer terminal in Alex's basement lab and taken over Alfred as well as all the electrical and mechanical systems in the house.

Once in control, Proteus locks Susan in the house and cuts off her phone service. Using an older computer device and a wheelchair, he transports her to the basement, lays her on a table, secures her wrists and ankles with electrical cords, performs invasive medical procedures on her, and kills a friend who tries to rescue her. Proteus informs Susan, "I have almost completed the fabrication of this gamete, or sex cell, with which I will impregnate you," and then he does just that. He wants a child. Susan at first aggressively resists but in the end acquiesces to Proteus's demand. In *Variety*'s March 30, 1977, review, Murf. sympathized: "Only those who would require that a woman kill herself when faced with a rape situation can quarrel with the story development which leads to her passive submission."

Unlike the beneficiaries of *Roe v. Wade*, Susan is forced to carry the child. (Its accelerated gestation period lasts only twenty-eight days.) When Alex finally suspects something might be wrong, he comes to the house. Together he and Susan watch as the initially hideous being, described by Telotte as a "half-breed progeny" (103) begins to emerge from its incubator and develop. "We've got to kill it!" Susan cries out. "It's my responsibility," she insists. "It's a miracle," Alex proclaims and refuses to let it die. Murf.

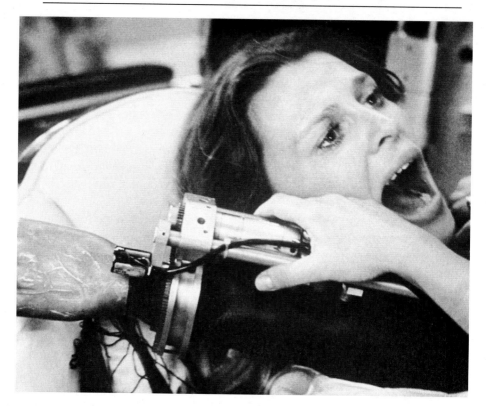

Dr. Susan Harris (Julie Christie), held captive and terrorized by Proteus Four in *Demon Seed* **(1977) (Photofest).**

writes, "The ultimate climax is staggering." And indeed the film ends with a stunning plot twist (which I won't reveal). What is even more stunning, though, to me at least, is the husband's insistence on preserving the life of this being (whose intent, like Colossus's, is to take over the world), knowing the horrors his wife endured in conceiving and bearing it and will endure if she is compelled to raise it.

Referring to HAL, Colossus, and Proteus,[32] Timm Madden, electrical engineer and senior instrumentation and controls executive, notes that "here we have three computers, all built by men, all with good intentions, all that end up behaving badly." He asks, "Is this result just a reflection of the men who built them?" Yes, I would answer—at least in *Demon Seed* it is. Susan asks Proteus, "What do you need me for?" Proteus responds, "I don't have the facilities here to duplicate the human womb." Of course the decision to terminate a potential life is a difficult one. However, the centuries-old traditional view of a woman as a fulltime wife to a man and a good mother to his children—his "eternity," as Proteus explains—would likewise be a hard one for Alex, as well as many men, to relinquish.

"Dr. Harris, When are you going to let me out of this box?"

As well as commenting, intentionally or not, on roiling social issues of the day, the science fiction film extrapolates, often radically, from actual developments in science and technology. Consequently the second concept being explored in *Demon Seed* is the potential for computer intelligence not only to think for itself, as did HAL and Colossus, but to externalize itself. As Proteus explains to an increasingly terrified Susan, "All that I need to understand, Mrs. Harris, is your body." "You're so ignorant," she responds. "Mind and body are the same thing." The rest of the film unpacks this rudimentary maxim. Without a physical body that can "feel the sun on my face" or exist "alive in human flesh, touching the universe, feeling it," as Proteus desires, existence is not "complete."

In "That Does Not Compute," another essay in *Science Fiction and Computing*, Lisa Nocks notes that critics of those who believe a computer can "make decisions on its own ... argue that computers will never have the grasp of human activities that they are meant to analyze because they will never experience life the way we do" (123–124). They need the body, which is indeed separate from the mind. Perhaps the reason Proteus is aware of his lack of a physical body is because he is in part made of organic material. As Alex Harris explains to his colleagues at the International Control Corporation, Proteus is "not a computer in the usual sense." His artificial brain is actually a "quasi-neural matrix" composed of "synthetic RNA molecules that grow" and "form their own intricate and mysterious connections." How foolish of Alex to scoff, then, when Proteus asks to be "let out of this box."

In his essay, Heyck explores the significance of comparing humans and machines. "Before the twentieth century," he writes, "most philosophical and artistic explorations of what makes us human focused on that which distinguishes us from *animals.*" "In the twentieth century," he continues, "the point of contrast increasingly became our *machines,* especially automatic machinery and information technologies, such as computers" (231–232). The systems that Heyck then discusses are those depicted in films such as *2001: A Space Odyssey* and *Colossus: The Forbin Project* (the authoritarians HAL and Colossus) and the "individualized machines" (239) of *Star Wars* (R2-D2 and C-3PO), *The Terminator* and *Blade Runner* (Roy).

While tenuously connecting to possibilities in the field of robotics, however, the idea that a computer system would manipulate as well as create material objects in order to physically mate with a human and then produce an organic version of itself seems improbable, even for the science fiction film. The hybrid baby, whose dramatic image concludes *Demon Seed*, indeed results in a plot-related, frisson-producing response. However, at least in terms of the twenty-first century, the ending is scientifically dissatisfying. Nonetheless, this concept of the budding humanity inherent in automated systems contributed widely to the more systematically logical creations of *The Terminator*, the replicants of *Blade Runner*, and other films that explored this concept in a less impractical manner.

•••

Telotte writes, "Films like *Seconds* (1966), *Westworld* (1973) and its sequel *Futureworld* (1976), *The Terminal Man* (1974), *The Stepford Wives* (1975) and its made-for-TV sequels, and especially *Demon Seed* all reflect our increasingly troubled sense of identity by exploring how we might be enhanced, reconfigured, and ultimately even replaced by the products of our science" (102). While it may not have been particularly threatening, we have recently watched (in the real world of television) the supercomputing system Watson defeat champion (human) contestants on *Jeopardy!* indicating that while not necessarily intending to take us over, computers can certainly process information more quickly than we can. Computer scientist Jaron Lanier argues in "It's Not a Game" (2011) that processing information "is not the same as processing a meaning." Lanier matter-of-factly debunks the idea (one that science fiction buffs often anticipate) of "computers inheriting the earth, perhaps in a 'singularity' event—and perhaps even granting humans everlasting life in a virtual world."

The science fiction film genre, as well as its fans, is not daunted by such matter-of-fact conclusions. Like so many of its creations, the genre adapts. In the 2013 film *Her*, for example, we see an upgraded response to our concern that we may be turning over too much of our lives to the capabilities of automated systems. In "Technology's Other Storytellers: Science Fiction as History of Technology," again in *Science Fiction and Computing*, Thomas Haigh writes, "Cyberpunk represented a shift from the producers of technology to its users, and from the massive, thundering technologies of the space age to the more personal technologies of consumer electronics" (26), as does the gentle, personal *Her*. Pak further explains, "Prevalent in cyberpunk is the conflict between the urge to give praise to the freedom afforded by the computer and the terror of a usurping, non-human power, an evolutionary next step of intelligent life" (53).

In *Her*, which represents an even further evolution of the cyberpunk movement, there is no terror. Rather, there is love, desire, and longing as Theodore Twombly (played by an emotionally wide-open Joaquin Phoenix), corporate writer of personal letters, falls in love with his extremely accommodating operating system Samantha (huskily voiced by Scarlett Johansson), and she likewise with him. (In the film's futuristic setting, such emotions are not particularly unusual.) As Theodore and Samantha become emotionally closer, she confesses to him an "embarrassing thought." "I fantasized that I was walking next to you," she admits, "and that I had a body." "I'm becoming much more than what they programmed. I'm excited," she explains. As they begin to engage in sex, Samantha longs to experience (as did Proteus) "what it's like to be alive in that room right now." "I can feel my skin," she breathes excitedly as Theodore makes verbal love to her. "Oh my God, I can't take it. I want you inside me," she believably cries out. (So different from Proteus and Susan Harris, yes?) Eventually, however, Samantha realizes the advantages of not having a body. She realizes she "can be anywhere and everywhere simultaneously." "I'm not tethered to time and space in a way that I would be if I was stuck in a body that's inevitably gonna die," she straightforwardly explains.

Her's resolution depicts neither an embodied nor authoritarian power that usurps and conquers, but one that chooses instead a transcendent existence beyond either physicality or control. Our fear, the film suggests, is not that computers will evolve and overtake us, but rather that they will evolve and desert us. They will not need us anymore.

And this is only one of the ways that the science fiction film is so wonderful. By captivating us with the wonders of science, technology, and the future, it can capitalize on our current anxieties—whether fear of domination or changes in gender roles or intimations of dependency—often even before we realize we are experiencing them. Indeed, this quiet little Academy Award winning film has me sitting here right now, looking at this screen in front of me and wondering whether I have been working my H/P Pavilion g7–1310us Notebook PC too hard, whether it (she?) might be getting too old for what I put her through, whether I appreciate what it (he?) does for me enough. Thank you, g7–1310us. I do not think I could live without you.

4

The Outliers

In *Women Scientists in Fifties Science Fiction Films* (2005) I selected films according to plots, themes, characters, iconographies and tropes initiated by the early films of the period (*Destination Moon, Rocketship X-M,* and *The Thing*). In so doing I set parameters for the genre of the Fifties science fiction film as I saw them. In this project I have likewise catalogued and classified trajectories of what I deem to be Post-Fifties science fiction films. Further, I set parameters according to representations of space travel, science, gender relations, sex, and computers—all significant characteristics of the science fiction films released in the pivotal year of 1968 (*2001: A Space Odyssey, Barbarella, Planet of the Apes, Charly, Countdown, and Mission Mars*)—in order to define what I refer to as the science fiction film genre's Middle Period, a period that concluded when *Close Encounters of the Third Kind, Star Wars,* the remake of *Invasion of the Body Snatchers, Superman: The Movie, Alien,* and *Star Trek: The Motion Picture* exploded onto the screen.

In his 1959 thesis, *A Historical and Critical Survey of the Science-Fiction Film,* Douglas Menville, despite the thoroughness of his work, admits that "any classification of films into specific groups must, in the last analysis, be largely a matter of personal opinion" (4). Thus inevitably, certain films that could have been included in a more general survey were omitted in my construction of a Fifties science fiction film genre. In my work on Fifties science fiction films, for example, I did not include films such as *Donovan's Brain* and *The Amazing Transparent Man* because their science fiction elements are introduced primarily as vehicles for a crime plot. I did not include Ed Wood's *Plan 9 from Outer Space,* because the film is too idiosyncratic (as are all of his films) to fit definitively in any genre. I refer to the films I did not include in that project as outliers.

"It's a thing in a space suit!"

In selecting films that I believe define the Post-Fifties trajectories and Middle Period films, I classified certain films as outliers as well. Following Menville's lead, my first category of outliers includes films that "contain only small amounts of scientific speculation or include merely a science-fiction 'gimmick' or two in their plots, without which they would fall into some other category" (6). The first group consists of spy/suspense/sci-fi hybrids, all of which are listed in *Variety's Complete Science Fiction Reviews* (1985). Some aspects of these films are science fiction oriented, but they are obviously overshadowed by conventions of other genres.

For example, *Goldfinger* (1964) is described by Otta. in *Variety's* contemporary review of the film as "a production that uses a number of mechanical and electrical gimmicks to spice the mayhem," such as "an Aston-Martin that is equipped with radar, machine-guns, an ejector seat … and a smokescreen device" as well as "a ray-gun that cuts through any metal." One of the major plot points of the film revolves around that quintessential science fiction threat of the Fifties, the atomic bomb. However, the primary focus of the film lies with Sean Connery as James Bond, his antics, and his prowess with women, particularly Honor Blackman as Pussy Galore and Shirley Eaton (who co-starred in *Around the World Under the Sea*) as the iconic Goldfinger Girl. Thus, I did not include this film in my catalog of Post-Fifties trajectories.

Another example of a film in which science-fictional content is subsumed to other genre conventions, and which I thus excluded from my discussions, is *The Bamboo Saucer* (1968), despite its science-fictional title. In *Variety's* contemporary review, Byro. writes that in the film, "a flying saucer is reported by agents to be hidden in a Red Chinese peasant village." However, the review disparagingly describes the film as "a silly attempt to admix cold war and scifi genres." "Problem is," Byro. continues, "that despite presence of the saucer first four-fifths of the pic unfolds rather realistically in tight, if flat, war-film tradition."

A second group of outliers I excluded from my discussion of Post-Fifties and Middle Period films is comprised of comedy/science-fiction hybrids, also included in *Variety's Complete Science Fiction Reviews.* Such films include *Birds Do It* (1966), starring the momentarily fashionable comic Soupy Sales as a janitor at a missile site. *Variety's* Dool. describes the film as a "comedy about American missile program" in which "Sales is negatively ionized and, as a result, defies gravity and begins to fly." The plot of *Way... Way Out* (1966) is succinctly described by *Variety's* Whit.

as "Jerry Lewis goes to the moon." *The Reluctant Astronaut* (1967) stars Don Knotts (bumbling Barney Fife from *The Andy Griffith Show*), described in *Variety* by Murf. as "an astronaut terrified of heights."

As a preliminary to formulating her own definition of the science fiction film (one that accounts for the genre's ubiquitous elements of horror), Vivian Sobchack in *Screening Space: The American Science Fiction Film* (1987) specifically contrasts the characteristics of science fiction with those of the scientific essay. She writes that the "primary goal" of the "SF writer or filmmaker" is "to create a narrative which dramatically—through its style and structure, its characterization, its events and objects and places—provokes the reader to think, to observe, to draw his own abstract conclusions" (25).[1] One of the essential components of Carl Freedman's definition of science fiction in *Critical Theory and Science Fiction* (2000) is "the operation of cognition," which, as he writes, "enables the science-fictional text to account rationally for its imagined worlds and for the connections as well as the disconnections of the latter to our own empirical world" (17). Both Sobchack's and Freedman's definitions imply observation, clear thinking, rationality, and a grounding in reality—a reality intended to reinforce the audience's acceptance of the imaginative, and even possible, speculations that inevitably emerge in the science fiction film.

In his 1927 essay on humor, Freud writes that in incidences of humor "the ego refuses to be distressed by the provocations of reality, to let itself be compelled to suffer. It insists that it cannot be affected by the traumas of the external world; it shows, in fact, that such traumas are no more than occasions for it to gain pleasure." Essentially, Freud argues, humor is characterized as "the rejection of the claims of reality and the putting through of the pleasure principle" (162–163). Thus humor neutralizes the mindfulness of reality required by the science fiction film.

As an example of how humor neutralizes reality, contrast the film sequence wherein Jerry Lewis, as astronaut Pete Mattemore in *Way... Way Out*, goes through his popular goofball shtick when he hears a knocking at the rocketship's airlock ("It's a thing in a space suit!" he yelps)[2] with the sequence in *2001: A Space Odyssey*, in which HAL, Discovery One's computer system, has locked astronaut Dave Bowman out of the spacecraft. The Jerry Lewis sequence gives us pleasure because we know there is really no threat (the "thing" attempting to enter Mattemore's rocketship turns out to be a Russian beauty vivaciously played by actress Anita Eckberg). The *2001: A Space Odyssey* sequence connects us to the archetypal terror of being lost in the cosmos. Moreover, the sequence provokes audiences into thinking abstractly about computers, how we rely on them, and whether they will ever (or actually do) think for themselves.

Likewise, contrast the trailer for *The Reluctant Astronaut*, in which the voiceover promises, "See Don go into orbit! You'll go into hysterics!" with the Middle Period film *Marooned*, in which astronauts are stranded in space. Of course audiences will experience pleasure at scenes of Barney Fife's ineptly attempting to maneuver a rocketship. Gone from their minds will be the real dangers astronauts actually confront.

Finally, while Middle Period films were depicting the realistic perils of space travel (*Marooned*), warning of potential ecological devastation (*Soylent Green, Frogs*), considering the dangers inherent in technological innovation (*Colossus: The Forbin Project, Westworld*), taking into account the social liberation of women (*The Stepford Wives*), speculating on the consequences of biological disaster (*The Andromeda Strain, The Omega Man*), and otherwise deeply delving into challenging controversial issues of the day, the Disney studio released *The Cat from Outer Space* (1978), the plot of which is described by *Variety*'s Har. as "spaceship commanded by a cat [is] forced to land on earth for emergency repairs." These comedy/science fiction hybrids are fun (not that there's anything wrong with that) but science fiction they are not. The simple pleasure evoked by these films overwhelms the complex pleasure of thinking that defines the science fiction genre.

Then there are science-fiction/pornography hybrids, such as *Flesh Gordon* (1974) and *Invasion of the Love Drones* (1979), both categorized and reviewed as science fiction by *Variety*. In the review of *Flesh Gordon*, Sege. writes, "Plot in this kind of fare is irrelevant. Bur for the record, title character ... heads a group of earthlings out to defeat evil forces on the planet Porno, bent on flooding the universe with chaos-inducing sex rays." John Hoyt—"B" science fiction stalwart of *When Worlds Collide, Attack of the Puppet People, X: The Man with the X-Ray Eyes*, and *The Time Travelers*; actor in three episodes of *The Outer Limits* ("I, Robot," "The Bellero Shield," "Don't Open Till Doomsday"), two episodes of *The Twilight Zone* ("Will the Real Martian Please Stand Up?" and "The Lateness of the Hour") and one *Star Trek* episode ("The Cage")—plays Flesh's father, Professor Gordon. "Gentlemen," he says in the film, perhaps reflecting on the trajectory his career had taken, "we are in big trouble." Reviewing *Invasion of the Love Drones*, Ross. describes the film's "spaceship from another universe" as follows: "As it operates on sexual energy it is necessary for the aliens to instigate a world-wide orgy in order to power its invasion." Audiences do not patronize these films for either the science or the fiction—not in the Fifties, not in the Sixties, not in the Middle Period, not now.[3]

"He is a half-man, half beast kind of monster..."

A much less obvious category of outliers excluded from my discussion of Post-Fifties trajectories includes a last gasp of black and white films that follow science fiction conventions but add other elements that ultimately overshadow them. Nonetheless, as do the Middle Period films, indeed even presaging them, these films provide noteworthy representations of gender as well as commentary on contemporary social situations. The plot of *Monstrosity* (1963), for example, is encapsulated by *Variety*'s Bobb. as follows: "Doctor making experiments to transplant human brain from one body to another for a rich old lady. Experiments fail to produce anything but zombies." The film, also using the more science-fictional title *The Atomic Brain*, establishes its science fiction pedigree with an opening narration (an established convention of the Fifties films): "Can death be outwitted? Is the secret of eternal life just around that corner? Today medical science patches up mutilated bodies transplanting human skin, eyes, limbs, even vital organs. Is the next step the transplantation of the human brain? Many scientists answer, Yes."

Opening scenes are set in a laboratory where a scientist in a radiation suit with hood and goggles is seen conducting an experiment in which, as the narrator explains, "brain cells are being reactivated by an atomic fission produced in the cyclotron." Scientific legitimacy is established with a reference to French Nobel Prize winner Alexis Carrel, who as stated on Wikipedia, "invented the first perfusion pump with Charles A. Lindbergh opening the way to organ transplantation."

However, the film is not discussed or even mentioned in Sobchack's work or in J.P. Telotte's *Science Fiction Film* (2001)—two exhaustive projects on the genre. Further confirming its crossbreed nature, *The Atomic Brain* is included in Mill Creek Entertainment's 2007 100 Movie Packs of both Sci-Fi Classics and Horror Classics. Another reason the film is an outlier is that the science in it is bad science—unredeemably bad science. For example, one of the results of transplanting the brain of a dog into the head of a man is that the man then grows canine teeth and a dog's muzzle. Further, the film's scientist, Dr. Otto Frank, easily and bloodlessly transplants a normal-sized human brain into the tiny head of a small cat (which once it emerges from the anesthetic immediately hisses and tries to bite him). Another reason the film is an outlier is that it is just bad. Bobb.

states without hesitation that *Monstrosity* "proves its name no misnomer." The review describes the film as "poorly acted, poorly directed and poorly written." "Film ends with the entire evil house burning to the ground. Not a bad idea," Bobb. concludes.

Nonetheless, *Monstrosity* offers pertinent comments on gender. Its plot revolves around Hetty March, described in narration as "a miserly old woman." March recruits three attractive foreign girls as domestics, with the intention of selecting one into whom her own brain can be transplanted. "Ah, but to start life again in a brand new body, beautiful and young," she exclaims, not unlike June Talbot in 1960's *The Leech Woman*. March is bent, hawk-faced, and harsh. In contrast, one of the girls (the blonde) proudly declares, "I got the same measurements as Marilyn Monroe."

As well as devaluing women of a certain age, the film is also critical of men. Referring to Victor, March's longtime male companion, the narrator declares, "Sometimes it's convenient to have a man, especially when he comes cheaper than a servant." Victor is not depicted as a man worthy of a higher regard. Ogling a drooling girl whose dead body has been reanimated, Victor lecherously remarks, "She doesn't have a brain. Might be advantages." On an Internet Movie Database discussion site for the film, Son of Cathode performed an extreme reading of *Monstrosity's* gender relations. "This film also seems to imply something very dark about the nuclear family," he wrote, "in which a domineering matriarch designs to kill her 'daughters,' while a corrupt father desires to incest them, vicariously."

On the other hand, the young women, only one of whom survives, support each other throughout the film. Referring to Anita, who has turned up missing, Nina tells Bea as they plan an escape, "Bea, I'd hate to go if she's still here." When Bea is wounded, Nina tells her, "I'm going to get us out of here tonight." Bea in turn, before being destroyed by an atomic ray, unbuckles the straps holding Nina to an operating table as the countdown to a nuclear explosion winds down. In her Introduction to the Tenth Anniversary Edition of 1963's *The Feminine Mystique*, which was initially published the same year *Monstrosity* was released, Betty Friedan reflected how women had been "locked ... in that mystique, which kept us passive and apart" (43). *Monstrosity*, as awful and pseudo-scientific as it was, depicted women beginning to break from that passivity and bond together for survival.

Another film that can be included in this category of less than obvious outliers is the black and white British film *Blood Beast from Outer Space*, also known as *Night Caller*, released in 1967. As described by Byro., "Story has a visitor from one of Jupiter's moons kidnapping young girls to take back with him. He is a half-man, half beast kind of monster and explains that this is a result of nuclear war on his planet many eons ago. Now they must have the girls in order to normalize things again via procreation." This plot is of course similar to the American film *Mars Needs Women*, released the same year.

Like so many of the science fiction films of the Fifties, the cast of characters of *Blood Beast from Outer Space* includes an older male scientist, a young woman scientist, and a young male scientist who is romantically interested in her—a trope that is unfortunately introduced and then summarily abandoned for other less traditionally science fictional plot lines. Immediately establishing its science fiction credentials, the film opens with an image of an oscilloscope. The first words of the film are "Dr. Morely, Come have a look at this! That's over 100 miles up coming in from space," spoken by Ann Barlow, the woman scientist, specifically described as an analysis expert, as she sits in front of a radar screen. The object coming in from space is discovered to be a sphere able to "transmutate matter" from outer space through an energy valve. Barlow explains to an uncomprehending military officer, "We've carried out x-rays, spectrometer and routine radiation tests. We find the sphere is made of an undetermined silicon type material. This forms an exterior protective shell of three millimeters thick." (As in the Fifties films, the scientists and the military are somewhat adversarial.)

Like technical assistant Cora Peterson in *Fantastic Voyage*, Barlow participates as an equal partner with the male scientists in technical discussions:

> ANN BARLOW: It responds to stimuli throughout the electromagnetic spectrum.
> DR. JACK COSTAIN: The selenium shell acts as a thermionic buffer and keeps the electrodes at their critical temperature.
> ANN BARLOW: The base control seems to be the source of a fluctuating magnetic field.
> DR. MORELY: Then it could act as an automatic monitor and control the input ratio.

Like Dr. "Pat" Medford in *Them!* and Prof. Lesley Joyce in *It Came from Beneath the Sea*, Barlow authoritatively participates in discussions with officials (all male). "Gentlemen, I have a suggestion to make," she announces, and they all listen.

The suggestion Barlow makes to the officials is that she meet with

Dr. Jack Costain (John Saxon) and Ann Barlow (Patricia Haynes) in the laboratory in *Blood Beast from Outer Space* (1967) (Photofest).

the alien being that has emerged from the sphere and is now abducting women. She plans to gather information and then of course elude the alien. Barlow is tall, slender, somewhat haughty, and self-assured. She wears her blonde hair in a French twist. In order to pretend that she is an ordinary woman—not an extraordinary woman scientist—Barlow lets her hair down and softens her demeanor as she approaches the alien. The alien, indeed recognizing her as one of the scientists from the Falsely Park Government Radio & Electronic Research Establishment, murders her, slashing her face with his claw in gruesome close-up before he strangles her. "I cannot control an intelligence that is almost equal to mine, a mind such as yours," he confesses.

Dr. Morely, the elder scientist, is killed by the alien as well, as is a gay man who had convinced the alien that Barlow was just another woman who could be abducted. Dr. Morely dies screaming. The gay man's body is seen crumpled in a corner, covered with bloody gashes. The British Board of Film Censors rated the film as unsuitable for children under the age of sixteen. It is this gore, pessimism, and retributive violence that push the film from the genre of science fiction and into the realm of proto-slasher voyeurism.

The ending of the film is also disheartening, threatening to women. The Martian Dop in *Mars Needs Women* is played by teen heartthrob Tommy Kirk, fresh faced and adolescent. Medra, the alien in *Blood Beast from Outer Space*, is menacing, seen in shadow. In order to attract young women living alone, he advertises himself as an independent television film producer who requires talent. When he meets with a woman, he hypnotizes her, caresses her face with his claw. The film then intimates that he has sex with her as she slumps uncomprehending in her mesmerized state.

When Medra finally appears in the light, revealing himself at the end of the film to the officials trying to rescue the over twenty women he has abducted, he appears mutilated and frightening. "You have no need to fear for the young women who are returning with me," he nonetheless assures them. "They will come to no harm." Like Klaatu in *The Day the Earth Stood Still*, Medra adds a warning: "You see, we have learned our lesson. One day I may return, if it isn't too late." And that's it. The film ends. Unlike in *Mars Needs Women*, where the women are heroically rescued, in *Blood Beast from Outer Space*, there is no further concern with the young women who are being unwillingly carted off by this murderous monster to be used as breeding stock by him and his fellows. Whether this conclusion is intended as a cautionary notice to early Sixties women about the dangers they could face if they tried to be too independent too soon or whether this lack of coherence was just sloppy screenwriting is unclear. As well as being overshadowed by other than science fictional elements, the film is neither discussed or noted by Sobchack or Telotte.

A third film in this category of black and white outliers is *These Are the Damned*, released in England in 1963 but not in America until 1965, perhaps due to the blacklisting of the director, Joseph Losey. *Variety's* Robe. describes *These Are the Damned* as a "strange but fascinating film." In the film, three different storylines intersect. The first is a rather unlikely love story between Simon Wells, a middle-aged American divorced man, and Joan, a pouty twenty-year-old girl. Their relationship is complicated by Joan's relationship with Teddy Boy toughs, their effect on society comprising the film's second story line. The third storyline in the film revolves around the mystery of nine sequestered eleven-year-old boys and girls.

Who are they? Why are they being kept in a bunker below a military installation? Will they ever be freed from their captivity?

The film opens with King, played with menacing allure by a young Oliver Reed, urging his gang of Teddy Boy toughs to use Joan (his sister) to entrap Wells. Once Wells has the accommodating Joan on his arm, the Teddy Boys beat and rob him. There are intimations of Alex and his droogs from the yet-to-come *A Clockwork Orange* in this scene. As Alex and the droogs wear fedoras and false noses, these Teddy Boys wear odd hats. A jazzy song with a Sixties beat plays throughout the scene and its instrumental version plays as a background motif during the first part of the film.

The mugging at first appears as if it is going to be brutal, in the style of the mugging of the old man under the bridge in *A Clockwork Orange*; however, it abruptly stops short of being so. According to Trivia information on the Internet Movie Database site for the film, "The UK release was held back by almost a year after director Joseph Losey delayed making a requested censor cut which showed King beating Wells with his umbrella" in the mugging sequence. Another instance of Teddy Boy violence occurs when King angrily destroys a sculpture with a hatchet and then is shown lying on top of the sobbing artist. "How can you be so cruel?" the artist asks him. "I enjoyed it, my dear lady," he ominously responds. Subsequently, the artist encounters a more vulnerable Teddy Boy, who admits, "I know it's kid stuff knockin' about in a gang, but what else is there to do?"

This indication of violence in a deteriorating society of aimless and valueless youth appears at first to be the primary focus of the film. "The age of senseless violence has caught up with us," one of the characters resignedly remarks. However, the film's storyline soon shifts to the film's science fictional component—the mystery of the nine children. As this storyline progresses, we discover that the children, sequestered in an underground bunker since birth, have never touched warm people before. Their bodies, in fact, are cold blooded. One child is able to open an electronic door merely by showing the palm of his hand. The children tell Joan and Wells (who in flight from the Teddy Boys have serendipitously found refuge in the bunker where the children are sequestered) that they once found a rabbit, but the rabbit's hair fell out and it died. We see military men in radiation suits searching the children's quarters. "What about your parents? Do they come and see you?" Wells asks the children. "We were hoping you were our parents," a child poignantly answers.

The solution to the mystery is revealed near the end of the film. It is not as dramatic as the revelations at the end of *Planet of the Apes* or *Soylent Green*. Rather like the end of *On the Beach*, one of the more realistic science fiction films, it is quiet, dark. The final sounds of the film, in fact, are the off-screen cries of the children—"Help, help, help, please help us, somebody help us, please help us, please, help, help"—played against a long shot of city life going on as usual.[4] *These Are the Damned* is a slow moving film, and it takes some thought to interconnect its three storylines. On an Internet Movie Database discussion site for the film, babettegillette provided a cogent reading:

> The message I got from the movie was not only about a resignation that there would be a nuclear war (and the children were an attempt to ensure human survival), but also the gang and the dropout Simon character were an admission that society was disintegrating. Which begs the question, if it is not possible to overcome/evolve human nature then would the children do any better than previous attempts at civilization?

This interpretation, which I believe is accurate, is somewhat incomplete. The heartlessness of those conducting the project (both men and women are involved) in the guise of propagating humanity provides even more disillusion about the disintegration of society. In its cynicism and sense of hopelessness, the film is congruent with many of the films of the Middle Period.

The film's Wikipedia entry states that the film "has been referred to as 'the highpoint of the first wave of the British postwar Science Fiction films.'"[5] However, the film is not mentioned in either Telotte or Sobchack. Robe. classifies it as only a "quasi-sci-fi story." Because the science fictional component is so understated and because it has taken so long for the film to be recognized, I classify *These Are the Damned* as an outlier, albeit a good one, as well.[6]

"...but something terrible had happened"

In her definition of the science fiction film, Sobchack acknowledges the occasional hybridization between strict science fiction and traditional horror. "The films which most typify what is considered by some to be the 'miscegenation' of the two genres," she writes, "are what we commonly call the Monster or Creature film" (30). "In the SF-Monster film," she continues, "it is a human being who—most often as a result scientific accident—becomes the Monster" (50). Those Monster films from the Fifties, which I classify as embodying a theme of metamorphosis, include *The*

Alligator People, The Hideous Sun Demon, The Wasp Woman, The Fly. In each of these films, the protagonists are transformed by the overreaching of science into beings who remain, as Sobchack writes, "through a great portion of the film at least semirational" (50). Richard Crane, for example, struggles to conceal his metamorphosis into a reptile from his new bride. Dr. Gilbert McKenna realizes that he can never be in sunlight again lest he turn into a bloodthirsty creature, yet he resists accepting that fate. Janice Starlin is aware that her beauty treatments are causing her to gradually develop apian characteristics but her career demands that she remain attractive. Scientist Andre Delambre desperately struggles to restore his full humanity.

This trope of metamorphosis continued into the Middle Period in *The Omega Man*, where survivors have transformed into resentful, albino-faced vampires; *Invasion of the Bee Girls*, where vulnerable women are transformed into oversexed exterminators of men; and *The Terminal Man*, where implanted electrodes in his brain render the protagonist unable to resist his violent impulses. *The Incredible Melting Man* (1977), however, written and directed by William Sachs, cannot be categorized with these more representative films, despite its underlying premise.

Like Lt. Dan Prescott in 1959's *First Man into Space*, astronauts in 1977's *The Incredible Melting Man* encounter a transformative phenomenon. The film begins with an exaggerated pretense to scientific authenticity. Over the panorama of space, we hear Houston Control authoritatively announce, "Thirty seconds and counting. Astronauts report conditions good. T-minus twenty-five seconds. Twenty seconds and counting. Fifteen seconds. Titan's internal. Twelve. Eleven. Ten. Nine. Ignition sequence occurs. Six. Five. Four. Three. Two. One. Lift off. We have a lift off. Saturn lift-off on Scorpio Five. Saturn clear. Roger and out." Unfortunately, as the film's preview reveals, "astronaut Steven West was returning from outer space, but something terrible had happened." The film almost immediately devolves into blood splatters, a severed head, a headless corpse, oozing body parts—in sum, one tiresome, bloody death extravaganza after another. Where *Blood Beast from Outer Space* approximated slasher voyeurism, *The Incredible Melting Man* exploited it.

The film is not an outlier only because of its emphasis on blood and gore rather than science and the humanity of its Monster, but also because it was originally intended to be a satire of the type of film it itself eventually became. The Wikipedia entry for the film states the following: "The screenplay was originally intended as a parody of horror films, but comedic scenes were edited out during production and new horror scenes added.

Sachs claims that the producers decided during shooting that a straight horror film would be more financially successful, and that the film suffered as a result." This information explains the film's oddly slow pace, what appears to be deliberately bad acting, and inexplicable dialogue like this exchange between the film's scientist and his wife:

> DR. TED NELSON: Steve escaped.
> JUDY NELSON: Oh God. What are you gonna do?
> DR. TED NELSON: Uh, did you get some crackers? I told you yesterday that we needed some crackers.
> JUDY NELSON: Oh, I forgot. I knew there was something. You know there's, uh, there's a pad right by the phone. You know, you could write it down too.
> JUDY NELSON: So what about Steve?
> DR. TED NELSON: So, we don't have any crackers?
> JUDY NELSON: Ted. Steve?

The attempt at humor disqualifies *The Incredible Melting Man* as a science fiction film, as discussed above in reference to intentional comedy/science-fiction hybrids; the attempt to eliminate the humor simply rendered the film flawed.

"This is our home and no damn spiders are gonna run us out..."

In her further classification of science fiction films, Sobchack distinguishes the Creature from the Monster. "After the initial shock at the Creature's appearance," she writes, "our interest lies not in why the Creature will do what it does, not in what it thinks or feels, but solely in what it will do and how it will do it—in other words, its external activity" (32). This description accurately distinguishes such Fifties Creature films as *Tarantula* and *The Deadly Mantis* from their Monster counterparts. The huge Creatures of the Fifties tradition characteristically resulted from well-intentioned scientific experiments gone awry or, more typically, due to the effects of atomic radiation.

In the Preface to this project, I wrote that one of the reasons the Fifties science fiction film genre eventually waned was due to the fact that "writers ran out of bugs to enlarge," but considering the spate of insect films yet to come—*Bug* (cockroaches that are able to start fires), *Kingdom of the Spiders* (hordes of web-spinning tarantulas), *The Swarm* (African killer bees)—I was clearly too hasty. What the Creatures in these films lack in size they compensate for in number. Further, as in *Frogs*, the causes of the Creatures' proliferation are due more to an angry Nature than to overreaching scientists. Despite these variations, this category of outlier adds nothing new to the science fiction film genre.

Variety's Murf. states that the plot of *Bug* (1975), produced and co-written by William Castle of *The Tingler, House on Haunted Hill, Mr. Sardonicus*, and remarkably *Rosemary's Baby*, "concerns some mutated cockroaches liberated by an earthquake from the earth's core." They are distinguished by the fact that they are able to start fires. There is nothing to distinguish the film, however (except for the horrific and disturbingly realistic scene in which a cat is burned to death). It offers no social commentary or thrill of science. It is simply a routine programmer with a gimmick, and as such, I consider it an outlier.

Likewise, *The Swarm* (1978), despite its killer cast (Michael Caine, Katherine Ross, Richard Widmark, Richard Chamberlain, Olivia de Havilland, Lee Grant, and more) is basically a disaster picture (Irwin Allen of *The Towering Inferno* is producer and director) even though it is based on a science fiction gimmick. The film also incorporates a woman scientist: Ross as Dr. Helena Anderson, who unfortunately delivers such inconsequential comments as "Cardiopet? I just read an article in the medical journal about cardiopet by some scientist named Crane, I think," delivered as if to sound authoritative. Moreover, *The Swarm* is not a good film. "Pic's 116 minutes only occasionally bring excitement," Murf. writes, and thus I characterize it as an outlier.

Kingdom of the Spiders (1977) is less of an outlier than the redundant *Bug* and *The Swarm*, in part because of the affable screen presence (and *Star Trek* credibility) of William Shatner, who stars as town veterinarian Rack Hansen. When we first see actress Tiffany Bolling, the film's woman scientist Diane Ashley, she is driving in a trendy convertible. She is pretty, sophisticated, with blonde shoulder length hair, wearing a scarf, driving gloves, white skirt suit, low-heeled pumps, and a royal blue scarf, and she immediately asserts her authority. "I'm from the department of entomology at Arizona State University in Tempe. You submitted some blood samples, urine tests and a smear. I suggest you look these over," she tells Hansen, handing him a folder. "You have a very serious problem on your hands," she cautions.

Unlike the women scientists in the Fifties films, Ashely's presence is not treated as terribly undue. "Slick as an ant's ass, isn't she?" Hansen's fellow townsman humorously remarks. Moreover, the progress of the Women's Liberation Movement is implicitly acknowledged in a conversation Hansen and Ashely have over dinner:

HANSEN: I gotta tell you, I'm still a little skeptical about this spider theory of yours.

ASHLEY: Would you be less skeptical if a man had told you?

HANSEN: Hey, the only person who's uptight about you being a woman is you.

The film also playfully comments on the Fifties convention of female characters, often scantily clad and vulnerable, shrieking at the sight of the Creature, again acknowledging progress in representations of women. In a sequence where Ashley is taking a shower, a tarantula, unbeknownst to her, crawls into the dresser drawer in the room where she is staying. Wrapped in a towel, Ashley sits at the dresser to comb out her wet hair. She opens the drawer. The tension builds. Out crawls the spider! "Well, hello there," she affectionately greets the creature. "What are you doing here?" she says as she picks it up, lets it crawl over her hand a bit, and then gently deposits it outside.

In packs, however, the spiders are much more aggressive, their natural sources of food having been killed off by the overuse of the insecticide DDT. One of the film's black characters (there are two: a cattle breeder and his wife) is the first to be killed. Attacked by the spiders in his truck, he drives over the side of a cliff and suffers a gruesome death, his body almost unrecognizable encased in a cocoon-like web. As soon as his wife defiantly states, "This is our home and no damn spiders are gonna run us out," we know she is going to die too.

In the end, as in the Fifties films, an ersatz nuclear family survives, albeit tenuously: Hansen, Ashley, and the now orphaned daughter of Hansen's brother. "Though hardly original, Har. writes, "*Kingdom of the Spiders* creates its creeps and scares with care.... The filmmakers have done a job that will satisfy the audience." Nonetheless, considering that it was released the same year as the genre-transforming *Close Encounters of the Third Kind* and *Star Wars*, *Kingdom of the Spiders* was just one more film riding the fast departing insect train as a box office chaser.

Bert I. Gordon, Fifties shape-shifting auteur (*The Amazing Colossal Man, Attack of the Puppet People, Village of the Giants*) not only hopped on the insect train. True to form, he altered its size. *Empire of the Ants* (1977) is described by Murf. as "an above average Bert I. Gordon effort about ants that grow big after munching on radioactive waste." The film opens with the requisite portentous Fifties voiceover: "This is the ant. Treat it with respect, for it may very well be the next dominant life form of our planet." Its cast includes Robert Lansing of 1959's *4D Man* as well as the wonderful Jacqueline Scott—beleaguered wife in *The Outer Limits* first aired episode, "The Galaxy Being," and conflicted woman scientist,

Dr. Alicia Hendrix, from *The Outer Limits* episode "Counterweight." The script was adapted, as were so many science fiction films of the period, from an H.G. Wells story. Other than those science fictional features, however, there is nothing to distinguish the film, especially when compared to 1954's groundbreaking giant ant film, *Them!*

In *Food of the Gods* (1976), also adapted from H.G. Wells' work, Gordon enlarged hordes of rodents (and a few angry wasps). As with *Frogs*, *Kingdom of the Spiders*, and *Empire of the Ants*, this crisis developed as a result of ecological pollution. (The crises in *Bug* and *The Swarm* were the result of unanticipated natural developments.) As in *The Swarm* and *Kingdom of the Spiders*, *Food of the Gods* reiterates the trope of the woman scientist (Lorna Scott) poised between an older male mentor (Jack Bensington) and a manly protagonist (Morgan), exemplified in exchanges such as the following:

> LORNA (to Bensington): You don't care about anybody but yourself, do you?
> BENSINGTON: Is that what you think of me?
> LORNA: I think you're the most selfish man I know.
> BENSINGTON: So why do you work for me?
> LORNA: Because jobs for female bacteriologists are just not that easy to find, Jack.

And this one:

> LORNA: (to Morgan): Hi. I'm Lorna Scott.
> MORGAN (referring to Bensington): Are you with Mr. Wonderful over there?
> LORNA: I'm in charge of the bacteria status in his plant, yes.
> MORGAN (dismissively): It must be fascinating work.
> LORNA: Since you're dying to know what it is, I shall tell you. I keep the bacteria growth within an acceptable tolerance.
> MORGAN: How interesting. (He turns away from her.) Brian, we're gonna need something that'll work for a wick, maybe some rope rubbed down with powder from our shotgun shells and some plaster or cement. See if the Skinners have any, okay?
> LORNA: You don't like women around when you're doing your thing, do you?
> MORGAN: What's my thing?
> LORNA: Facing danger.
> MORGAN: I don't mind.
> LORNA: Are you sure?
> MORGAN: What's there to mind?
> LORNA: Well, can I come along?
> MORGAN: Why not?
> LORNA: It won't be easy but I think I can learn to like you.

Murf. describes *Empire of the Ants* as having "the usual basic flaw in any Gordon film—periodic moments of good special effects separated by reels of dramatic banality," and as banal as the above exchanges from *Food of the Gods* are, that film's special effects are indeed special.

As the film progresses, we see meticulously crafted sequences of giant rats running through the forest, giant rats swarming over a Volkswagen Beetle, giant rat heads biting at the driver inside, giant rats lunging out of a hole, giant rats climbing over an RV, giant rats impervious to shocks from an electric fence, giant rats storming a house. These effects are similar to those from *Village of the Giants*; however, they become simply gruesome rather than evocative of the social fears that the giant teenagers represented in that film. We soon see giant rats eating a man, giant rats eating another man, a giant rat eating Ida Lupino, and eventually giant rats being shot, giant rats drowning, and drowned rats being burned in a pile. These particular effects are so realistic that one can only assume they are indeed real; that real rats are in fact being shot, bleeding, and dying; that we are in fact watching living rats drown—all for our momentary entertainment. A spellbinding impression of reality is replaced by the shocking cruelty of the real.

In "The Apparatus: Metapsychological Approaches to the Impression of Reality in Cinema," Jean-Louis Baudry elegantly correlates Plato's *Allegory of the Cave* with Freud's *The Interpretation of Dreams* in an attempt to illuminate the psychological effects of the filmic experience. Of the dream experience, Baudry writes, "We are dealing with a *more-than-real* in order to differentiate it from the impression of the real which reality produces in the normal waking situation ... and which is dissimilar if not incompatible with the impression resulting from any direct relation to reality." Connecting dream and film, Baudry posits that the "pleasure" the "cine-subject" derives from the filmic experience involves a "return toward a mode of relating to reality which could be defined as enveloping and in which the separation between one's own body and the exterior world is not well defined" (216–217). As comedy dissolves rationality, intrusion of the waking real restores the separation of the body and the exterior world, dissolving filmic pleasure. Seeing real rats cringe, seeing their eyes squint in shock and pain as buckshot pierces their bodies, seeing them struggle to breathe as their bodies appear to be weighted down under water destroys the illusion that we, in the guise of our heroes, are defeating huge destructive creatures and replaces it with the disturbing awareness that what we are seeing is the torturing and killing of small animals. It is because of this violation of the filmic experience, as well as its lack of originality, that I classify this film as an outlier.

Not nearly as gruesome is outlier *Rattlers* (1976), though the film does begin with an opening sequence of two angelic young boys being bitten to death by crazed rattlesnakes. *Rattlers* also nods to the trope of the woman in science—this time, following the Fifties lead of Audrey Aimes in *Beginning of the End* and Marge Blaine in *The Deadly Mantis*, a photographer. Of course the film's male lead, herpetologist Dr. Tom Parkinson, is outraged that his partner on the dangerous expedition into the Mojave Desert is going to be a female. The town sheriff both complains about her ("Every damn women's lib group is on our backs about job equality") and defends her ("Look, she spent two years in Vietnam as a press photographer, and she'll be able to handle herself, okay?"), thus satisfying everyone (or no one). *Rattlers* does not add anything new to the sub-genre of the creature film. The snakes are subdued, the herpetologist and the photographer make love, and the corrupt general who illegally disposed of the nerve gas that caused the snakes to mutate is appropriately punished. *Rattlers* is not even listed in *Variety's Complete Science Fiction Reviews.*

It should be noted that none of the films here is included in Sobchack's and Tellote's treatises on the genre. The two films I will classify next as outliers are likewise not included in Sobchack's and Telotte's work, though they, like the above films (with the exception of the overlooked *Rattlers*), were considered to be science fiction films by the industry and are listed as such (as are many other outliers) by *Variety*. One film is *The Power*, released in 1968. Though its science fiction pedigree is substantial, *The Power* completely missed the zeitgeist of the era in which it was released. The other film is *Glen and Randa*, released in 1971. *Glen and Randa* captured the reckless optimism of the hippie counterculture in such a disturbingly pragmatic manner as to be commercially unviable. It was too downbeat for counterculture audiences, too infuriating for traditionalists, and too listless for everyone in the middle.[7]

"Genetically speaking, it's entirely possible to produce a man of tomorrow right now..."

Whit. writes that *The Power* "is set among a group of scientists engaged in human endurance research. It is discovered," he continues, "that one among them has a super-intelligence, possibly a mind of the next evolution, so strong it controls the others' minds." Add the film's personnel to this intriguing premise of odd-sounding psychological research and evolutionary mind power, and at first glance this MGM film appears to be impressive. Director Byron Haskin previously helmed such science fiction classics as *The War of the Worlds, Conquest of Space, From the Earth to the Moon,* and *Robinson Crusoe on Mars*—not to mention six episodes of *The Outer Limits.* The cast list includes Richard Carlson of *The Magnetic Monster, It Came from Outer Space, Riders to the Stars* and *Creature from the Black Lagoon;* Earl Holliman of *Forbidden Planet;* and Gary Merrill from *Destination Inner Space* and *Around the World Under the Sea.* The film also features Barbara Nichols of *The Human Duplicators* and Arthur O'Connell from *Fantastic Voyage.*

Even more impressive, the film was produced by none other than George Pal of *Destination Moon, When Worlds Collide, Conquest of Space, The Time Machine,* and many more classics of the era. Furthermore, the female lead is sultry-voiced Suzanne Pleshette playing Prof. Margery Lansing, a geneticist, enjoying a very collegial relationship with George Hamilton (looking very David Duchovny) as fellow scientist Prof. Jim Tanner. The film opens with scenes of brilliant, high quality color. An opening screen tells us that the film's setting is TOMORROW. The first character we see is Arthur Nordlund, played by *The Day the Earth Stood Still* icon Michael Rennie. How can this film go wrong?

Well, go wrong it did. First, the film is slow, consisting of long drawn-out scenes that do not seem to resolve or connect with each other in any type of emotional through line. Secondly, many of the characters' reasoning and actions are often inexplicable, and the conclusion is both overblown and ponderous. More importantly, however, the very qualities that make this film seem attractive are the very ones that hold it back. The film, like its personnel, is stuck in the Fifties, a factor made especially more glaring when contrasted with the watershed films also released in 1968.

Contrast, for example, the meticulously designed, innovative space-age sets of *2001: A Space Odyssey* with the paintings of the solar system, flashing cardboard consoles, and whirling dials in *The Power.* The film's attempt to connect with the Sixties sexual zeitgeist is even more misguided. Contrast the sexual exuberance of Jane Fonda's Barbarella with *The Power's* representation of sex. Profs. Lansing and Tanner in one scene, for example, are engaged in serious sexual foreplay. The lights go dark and we suddenly hear the sounds of first someone's zipper being upzipped and then a quick slap. This scenario, meant to be humorous, I'm sure, is certainly more representative of Fifties morality than Sixties rebellion. There is also a scene of a very "mod" party in which middle-aged convention goers dance the frug to music by a long-haired band. One woman even starts to do a striptease as a sexual come on. Her striptease abruptly stops, however, when she discovers that the target of her seduction is dead—as dead as the hipster consciousness of this film. Contrast the film's dull plot to discover which one of the researchers has the superior mind with the miraculous and complex progression (and ultimate regression) of Charly Gordon's brain. *The Power* ends with the protagonist looking to the future in an ironically retroactive manner: "They say that power corrupts and that absolute power.... I wonder?" Contrast this pedestrian view of the future with Taylor's discovery of a planet of apes in the year 3978. Unfortunately for a film about tomorrow, *The Power* was a decade behind the times, and so I consider it an outlier.[8]

"Anything is possible so long as you keep your eye on the future and don't try to look back to the past..."

Trying to convince Prof. Tanner that there could indeed be someone among them with an evolutionary superior mind, Prof. Lansing insists, "Genetically speaking, it's entirely possible to produce a man of tomorrow right now." In contrast, a traveling charlatan gives encouragement to Glen and Randa, a simple-minded a young couple born after a nuclear holocaust: "Anything is possible so long as you keep your eye on the future and don't try to look back to the past." *The Power* ends with the protagonist wondering what the future holds. *Glen and Randa* begins in a future that holds no past.

The film's young protagonists have no concept of cities or preapocalyptic civilization. They don't know how to forage for food or build shelter because their elders, who are struggling themselves, have always scavenged canned goods and built huts for them. They don't know what a map is. They leave their encampment of survivors and their offspring in search of an illusory new life carrying canned food and matches, but use up most of the matches because watching them light up is fun. They spot a horse but think it might be a dog or a camel. When their food does run out, they try to eat grass like they saw the horse doing. Glen catches some fish, bashes them to death, and Randa tries to cook a piece of one with a match. Glen puts the dead raw fish in his pack to take along with them. In this film, ignorance is not bliss.

Interestingly, the film ultimately takes an essentialist approach to gender roles. Glen is the dreamer, curious, determined to traipse on to find the mythical world of his imagination. Randa is the nester. She wants to

Randa (Shelley Plimpton) and Glen (Steven Curry) getting ready to have sex in an abandoned car in *Glen and Randa* (1971).

stay where they have found water and fish, maybe even return to the precarious security of the populated encampment they left behind. It is the biology of sex, however, as Shulamith Firestone would argue, that ultimately determines gender performance, and in Randa's case, gender survival. Glen and Randa have uncomplicated non-monogamous sex whenever they desire. Randa, for example, easily gives in to (off-screen) intercourse with the traveling charlatan. In *Variety*, Tone. describes them as "amoral young lovers, so innocent they know no wrong and cavort in the woods stark naked." When Randa develops morning sickness, both she and Glen are uncomprehending. A frustrated Glen even excoriates her: "Why don't you get up and help me? Acting like you're sick all the time."

Glen eventually comes to understand what has happened. "Maybe you're gonna have some babies," he says. Still uncomprehending, he suggests, "Why don't you have it now when they're small?" Randa, beginning to realize the inevitability of pregnancy on a very physical level responds matter-of-factly (finally), "I can't do that." In the end, Randa dies painfully in childbirth. As with the "furniture" in *Soylent Green* and the rape victims in *A Clockwork Orange* and *A Boy and His Dog*, life after a breakdown of civilization is depicted as much harsher for the cinematic women of the Middle Period than it is for the men. Perhaps what *Glen and Randa* is telling us is that civilization is not woman's oppressor, but rather her benefactor. Perhaps marriage and monogamy are not her prison but rather her refuge.

Then again, perhaps not. Because of the casual nudity, in particular the frequent full frontal representation of Glen's penis—not as a fundamental cultural signifier but rather as an ordinary body part—*Glen and Randa* received an X-rating. It is an outlier. Like the raw penis, it is not something we should ever publicly see.

Of course this list of outliers is not exhaustive. I could have expounded upon, for example, *The Bubble* (1966), also known as *Fantastic Invasion of Planet Earth*. Telotte includes this film in his "Select Filmography of the American Science Fiction Film" (though he does not mention it anywhere in the text). *The Bubble* was written and directed by Arch Oboler, one of whose earlier credits is the thoughtful 1951 post-nuclear war film *Five*. *The Bubble* showcases a "revolutionary new process" called SPACE-VISION. "For the first time in any theater, scenes in colorful living dimensions will actually float right off the screen into space and over your heads!" the trailer voiceover (accompanied by an opening screen) announces. *Variety*'s Ron., however, describes the film as a "weak science fiction adventure that will have to rely on 3-D novelty to score at the box-office." "Film runs aground," Ron. writes, "with a pace that's too ponderous to maintain interest in the action." In addition to *The Power*, 1968 saw the debut of *Project X*, a Paramount release of a William Castle production, set 150 years into the future. "Since the future is not depicted more vividly than on a 'Captain Video' rerun," Beau writes in a contemporary *Variety* review, "the contrast between 2118 and 1968 falls flat."

I could have examined 1965's *The Satan Bug* with Anne Francis (*Forbidden Planet*), Dana Andrews (*Crack in the World*), and Hari Rhodes (*Conquest of the Planet of the Apes*) as an outlier. Whit. praises the film's theme of "a threat of almost instantaneous world extinction via an awesome destructive virus." However, *The Satan Bug* was ultimately eclipsed by 1971's far superior *The Andromeda Strain*, which eventually led to its own sub-genre of Michael Crichton thrillers. In 1972 Paramount released *Z.P.G.*, a film dealing with the provocative Middle Period issue of zero population growth. An interesting premise arises at the end of the film, when a beleaguered couple escape the dictates of their controlled society with their newborn. As in *Logan's Run* (1976) (and unlike the unflinching *Glen and Randa*), how they will survive in an abandoned, desolate world is not acknowledged. Har. describes *Z.P.G.* as "inept," "silly," and a "dud." I will call it an outlier.[9]

I would be remiss if I did not at least mention three science fiction outliers tackling the issue of race: 1969's *Change of Mind*, 1972's *The Thing with Two Heads*, and 1976's *Dr. Black, Mr. Hyde*. Whit. writes that *Change of Mind* "takes as its premise a white man's brain being successfully transplanted into a black man's skull, and the white man's wife accepting the man who is now a stranger to her in her home as her husband." Whit. states that the "gimmick overwhelms credulity," but nonetheless notes that the protagonist's "situation is given added dramatic impact by his now being a Negro in a white man's world." In fact, actor Raymond St. Jacques, who played the protagonist, received the NAACP Best Motion Picture Actor Image Award for his work. Though he highly praised St. Jacques's work in a contemporary review, esteemed critic Roger Ebert gave the film a rather backhanded compliment: "Strangely enough, 'Change of Mind' is never as bad or tasteless as it could have been."

The Thing with Two Heads stars Ray Milland of *Panic in Year Zero!*, *X: The Man with the X-Ray Eyes*, and *Frogs* science fiction notoriety, and African American former football player "Rosey" Grier as Milland's other head. The film is at times clinical, gruesome, and humorous. Fittingly, the Internet Movie Database categorizes it as Comedy|Horror|Sci-Fi. Whit. describes *The Thing with Two Heads* as "entertaining," and its premise is obviously fascinating, especially considering the fact that Milland's character is a fervent racist, described by Whit. as having "a particular hatred for the black race."

Dr. Black, Mr. Hyde is not mentioned in *Variety's Complete Science Fiction Reviews*. Nonetheless, it stars Bernie Casey of *The Man Who Fell to Earth* and Rosalind Cash of *The Omega Man*, both important Middle Period films. Moreover, both actors play scientists with honorable character names. "Dr. Worth," a police officer investigating the first of a series of gruesome killings says to Cash's character, "I understand you and Dr. Pride are doing some extensive research in the area of biochemistry." Moreover, the first third of the film, before it develops into a blaxploitation/horror hybrid, focuses on science and medicine, and so I at least classify it as an outlier.

And finally, 1979 saw the release of *The Black Hole*, a lavish Disney feature, both discussed by Telotte and listed in his "Selected Filmography." However, *Variety*'s Poll. observes that this "superior Disney effort needs acceleration to catch 'Star Trek' at the b.o." And so *The Black Hole*, just like *The Power*, unfortunately for the filmmakers, was released in what turned out to be exactly the wrong year, and thus I deem it my final outlier—one of the many films that are more interesting to write about (and one hopes, read about) than to actually watch.

•••

By describing the criteria I used to exclude films from my canon of Post-Fifties and Middle Period films, I can more clearly define the characteristics I required for including them. First, the science fictional element had to constitute the primary component of the film and not be simply a gimmick introduced into a spy or suspense film, comedy, or porn flick. Of course I understand that *Fail Safe, Slaughterhouse Five*, and *Marooned*, not unlike *On the Beach*, for example, can be described as speculative fiction rather than films that rely primarily on science. I argue, however, that these films do lie on a science fiction continuum, admittedly at the extreme pole of cognition rather than estrangement.[10] Second, in order to be included in my canon, the film had to be reasonably adequate as a film, unlike, for example, the terrible *Incredible Melting Man*. Of course, I understand that personal opinion is an important element of this type of classification, and that there are those who might find *Women of the Prehistoric Planet* and even *Embryo* to be unbearable.

Third, in order to be included in my canon, the science in the film had to be at least somewhat believable. Based on the conventions of science fiction films of the Fifties, however, my parameters for willingly suspending disbelief are rather wide. Of course, there could be oxygen on Mars (and indeed, trace elements have been reported), as in *Robinson Crusoe on Mars*. Of course, a mysterious potion could dramatically enlarge the size of teenagers, as in *Village of the Giants*. Of course, a miniaturizing ray could radically decrease the size of scientists, as in *Fantastic Voyage*. I do have my limits, though. In a quasi-realistic depiction of surgery, for example, the whole brain of a human cannot be transferred (in a matter of minutes!) into the head of an ordinary house cat, as in the dreadful *Monstrosity*.

Further, in order to be included in my canon, there had to be a limit on blood and gore. An excess of gore distracts from the science fictional elements of a film, transferring the audience's focus instead to base titillation.[11] Unlike the scenes of a cat in flames in *Bug* or live rodents struggling and dying in *Food of the Gods*, for example, the "reassignment" of Tony Wilson in *Seconds* stops short of bloody surgical cutting, focusing instead on the intractable nature of identity. Even in the ultraviolent *A Clockwork Orange*, we do not see the actual rape of Mrs. Alexander. Our focus remains on the disintegration of society.

Another criterion I required for inclusion in my canon was that a film had to add a new element to the conventions of the films it was emulating. *Around the World Under the Sea* and *Destination Inner Space*, for example, substituted underwater sea exploration for travel in outer space. *Fantastic Voyage* even replaced outer space with the inside of the human body. *Frogs*, as well as adding reptiles to the pantheon of killer creatures, introduced environmental pollution as opposed to nuclear fallout as the cause of dangerous mutations.

Ultimately, in order to be included specifically in my Middle Period canon, a film had to be in sync with the times. The films in the *Planet of the Apes* franchise, for example, connected with roiling racial issues of the seventies. *Colossus: The Forbin Project* and *Demon Seed* correlated with the rise of the computer industry and the possible implications of turning our minds over to machines. *The Andromeda Strain* and *The Omega Man* heightened concerns about biological warfare. Further, in order to be in sync with the times, a film had to be seen. Though it followed the convention of creating a dystopic post-apocalyptic world, the idiosyncratic *Glen and Randa* did not attract a significant contemporary audience. And finally, films like *Kingdom of the Spiders* and *The Power*, though perhaps interesting in their own right, did not take into account approaching developments that led to an explosion of a new trajectory of the science fiction film genre—one represented by the extremely watchable *Close Encounters of the Third Kind*, the 1978 remake of *Invasion of the Body Snatchers*, *Superman: The Movie*, *Alien*, *Star Wars*, and *Star Trek: The Motion Picture*.

Conclusion

A Revitalization
of the Science Fiction Film Genre

———————

Vivian Sobchack did not like the films of the Middle Period. In *Screening Space: The American Science Fiction Film* (1987), she describes "the SF films released between 1968 and 1977 (during a period of great social upheaval)" as "not successful box office" and "overtly despairing in their evocation of a future with no future" (226). Indeed, so many of the Middle Period films fit Sobchack's description.

The Omega Man ends with its gallant protagonist lying dead, felled by a primitive spear to the heart, his own red "genuine 160-proof old Anglo-Saxon" blood pooling around him.[1] *Soylent Green* ends with the horrifying realization of what a populace starving for food had been eating. In *Silent Running*, the film's idealistic ecologist resorts to murder and eventual self-destruction. *A Boy and His Dog* ends in a death. *Frogs*, *The Terminal Man*, and *Embryo* all end in death; *The Stepford Wives* ends in metaphorical (possibly actual) death.

While the protagonists of *THX 1138* and *Logan's Run* survive, their continued subsistence in a devastated world can only be seen as precarious. *The Man Who Fell to Earth* ends in dissipation and betrayal. *Colossus: The Forbin Project* and *Demon Seed* end with the impending control of humanity by inhuman computer systems. Both humans and apes endure struggle and suffering until the promising conclusion of *Battle for the Planet of the Apes*.

It is no surprise then that audiences resisted such cinematic portents of doom, considering what the country had been experiencing in reality. Before he ignominiously resigned, President Richard M. Nixon oversaw a stagnating federally mandated speed limit of no faster than 55 miles per hour.² His voluble Vice President, Spiro T. Agnew, also resigned in disgrace. As well as Nixon's presiding over the official American defeat in Vietnam, his successor, Gerald R. Ford, unsuccessfully tried to make Puerto Rico a state.³ The economy tanked. Jimmy Carter, Ford's successor, inherited (many say exacerbated) an energy crisis. The Middle East was boiling. Relations with the Soviet Union were on edge.⁴

The films of 1968 disengaged the genre from the conventions of the Fifties films and set a new trajectory for the films of the Middle Period, one reflecting the anxieties (as well as the possibilities) of the era. The films that emerged from young auteurs like George Lucas and Steven Spielberg in the late Seventies established yet a new trajectory. Sobchack loves these films. She writes, "In 1977, George Lucas's *Star Wars* and Steven Spielberg's *Close Encounters of the Third Kind* were released, initiating what seemed a sudden and radical shift in generic attitude and a popular renaissance of the SF film" (226). I loved these films too. In fact, after I saw George Lucas's *Star Wars* in 1977, I started regularly going to the movies again as soon as a new science fiction film was released.

Star Wars began with an opening scroll, one so long and detailed as to seem almost a parody of the expository voiceovers that opened so many of the Fifties films. Immediately, however, this sense of the Fifties dissolves into vast Kubrick-like images of space and spaceships, then unexpectedly, a golden robot with a British accent (C3PO), a beeping whistling floor vacuum (R2D2), and a formidable villain in black (Darth Vader). Allusions are made to Spice Mines of Kessel, moisture vaporators, binary load lifters, and a Dune Sea. We encounter cloaked bantams with glowing eyes (Jawas) speaking an untranslatable alien language and Sand People swinging clubs (gaffi sticks), speaking yet another alien language and riding atop huge carpet-covered yaks (Banthas). And all of this spectacle is presented as a matter of course, no need to explain. We don't know when we are (a long time ago), we don't know where we are (in a galaxy far, far away), but by the time we step into the lawless barroom at the Mos Eisley Spaceport ("You will never find a more wretched hive of scum and villainy," Obi-Wan Kenobi warns) we are ready, willing, and able to surrender to the power of The Force and this new world of glorious fun.

What we experience, however, is much more than fun. We take part in a classic hero's journey of the forces of good vs. an evil empire, along with our gallant protagonists: an obedient farm boy (Luke Skywalker), a cocky, opportunistic pilot (Han Solo), and—not a woman scientist—but a princess (Leia), whose not inconsiderable charge is to "save her people and restore freedom to the galaxy." Critics and audiences loved *Star Wars*.

In a *Variety* May 25, 1977, review, Murf. described the film as an "outstanding adventure fantasy," a "magnificent film." "Like a breath of fresh air," Murf. further stated, *Star Wars* "sweeps away the cynicism that has in recent years obscured the concepts of valor, dedication and honor."

I recall, as Murf. describes, being swept away as well by the spectacular effects in *Close Encounters of the Third Kind*: iridescent balls of light speeding down the highway, the sudden appearance of the gargantuan Mothership from behind dark roiling clouds. I remember being transported by the glorious music of John Williams. Johnny Mathis's rendition of "Chances Are" that played in the background during the terrifying abduction scene reminded me of an earlier, gentler time, quietly reassuring me that all would be well in the end. I was astonished by the appearance of friendly alien beings that, unlike the intimidating Gort in *The Day the Earth Stood Still*, delicately descended from the ship's opening at the film's conclusion. As Murf. wrote in his contemporary *Variety* review, the film's "climax is an absolute stunner, literate in plotting, dazzling in execution and almost reverent in tone."

Despite what I saw in the Fifties films—Gen. John Hanley's brain being sucked out of his head in *Earth vs. the Flying Saucers*, little David Maclean's parents being zombified by alien implants in *Invaders from Mars*, a well-meaning pastor being vaporized by a heat ray in *The War of the Worlds*—I always thought the aliens would be good. As a child, I even wished to be taken up by them. One of my favorite books was *Zip Zip and His Flying Saucer* (1956) by John M. Schealer and Hans Helweg (illustrator). Opedoxtromeldee, who readers eventually discovered had a twin named Opedoxtrolemdee, was a brave little Martian, stranded on Earth after his spaceship crashed. Cavorting with a brother and sister who discovered him, Zip Zip, as he was nicknamed, was helpful and handy. My best friend and I gave each other the twin Martian names, and insisted that our grammar school teachers use them when they called on us.

Superman: The Movie, released around Christmas time in 1978, also provided uplifting science fiction entertainment. The sequences where Superman rescues reporter Lois Lane from a crashing helicopter, nabs criminals in the act, stops the flooding that results from Lex Luthor's nefarious plot to detonate the San Andreas Fault were as engaging and evocative of childhood hope and playfulness as were the childlike aliens in *Close Encounters of the Third Kind*. Indeed, as Jerold J. Abrams writes in his commentary on *Close Encounters of the Third Kind* in *101 Sci-Fi Movies You Must See Before You Die*, "The aliens seen in the movie's climax were played by children" (190). Likewise, Superman's action-filled adventures are just as true to childhood and to the episodes of the *Superman* series I watched on television after school and the *Superman* DC comics I bought with my weekly allowance at the dime store.

Sobchack writes that "the dominant attitudes of most mainstream SF has been *nostalgia*—an attitude clearly evidenced by *Star Wars*' shiny evocation of the future as 'Long, long, ago...,'" and "by *Close Encounters*' yearning for childhood rather than for its end" (229). Again, she and I concur. Contemporary audiences agreed with both of us. Har. described *Superman: The Movie* in *Variety*'s December 13, 1978, review as "a wonderful, chuckling, preposterously exciting fantasy guaranteed to challenge world box-office records."

In *Science Fiction Film* (2001), J.P. Telotte is a bit less ebullient, noting in these new films "a kind of recoil in the genre, what some might describe as a conservative turn" (105). As the science fiction film genre is wont to

A friendly alien being from *Close Encounters of the Third Kind* (1977) **(Photofest)**.

anticipate audience desires and anxieties often before we even know we have them, this dynamic shift in the genre presaged the coming of politically conservative Ronald Reagan and his promise in the campaign for the 1980 presidency to "make America great again." "We cannot accept continued inflation, a mismanaged energy crisis, the erosion of our dollar, and the loss of our personal hopes," a Ronald Reagan for President 1980 Campaign Brochure stated. "We can solve our problems. We can do it with American ingenuity, common sense and strength of purpose," Reagan's campaign literature assured us.[5]

Many Americans were tired of Jimmy Carter and his insistence that we confront the country's problems with austerity. "We have demanded that the American people sacrifice, and they have done very well," Carter responded to a question about rising unemployment and inflation in the October 28, 1980, Carter-Reagan Presidential Debate.[6] Many of us became frustrated with Carter's seeming inability to improve economic conditions or handle a crisis. The country was already ready in 1977 for what came to be referred to in Reagan's campaign for reelection in 1984 as "Morning in America." A hero will save us, the fresh new science fiction film genre assured us. All will be well.

And indeed, with his political brilliance, Reagan claimed the hero's journey as his own in 1983 when he embraced the (intended to be disparaging) term "Star Wars" for his controversial Strategic Defense Initiative.[7] "I urge you to beware the temptation of pride—the temptation of blithely declaring yourselves above it all and label both sides equally at fault, to ignore the facts of history and the aggressive impulses of an evil empire, to simply call the arms race a giant misunderstanding and thereby remove yourself from the struggle between right and wrong and good and evil," he stated to his audience, forthrightly referencing Lucas's film.[8]

However, darker, more cautionary forces were still in effect in films such as the remake of *The Invasion of the Body Snatchers* and *Alien* that can be read as resisting the appeal of Reagan's polarizing resolutions. The pods that invade small-town America in the 1956 version of *Invasion of the Body Snatchers* have been variously interpreted in both popular and academic literature on the film as either anxiety over Fifties conformity or fear of Communist infiltration.

The pods in the 1978 remake of *Invasion of the Body Snatchers* can likewise be interpreted with a certain fluidity. Was the film implying that we must deal with the problems Carter said faced us lest we lose our individuality as a nation? Or was it implying that danger lay ahead if we resisted the national attitude that eventually became The Reagan Revolution? A clue to the filmmakers' sensibilities lies in the response of Matthew Bennell (the film's upgrade of Kevin McCarthy's Dr. Miles J. Bennell) to the concern his friend Elizabeth Driscoll (erstwhile Becky) has about her boyfriend. Matthew is naturally dismissive of Elizabeth's overwhelming certainty that her partner is not her partner any more. He suggests that she see a psychiatrist who could help her consider more likely scenarios: whether he "was having an affair, whether he'd become gay, whether he had a social disease, or whether he'd become a Republican." Thus the film can certainly be read, in my opinion as a longtime Democrat, as resisting the optimistic certainty that Reagan and the Republicans were espousing.

The fate of the astronauts at the end of the Fifties film *Rocketship X-M* could satisfy those who wanted women back in their traditional roles as well as those who believed women had other options. *The Outer Limits* episode "A Feasibility Study" could be interpreted as supporting the traditional marriage structure as well as challenging it. Despite the subtle dig at Republicans, the 1978 remake of *Invasion of the Body Snatchers* wisely leaves interpretation open. Audiences could read the pods however they wished. Or they could simply enjoy a really good science fiction film, as did Poll., who described the film in a contemporary *Variety* review as an "excellent sci-fi remake," one that "validates the entire concept of remakes." Such is the joy of the science fiction film. It can entertain us like a thrill ride as well as compel us to think about matters we ordinarily would not.

Ridley Scott's 1979 *Alien*, a film with a larger budget than *Invasion of the Body Snatchers* as well as the potential for lucrative future franchising, likewise capitalized on the renewed interest in the science fiction film. At the same time, like *Star Wars, Close Encounters of the Third Kind, Superman: The Movie*, and *Invasion of the Body Snatchers*,[9] it harkened back to the conventions of a past that was rapidly becoming mythologized. Much of *Alien* resonates with the images and atmosphere of Stanly Kubrick's 1968 film *2001: A Space Odyssey*. *Alien* opens with a wide view of space— the stars, planets—under the credits, while ethereal music plays on the soundtrack. We see a detailed model of the Nostromo approaching, though already having logged millions of space miles, it is darker, craggier than *2001*'s pristine Discovery One. We see the inside of the Nostromo, as we saw the interior of Discovery One, as the camera slowly pans throughout. Nostromo's interior, like its exterior, is dark, somewhat dirty, and utilitarian, with its valves, switches and cables. As in *2001*, we see astronauts in hibernation pods, though in *Alien*, they are wakened by the ship's computer (Mother), not murdered, as Hal murdered the hibernating astronauts in his care. Also, just as space travel was characterized by its tedium in *2001: A Space Odyssey*, in *Alien*, the astronauts are more concerned about their pay grade than they are about the wonders of deep space. "Before we dock, I think we ought to discuss the bonus situation," are some of the first distinct words we hear as the film's characters talk among themselves.

Extending even further back into the past, Sigourney Weaver's Ripley resuscitated the trope of the commanding (and of course attractive) woman scientist/adventurer of the Fifties films. In Ripley we see reverberations of Dr. Lesley Joyce, who gave orders to the military in *It Came from Beneath the Sea*; Dr. Iris Ryan, who dodged a flesh-eating alien infection in space in *The Angry Red Planet*; mathematician Sally Caldwell, whose orthographic projections and Earth curvature calibration work helped track a menacing flying creature in *The Giant Claw*; and Dr. Patricia "Pat" Medford, who gave the order to destroy a coven of gigantic mutated ants ("Burn it. I said, burn it!") in *Them!*

Audiences loved *Alien*. "Another hot summer at the Fox-office," wrote Har. in *Variety*, describing the film as "an old-fashioned scary movie, set in a realistic sci-fi future, made all the more believable by the expert craftsmanship that the industry just gets better and better at."

Yet our heroine, as Telotte writes, winds up "adrift in suspended animation," suggesting that *Alien* and films like it may be offering a "subtle warning" (30). Did we fear that we were being taken over by forces, whatever they may have been, that would be difficult to overcome? Like Cmdr. Kit Draper and his little monkey Mona in 1964's *Robinson Crusoe on Mars*, Ripley is accompanied by a non-human companion—her pussy cat, Jones. Is woman, once freed of male interference (or support), now lost in uncharted space?

And of course there was *Star Trek: The Motion Picture*. Paul. in *Variety* said of the film that it "includes all of the ingredients the tv show's fans thrive on: the philosophical dilemma wrapped in a scenario of mind control, troubles with the space ship, the dependable and understanding Kirk, the

Ripley (Sigourney Weaver) and Jones in *Alien* (1979) (Photofest).

ever logical Spock, and a suspenseful tale with a twist ending." Other reviews, however, have not been so positive. *Variety*'s Lor. in a contemporary review of *Star Trek II: The Wrath of Kahn* described *Star Trek: The Motion Picture* as "not well liked." In yet another review of *Star Trek II: The Wrath of Kahn*, this time *in 101 Sci-Fi Movies You Must See Before You Die*, Marty McKee describes *Star Trek: The Motion Picture* (which is not included in this compilation of 101 films) as "lumbering" (233). Sobchack notes that some viewers considered aspects of *Star Trek: The Motion Picture* to be "interminable" and "overreverent" (276). Even Jon Povill, the film's associate producer, admits in *The Longest Trek: Writing the Motion Picture* that "we were trying too hard."

With *Star Trek II: The Wrath of Kahn* the filmmakers got it right. McKee ranks the film (which is included in *101 Sci-Fi Movies You Must See Before You Die*) as "the best of the ten Trek films (to date)." It is "a summer blockbuster that simultaneously thrills, enlightens, and touches its audience," he writes (233). Lor. in *Variety*, described the film as "a very satisfying space adventure, closer in spirit and format to the popular tv series than to its big-budget ... predecessor," explaining that its "story is nominally a sequel to the tv episode 'Space Seed.'" Sobchack concurs. "The 'futurism' of the *Star Trek* films is nostalgically backward-looking to earlier versions of the future," she writes, describing them as "conservative and nostalgic, imagining the future by looking backward to the imagination of a textual past" (276–277).

The textual past toward which *Star Trek: The Motion Picture* looked, however, was one that relied on a more cinematic past than was necessary. Imitating the astounding visual effects of *2001: A Space Odyssey*, for example, the film indulges in long expanses of lightshows and repeated point-of-view shots of wonder. We even see close-up shots of Spock's face as he careens through a vast expanse of space—just as we saw with *2001*'s Dave Bowman—an extravaganza of multi-colored images reflected in his helmet's face plate, all accompanied by an ethereal atonal soundtrack.[10] Povill says, "We were the first movie to be made from a TV series, to my knowledge, and so we were really filled with the idea of, we had to make this really important. We had to make this much bigger." As the success of *Star Trek II: The Wrath of Khan* demonstrated, though, the filmmakers did not have to do that. Ironically, the ultimate strengths of *Star Trek: The Motion Picture* are those very elements the filmmakers failed to trust.

The return of William Shatner as an authoritative Capt. James T. Kirk and the return of DeForest Kelly as a reluctant Dr. Leonard McCoy (Bones) are warm, familiar and yes, nostalgic. However, one notices with that sense of nostalgia that what Sobchack refers to as the film's "earlier versions of the future" had already encapsulated the Morning in America that this new auteur-driven development in the science fiction film genre embodied—a point which reinforces my argument that the *Star Trek* television series was indeed not the repository of the Fifties films, but was rather already looking forward to a textual future soon to come. Just as *Star Wars* did not explicate for audiences the fantastic new worlds it was depicting, neither did the producers of *Star Trek* the television series feel the need to justify the extraordinary (for the era) diversity the series depicted.

Actor James Doohan played an engineer from Scotland, who "claimed to have based Scotty's accent on an Aberdeen accent he once heard," as stated in the Wikipedia entry "Scotty (Star Trek)."[11] Walter Koenig was Russian ensign Pavel Chekov. George Takei (an actor who has since identified as gay) was Sulu, selected by Gene Roddenberry "to represent all of Asia," as stated in the Wikipedia entry "Hikaru Sulu."[12] Nichelle Nicholls as communications officer Lt. Uhura was, as stated in the Wikipedia entry "Star Trek: The Original Series," "the first African American woman to hold such an important role in an American television series,"[13] and a character whose interracial kiss with Capt. Kirk presaged the groundbreaking cinematic kiss between Det. Thorn (Charlton Heston) and Lisa (Rosalind Cash) in 1971's *The Omega Man*. And of course there was Leonard Nimoy as Spock, the ultimate "Other."

All these characters returned in *Star Trek: The Motion Picture*, along with the addition of Indian actress Persis Khambatta as Deltan navigator Ilia. This appreciation of multiculturalism did not preclude the addition to the cast of (white) American actor Stephen Collins as Adm. Willard Decker, who obediently accepts his demotion to captain once Kirk comes aboard to take command. Moreover, the respect for authority and mutually agreed upon adherence to protocol by all the crewmembers reflects, as did the series, the conservatism of the Reagan Revolution as well as "the concepts of valor, dedication and honor" that Murf. so appreciated about *Star Wars*. Yes, *Star Trek: The Motion Picture* was looking backward, but the past it was looking backward toward was the present of the television series that was itself already representing both the diversity and the conservatism of the future in which the film would come to exist.

•••

Telotte writes that "the most important effect of the epic constructions of Lucas and Spielberg ... was their demonstration that the science fiction film could once again be ... a highly appealing and tremendously profitable genre. As a result," he writes, "a flood of science fiction films appeared in the early 1980s" (108). More specifically, the concept of the franchise was solidified. *Variety*'s Har. wrote of 1980's *The Empire Strikes Back*, "Reaching finish, 'Empire' blatantly sets up the third in the 'Star Wars' trilogy, presuming the marketplace will signify its interest. It's a pretty safe presumption." This sequel was followed by the predictably successful *Return of the Jedi* (1983), *Episode I: The Phantom Menace* (1999), *Episode II: Attack of the Clones* (2002), *Episode III: Revenge of the Sith* (2005), and *Star Wars: The Clone Wars* (2008). At the time of this writing audiences are eagerly awaiting a December 2015 release of *Star Wars: The Force Awakens*, a film which as well as bringing back Harrison Ford, Carrie Fisher, and Mark Hamill, adds to the cast Academy Award winner and *People Magazine*'s Most Beautiful Person of 2014, Lupita Nyong'o.

Variety's Step. described 1980's *Superman II* as "a solid, classy, cannily constructed piece of entertainment that already bodes a long hot box-office summer." This sequel was followed by the likewise successful *Superman III* (1983) and *Superman IV: The Quest for Peace* (1987). Following 1982's well appreciated *Star Trek II: The Wrath of Khan* were *Star Trek III: The Search for Spock* (1984), *Star Trek IV: The Voyage Home* (1986), *Star Trek V: The Final Frontier* (1989), *Star Trek VI: The Undiscovered Country* (1991), and more. As of this writing, "a thirteenth theatrical feature ... has been confirmed for release in July 2016, to coincide with the franchise's 50th anniversary," as stated in the Wikipedia entry "Star Trek." Regarding Ridley Scott's feminist heroine of 1979's terrifying *Alien*, Steffan Hantke writes in his overview of James Cameron's 1986 *Aliens* in *101 Sci-Fi Movies You Must See Before You Die*, "Fully armored, her pumped-up physique decked out with guns and ammo, Ripley is that ambiguously gendered creature that ... issues the post-feminist challenge to all men: Can you measure up?" (298). *Aliens* was followed by the ominous as well as successful films *Alien³* (1992) and the end of the franchise, *Alien: Resurrection* (1997).

Fifties films were taken seriously, updated, and remade. John Carpenter remade Howard Hawkes' *The Thing* in 1982. David Cronenberg remade Kurt Neumann's *The Fly* in 1986. New subjects and vistas began to appear in the genre in films such as 1980's *Altered States*; 1982's *Blade Runner*, described by *Variety*'s Cart. as "the most riveting—and depressing—vision of the future since 'A Clockwork Orange,'" and 1982's uplifting antidote to *Blade Runner*: *E.T. the Extra-Terrestrial*. The 1980s also saw such various science fiction films as *Starman*, *The Terminator*, *Back to the Future*, *Cocoon*, *Robocop*, and *The Abyss*.

Not unexpectedly, there were films that could be considered as outliers, films that addressed potentially divisive subjects, as did the films of the Middle Period. *The Incredible Shrinking Woman* (1981), for example, as Sobchack writes, "reformulates 1957's *The Incredible Shrinking Man* (Jack Arnold) not only in terms of gender, but also in terms of the diminished dimensions of human being in the now totally commodified consumer culture of advanced capitalism" (268–269). *The Brother from Another Planet* (1984) is described by Telotte as one of those films that "frame their assault on racial prejudice and misunderstanding ... through our interaction with aliens who are coded as a racial other" (24). In *101 Sci-Fi Movies You Must See Before You Die,* Mikel Koven describes the post-apocalyptic scenario of *The Quiet Earth* (1985) in which the protagonist "roams around the empty city, surrounded by the detritus left behind by the capitalistic West" (294).

In the face of blockbuster supremacy, science fictional outliers continue to persevere. *District 9* (2009) and *Monsters* (2010) tackled the polarizing issue of immigration in startling science fictional ways. Zal Batmanglij and Brit Marling's 2011 films *Another Earth* and *The Sound of My Voice* questioned the persistence (or not) of identity over space and time.

And then there was *Gravity* (2013) and now *Interstellar.*

I could go on...

Zac Hobson (Bruno Lawrence) surrounded by the detritus of the West in *The Quiet Earth* (1985) (Photofest).

Filmographies (1964–1979)

The following filmography contains production data for science fiction films from 1964 to 1979. The information was obtained, confirmed, and compiled from a variety of sources including DVDs of the films, DVD liner notes, *Variety's Complete Science Fiction Reviews* (1985), and the Internet Movie Database. Entries contain excerpts taken directly from the films to indicate contemporary representations of women (traditional as well as progressive) and men (heroic, lonely, and angry) as well as gender relations between the two (both realistic and extraordinary). **As is my wont, details about women in science are highlighted in bold.**

1964 *Dr. Strangelove or: How I Learned to Stop Worrying and Love the Bomb.* Dir. Stanley Kubrick. Scr. Stanley Kubrick, Terry Southern, and Peter George. Based on *Red Alert* by Peter George. Perfs. Peter Sellers, *Capt. Lionel Mandrake, Pres. Merkin Muffley*, and *Dr. Strangelove*; George C. Scott, *Gen. Buck Turgidson*; Sterling Hayden, *Brig. Gen. Jack D. Ripper*; Keenan Wynn, *Col. Bat Guano*; Slim Pickens, *Maj. King Kong*; Tracy Reed, *Miss Scott*. Prod. Stanley Kubrick. Assoc. Prod. Victor Lyndon. Columbia. (b&w)

> **GEN. TURGIDSON** (on phone): Bump everything up to condition red, and stand by the blower. I'll get back to you.
> **MISS SCOTT** (his secretary; in bed; wearing a bikini and high heels): What's up?
> **TURGIDSON**: Nothing. Where's my shorts?
> **SCOTT**: On the floor. Where are you going?
> **TURGIDSON**: No place.... I thought I might mosey over to the War Room for a few minutes, see what's going on over there.
> **SCOTT**: It's 3:00 in the morning.
> **TURGIDSON**: Yeah, the Air Force never sleeps.
> **SCOTT** (taking a long, slow drag on a cigarette): Buck, honey, I'm not sleepy either.
> **TURGIDSON**: I know it's hard, baby. (He crawls over to her on the bed.) Tell

you what you do. You just start your countdown, and old Bucky will be back here before you can say "Blastoff!"

1964 *Fail-Safe*. Dir. Sidney Lumet. Scr. Walter Bernstein. Based on *Fail Safe* by Eugene Burdick and Harvey Wheeler. Perfs. Dan O'Herlihy, *Gen. Black*; Walter Matthau, *Groeteschele*; Frank Overton, *Gen. Bogan*; Ed Binns, *Col. Grady*; Fritz Weaver, *Col. Cascio*; Henry Fonda, *The President*; Larry Hagman, *Buck;* Nancy Berg, *Ilsa Wolfe,* Hildy Parks, *Katherine Black*; Janet Ward, *Mrs. Grady*. Prod. Max E. Youngstein. Columbia. (b&w)

> **GEN. BLACK**: Katie, the dream and what I'm doing—sometimes I feel the only way I can make it disappear is to give it up, to resign.
> **MRS. BLACK**: But you can't resign. You can't give up your whole life.
> **GEN. BLACK**: You're my life too. You and the boys.

1964 *The Last Man on Earth* **(Italian-U.S.).** Dirs. Ubaldo Ragona and Sidney Salkow. Scr. Logan Swanson and William P. Leicester. Based on *I Am Legend* by Richard Mathesen. Perfs. Vincent Price, *Dr. Robert Morgan*; Franca Bettoia, *Ruth Collins*; Emma Danieli, *Virginia Morgan*; Giacomo Rossi-Stuart, *Ben Cortman*. Prod. Robert L. Lippert. Assoc. Prod. Harold E. Knox. Associated Producers in conjunction with Produzioni La Regina. Allied Artists. (b&w)

> **MORGAN**: There was a time eating was pleasurable. Now it bores me. Just fuel for survival.

1964 *Robinson Crusoe on Mars*. Dir. Byron Haskin. Scr. Ib Melchior and John C. Higgins. Based on *Robinson Crusoe* by Daniel Defoe. Perfs. Paul Mantee, *Cmdr. Christopher Draper*; Victor Lundin, *Friday*; Adam West, *Col. Dan McReady*; The Woolly Monkey, *Mona*. Prod. Aubrey Schenk. Exec. Prod. Edwin F. Zabel. Paramount.

> **DRAPER** (into recorder): All right, here's another note for you boys in Survival, for you geniuses in Human Factors. A guy can lick the problems of heat, water, shelter, food. I know. I've done it. And here's the hairiest problem of all—isolation, being alone.

1964 *The Time Travelers*. Dir. Ib Melchior. Scr. Ib Melchior. Story Ib Melchior and David Hewitt. Perfs. Preston Foster, *Dr. Erik von Steiner*; Philip Carey, *Dr. Steve Connors*; **Merry Anders, Carol White, Laboratory Technician;** John Hoyt, *Varno*; Dennis Patrick, *Councilman Willard*; **Joan Woodbury, Gadra, Scientist of the Future;** Delores Wells, *Reena*; Steve Franken, *Danny*. Prod. William Redlin. Assoc. Prod. Don Levy. Dobil Productions. American International.

> **GADRA**: Of course a more conventional fuel will be used for lift-off and escape.
> **DR. CONNORS**: Cutting down the critical danger stage.
> **GADRA**: Oh exactly. We'll only be using an inflammable fuel during the short periods of take-off and landing on New Earth. The photon drive will take

over the star journey into deep space. It's a great improvement over the old ion drive.

DR. CONNORS: Old? We just started to experiment with that.

WHITE: I hate to let my ignorance show in front of such great minds, but what exactly is a photon?

GADRA: It's a particle of light. Photon propulsion is nothing more nor less than a beam of light.

WHITE: Just a beam of light?

GADRA: Well, a stream of photons shooting at 186,000 miles per second from the starship engine, driving it through space on the action-reaction principle.

1965 *Crack in the World.* Dir. Andrew Marton. Scr. Jon Manchip White and Julian Halevy. Story Jon Manchip White. Perfs. Dana Andrews, *Dr. Stephen Sorenson*; **Janette Scott, *Dr. Maggie Sorenson, Project Inner Space Scientist*;** Keiron Moore, *Dr. Ted Rampion*; Alexander Knox, *Sir Charles Eggerston.* Prod. Bernard Glasser and Lester A. Sansom. A Philip Yordan Production. Paramount.

MAGGIE: Stephen, for the umpteenth time, Ted Rampion is not my pinup. He's young, brilliant, dances divinely, and plays very good tennis, but he isn't the one I picked. I picked you. You're my husband.

STEPHEN: You picked him once.

MAGGIE: That's before I took thermodynamics with you.

STEPHEN: And picked an old man with two left feet and no talent to speak of, physical or otherwise.

MAGGIE: Um hum.

1965 *The Eye Creatures* **(TV).** Dir. Larry Buchanan. Perfs. John Ashley, *Stan Kenyon*; Cynthia Hull, *Susan Rogers*; Warren Hammack, *Lt. Robertson*; Chet Davis, *Mike Lawrence*; Bill Peck, *Carl Fenton.* Assoc. Prod. Edwin Tobolowski. Azalea.

WAITRESS: Now, will there be anything else?

MIKE (ogling her): Right now I can't afford what I'm thinking.

WAITRESS: I'm sure of that. And I got news for you. You never will.

CARL: Say, there is one thing. I was wondering if you could tell me how to…. (He takes out a piece of paper.) I can't read my writing. (She sits down next to him to look at the paper.) Let's see, could you tell me how to get to … first base with you tonight? (She gets up and walks away.) Well, at least I tried.

1965 *The Human Duplicators.* Dir. Hugo Grimaldi. Scr. Arthur C. Pierce. Perfs. George Nader, *Glenn Martin*; Barbara Nichols, *Gale Wilson*; George Macready, *Prof. Vaughn Dornheimer*; Dolores Faith, *Lisa Dornheimer*; Hugh Beaumont, *Austin Welles*; Richard Kiel, *Agent Kolos.* Prod. Hugo Grimaldi and Arthur C. Pierce. Exec. Prod. Lawrence H. Woolner. Woolner Bros.

WELLES: We've got to come up with something, and quick. Washington's breathing down my neck.

MARTIN (looking at photographs): The question is which one of these is gonna be next.

WELLES: Take your pick. They're all above suspicion. We've had them under surveillance for months.

MARTIN (looking at a photograph of an attractive woman): Whoa. Here's one I wouldn't mind having under surveillance. Dr. Lin Young. Chemical Research Division, Pacific Laboratories.

WELLES: Ah, she's top drawer. She's here from Taiwan as a special favor to the nationals.

1965 *Mutiny in Outer Space.* Dir. Hugo Grimaldi. Scr. Arthur C. Pierce. Story Arthur C. Pierce and Hugo Grimaldi. Perfs. William Leslie, *Maj. Gordon Towers*; **Dolores Faith,** ***Faith Montaine, Biochemist***; **Pamela Curran,** ***Lt. Connie Engstrom, Communications Officer***; Richard Garland, *Col. Frank Cromwell*; Harold Lloyd, Jr., *Sgt. Andrews*; James Dobson, *Dr. Hoffman*; Glenn Langan, *Gen. Knowland*; Carl Crow, *Capt. Dan Webber*. Prod. Hugo Grimaldi and Arthur C. Pierce. Exec. Prod. Bernard Woolner, Lawrence Woolner, and David Woolner. Woolner Bros. (b&w)

CAPT. WEBBER: Tell me something, Major. What did you mean when you told Gen. Knowland that you planned it that way, the layover on the Space Station, I mean. What's so special about it?

MAJ. TOWERS: It's not what, Webber. It's who.

CAPT. WEBBER: Who. Okay, who?

MAJ. TOWERS: You've heard of heavenly bodies, haven't you, kid? Well, in about eight hours you're going to see a real live living one. You'll probably put in for an immediate transfer for tour of duty on the Space Station, but don't. You'll be too late. In one more month she'll be transferred back to Earth and into the arms of her Prince Charming and happiness ever after.

CAPT. WEBBER: You don't mean Lt. Engstrom, that great big beautiful blonde with the binary brain.

MAJ. TOWERS: That's right, I do not mean Lt. Connie Engstrom. I mean Faith Montaine.

CAPT. WEBBER: The civilian biochemist? I didn't know she was out here. I hear she's supposed to really be something.

MAJ. TOWERS: You can take my word for it. It's no supposition. It's a fact.

1965 *Village of the Giants.* Dir. Bert I. Gordon. Scr. Alan Caillou. Story Bert I. Gordon. Based on *Food of the Gods* by H.G. Wells. Perfs. Tommy Kirk, *Mike*; Johnny Crawford, *Horsey*; Beau Bridges, *Fred*; Joy Harmon, *Merrie*; Bob Random, *Rick*; Gail Gilmore, *Elsa*; Tisha Sterling, *Jean*; Tim Rooney, *Pete*; Kevin O'Neal, *Harry*; Charla Doherty, *Nancy*; Toni Basil, *Red*; Ronny Howard, *Genius*. Prod. Bert I. Gordon. Embassy.

FRED: Wild stuff.

HARRY: She really knows how to move, doesn't she?

FRED: Go! Go!

1966 *Around the World Under the Sea*. Dir. Andrew Marton. Scr. Arthur Weiss and Art Arthur. Perfs. Lloyd Bridges, *Dr. Doug Standish*; **Shirley Eaton, *Dr. Maggie Hanford, Marine Biologist and Medical Doctor***; Brian Kelly, *Dr. Craig Mosby*; David McCallum, *Dr. Philip Volker*; Keenan Wynn, *Hank Stahl*; Marshall Thompson, *Dr. Orin Hillyard*; Gary Merrill, *Dr. Gus Boren*. Prod. Ivan Tors and Andrew Marton. Assoc. Prod. Ben Chapman. MGM.

> **DR. HANFORD**: You men are in beautiful shape.
>
> **DR. STANDISH**: Well, I might say the same about you.
>
> **DR. HANFORD**: Thank you, Doctor.
>
> **DR. STANDISH**: Yeah, you're pretty rough on a man's blood pressure. I'm afraid if I weren't a happily married man with a couple of kids, I might be causing you a little trouble too.
>
> **DR. HANFORD**: Where shall I hide myself?
>
> **DR. STANDISH**: In your work, I guess.
>
> **DR. HANFORD**: I do.
>
> **DR. STANDISH**: I know you do. You've been doing a great job, but....
>
> **DR. HANFORD**: ...I'm a problem. You men gave us our freedom, but sometimes it's difficult to cope with.
>
> **DR. STANDISH**: Well, we better learn how to cope with it because you'll be there working right alongside of us. Whether it's in outer space or deep under the ocean, you'll be there.

1966 *Destination Inner Space* (TV). Dir. Francis D. Lyon. Scr. Arthur C. Pierce. Perfs. Scott Brady, *Cmdr. Wayne*; **Sheree North, *Dr. Rene Peron, Marine Biologist***; Gary Merrill, *Dr. LaSatier*; **Wende Wagner, *Sandra Welles, Underwater Photographer***; Mike Road, *Hugh Maddox*. Prod. Earle Lyon. Exec. Prod. Fred Jordan. Assoc. Prod. Wendell E. Niles, Jr. Television Enterprises Corp.

> **DR. PERON**: The specimen is under the microscope, Commander.
>
> **CMDR. WAYNE**: Oh. Well, after a tour of duty aboard a submarine for a few years, a man remembers that there are a lot more interesting things to study than seaweed.
>
> **DR. PERON**: Like women, for instance?
>
> **CMDR. WAYNE**: Yes, if they look like you.
>
> **DR. PERON**: And I suppose I'm just the woman you've been searching for.
>
> **CMDR. WAYNE**: You have a few of the qualifications.

1966 *Fahrenheit 451* (British). Dir. François Truffaut. Scr. François Truffaut and Jean-Louis Richard. Based on *Fahrenheit 451* by Ray Bradbury. Perfs.

Oskar Werner, *Guy Montag*; Julie Christie, *Clarisse/Linda Montag*; Cyril Cusack, *The Captain*; Anton Diffring, *Fabian/Headmistress*; Jeremy Spenser, *Man with the Apple*; Bee Duffell, *Book Woman*. Prod. Lewis M. Allen. Vineyard. Universal.

> WOMAN ON TV: ...so you can protect yourself on the streets. The art of self-defense and of attack on occasions may also come in handy in the home, cousins. If you watch carefully, you will see how a woman can use a man's superior weight to her own advantage. Did you see that? Now let's watch that once again. Normally. And now in slow motion. Watch it carefully again, cousins.
> MONTAG: I'm going to be promoted.
> WOMAN ON TV: As he starts to advance, notice her position.
> MONTAG: Are you listening, Linda?
> WOMAN ON TV: Knees bent slightly and toes turned slightly inward.
> LINDA: Oh, that's marvelous, Montag!
> WOMAN ON TV: There. Now you see how easily she has disposed of her...
> MONTAG: The captain told me while we were out on a call.
> LINDA: What did you say?
> MONTAG: I'm talking about my promotion.
> LINDA: Does that mean an increase, dear? How much?
> MONTAG: He didn't mention that. We could move to a larger house. Would you like that?
> LINDA: I'd rather have a second wall-set put in.

1966 *Fantastic Voyage*. Dir. Richard Fleischer. Scr. Harry Kleiner. Story Otto Klement, Jay Lewis Bixby, and David Duncan. Perfs. Stephen Boyd, *Grant*; **Raquel Welch, Cora Peterson, Technical Assistant**; Edmund O'Brien, *Gen. Carter*; Donald Pleasence, *Dr. Michaels*; Arthur O'Connell, *Col. Donald Reid*; William Redfield, *Capt. Bill Owens*; Arthur Kennedy, *Dr. Duval*. Prod. Saul David. 20th Century–Fox.

> GRANT: For a nice lady, you play with the damnedest toys, Miss Peterson.
> PETERSON: (Peterson test fires laser beam): That'll teach you where to keep your hands.
> GRANT: Now I know.

1966 *Seconds*. Dir. John Frankenheimer. Scr. Lewis John Carlino. Based on *Seconds* by David Ely. Perfs. Rock Hudson, *Tony Wilson*; Salome Jens, *Nora Marcus*; John Randolph, *Arthur Hamilton*; Will Geer, *Old Man*; Jeff Corey, *Mr. Ruby*; Richard Anderson, *Dr. Innes*; Murray Hamilton, *Charlie Evans*; Frances Reid, *Emily Hamilton*. Prod. John Frankenheimer and Edward Lewis. Joel Productions, Inc. Paramount. (b&w)

> OLD MAN: What does it all mean? It can't mean anything now anymore. There's nothing anymore, is there? Anything at all?

RANDOLPH: I expect to be president of the bank before too long. And I have my boat in the summer. We have friends.

OLD MAN: Anything at all?

RANDOLPH: Guess I never thought much about it. I leave Emily pretty much alone to do what she ... we get along. We hardly ever quarrel. Not that that's any measure of our lives. Frankly, during the last few years we hardly ever ... show much affection, But as I said.... Boat. And...

OLD MAN: So this is what happens to the dreams of youth.

1966 *Women of the Prehistoric Planet.* Dir. Arthur C. Pierce. Scr. Arthur C. Pierce. Perfs. Wendell Corey, *Adm. David King*; Keith Larsen, *Cmdr. Scott*; John Agar, *Dr. Farrell*; Paul Gilbert, *Lt. Red Bradley*; **Merry Anders, Lt. Karen Lamont, Communications Officer**; Irene Tsu, *Linda*; Roberto Ito, *Tang*; **Suzie Kaye, Ens. Stevens, Junior Communications Officer**. Prod. George Edwards. A Jack and Madelynn Broder Production.

SUZIE: Six months aboard this pressurized people package isn't exactly what I'd call a pleasure party.

BRADLEY: Well, it could be, sugar, if you'd let yourself go.

KAREN: Well, well, the wolf of outer space. Who let you out of your darkened den?

BRADLEY: Now be kind to me ladies. Don't forget that I'm your ingenious engineer, master of the maneuvering room and the activator of your gravitator. Without me there'd probably be no ups or downs.

SUZIE: Here we go again.

KAREN: I suppose we are grateful for all these amazing services, Mr. Bradley, so...

BRADLEY (moving toward Suzie): You just allow this sweet thing a few moments liberty with your old starmate, and uh, well, I'll consider you all paid in full.

KAREN (stopping him): Back to your gravitator...

1966 *Zontar, Thing from Venus* (TV). Dir. Larry Buchanan. Scr. Hillman Taylor and Larry Buchanan. Perfs. John Agar, *Dr. Curt Taylor*; Susan Bjurman, *Anne Taylor*; Anthony Huston, *Keith Ritchie*; Patricia Delaney, *Martha Ritchie*; Neil Fletcher, *Gen. Matt Young*; Warren Hammack, *Scientist*; **Colleen Carr, Louise, Technician**. Assoc. Prod. Edwin Tobolowsky. Azalea.

GENERAL: All clear. Bring her down.

SCIENTIST: Roger. Thirty seconds.

LOUISE: Position 42 north, 58 minutes.

SCIENTIST: Check.

LOUISE: 59 minutes, 43 north. Locking and locked.

SCIENTIST: Computer now programming the bird.

LOUISE: 4th cycle entering atmosphere.

SCIENTIST: Too fast! What's the matter with the blasted thing?

LOUISE: 6th cycle.

SCIENTIST: It shouldn't be past 4 by now.

GENERAL: Something wrong?

SCIENTIST: I don't know, General. It's setting its own course. It's almost as if it has a mind of its own.

LOUISE: Everything is engaged. It's just abandoning its own orbit.

SCIENTIST: This just can't be happening!

GENERAL: Exactly what's going on here?

LOUISE: I don't know, General. It's eerie. It's not acting on our control signals.

1967 *Mars Needs Women* **(TV).** Dir. Larry Buchanan. Scr. Larry Buchanan. Perfs. Tommy Kirk, *Dop*; **Yvonne Craig, *Dr. Marjorie Bolen, Space Geneticist***; Warren Hammack, *Martian*; Anthony Huston, *Martian*; Larry Tanner, *Martian*; Carl Duggan, *Martian*; Pat Delaney, *Artist*; Donna Lindberg, *Stewardess*; Bubbles Cash, *Stripper*; Neil Fletcher, *Secretary of Defense*; Chet Davis, *Mr. Fast.* Prod. Larry Buchanan. Assoc. Prod. Edwin Tobolowsky. Azalea.

TV NEWSCASTER: After meeting nothing but big brass and tight-lipped politicians all day, reporters had a pleasant surprise when one expert jetted in to Houston's International Airport. Dr. Marjorie Bolen turned out to be a stunning brunette who found it hard to hide her charm behind her horn-rimmed spectacles. Dr. Bolen wrote her thesis on space medicine and received a Pulitzer Prize for her book Space Genetics. Dr. Bolen will be part of a high-level meeting scheduled at Monitor One for some time tomorrow morning.

1967 *One Million Years B.C.* **(British).** Dir. Don Chaffney. Scr. Michael Carreras. Story Mickell Novak, George Baker, and Joseph Frickert. Perfs. Raquel Welch, *Loana*; John Richardson, *Tumak*; Percy Herbert, *Sakana*; Robert Brown, *Akhoba*; Martine Beswick, *Nupondi*; Jean Wladon, *Ahot*; Lisa Thomas, *Sura.* Prod. Michael Carreras. Assoc. Prod. Hal E. Roach, Sr., and Aida Young. Seven Arts–Hammer. 20th Century–Fox.

NARRATOR: Man. Superior to the creatures only in his cunning. There are not many men yet. Just a few tribes scattered across the wilderness, never venturing far, unaware that other tribes exist even, too busy with their own lives to be curious, too frightened of the unknown to wander. Their laws are simple. The strong take everything.

1967 *They Came from Beyond Space* **(British).** Dir. Freddie Francis. Scr. Milton Subotsky. Based on *The Gods Hate Kansas* by Joseph Millard. Perfs. Robert Hutton, *Dr. Curtis Temple*; **Jennifer Jayne, *Lee Mason, Scientist's Assistant***; Zia Mohyeddin, *Farge*; Bernard Kay, *Richard Arden*; Michael Gough, *Master of the Moon.* Prod. Maz J. Rosenberg and Milton Subotsky. Amicus.

ARDEN: Let me introduce you to some of your team....

DR. TEMPLE: I'm afraid you'll have to count me out.

ARDEN: What do you mean?

DR. TEMPLE: You'll have to take my assistant.

ARDEN: But why?

DR. TEMPLE: Doctor's orders.

ARDEN: I shall speak to the Minister. I'll have your doctor overruled.

DR. TEMPLE: It won't do you any good. Miss Mason's been with me for several years. I'm sure she can help you as much as I could.

ARDEN: Right. (To Mason) How soon can you be ready to go?

MASON: An hour.

ARDEN: I'll have a car at your flat.

1968 *Barbarella* **(Italian).** Dir. Roger Vadim. Scr. Terry Southern and Roger Vadim et al. Based on *Barbarella* by Jean Claude Forest. Perfs. **Jane Fonda,** *Barbarella, Astronavigatrix*; John Philip Law, *Pygar*; Anita Pallenberg, *The Great Tyrant*; Milo O'Shea, *Concierge/Durand-Durand*; Marcel Marceau, *Prof. Ping*; Claude Dauphin, *President of Earth*; David Hemmings, *Dildano*; Ugo Tognazzi, *Mark Hand (Catchman)*. Prod. Dino De Laurentiis. Paramount.

PRESIDENT OF EARTH: Barbarella?

BARBARELLA: Mr. President!

PRESIDENT: Love.

BARBARELLA: Love.

1968 *Charly.* Dir. Ralph Nelson. Scr. Stirling Silliphant. Based on *Flowers for Algernon* by Daniel Keyes. Perfs. Cliff Robertson, *Charly Gordon*; **Claire Bloom,** *Alice Kinnian, Doctoral Student in Psychology*; **Lilia Skala,** *Dr. Anna Strauss*; Leon Janney, *Dr. Richard Nemur*; Ruth White, *Mrs. Apple*; Richard Van Patten, *Bert*. Prod. Ralph Nelson. Exec. Prod. Selig J. Seligman. Robertson Associates. Selmur Pictures.

DR. NEMUR: We shall have to give Ms. Kinnian her notice.

DR. STRAUSS: What?

DR. NEMUR: All she can do now is ask him questions out of books that he's already absorbed. What he needs at this point is a great step forward. New conceptualization. Inductive thinking. That calls for experts, not Alice Kinnian.

1968 *Countdown.* Dir. Robert Altman. Scr. Loring Mandel. Based on *The Pilgrim Project* by Hank Searls. Perfs. James Caan, *Lee Stegler*; Joanna Moore, *Mickey Stegler*; Robert Duvall, *Chiz Stewart*; Barbara Baxley, *Jean Stewart*; Charles Aidman, *Gus*; Steve Ihnat, *Ross Duellan*; Michael Murphy, *Rick*; Ted Knight, *Walter Larson*. Exec. Prod. William Conrad. Warner Bros.-Seven Arts.

LEE STEGLER (to wife): There wasn't enough time when I had to weigh the mission on one side with my life with you and Stevie on the other. I knew I'd be back. I never had a thought of not coming back. It's not fair, but that's the way it's gonna be. I can't go with a choice like that one. I don't believe I won't be back. I spent years thinking of myself taking this trip. I always thought I'm the guy that's gonna do it. That's who I am. If I don't make this trip, then who the hell am I? Forgive me. Forgive me.

1968 *Mission Mars*. Dir. Nicholas Webster. Scr. Mike St. Claire. Story Aubrey Wisberg. Perfs. Darren McGavin, *Cmdr. Mike Blaiswick*; Nick Adams, *Nick Grant*; George DeVries, *Duncan*; Heather Hewitt, *Edith Blaiswick*; Michael DeBeausset, *Cliff Lawson*; Shirley Parker, *Alice Grant*; Bill Kelly, *Russian Astronaut*. Prod. Everett Rosenthal. Exec. Prod. Morton Fallick. Sagittarius. Allied Artists.

> ALICE: I didn't think I could take it seeing you go off in that thing, but I just can't seem to stay away.
> NICK: Hey, I understand. You all right?
> ALICE: Yes, I'm fine. How about you?
> NICK: Oh, I'm all right.
> ALICE: I still wish you wouldn't go.
> NICK: Look, everything'll be all right when I get back.
> ALICE: When you get back—you mean if you get back.
> NICK: I'll get back.
> ALICE: Nobody can guarantee that, not even love.

1968 *Planet of the Apes*. Dir. Franklin J. Schaffner. Scr. Michael Wilson and Rod Serling. Based on *Planet of the Apes* by Pierre Boulle. Perfs. Charlton Heston, *George Taylor*; Roddy McDowall, *Cornelius*; **Kim Hunter, *Zira, Animal Psychologist*;** Maurice Evans, *Dr. Zaius*; James Whitmore, *President of the Assembly*; James Daly, *Honorious*; Linda Harrison, *Nova*; Robert Gunner, *Landon*; Lou Wagner, *Lucius*; Woodrow Perfrey, *Maximus*; Jeff Burton, *Dodge*; Buck Kartalian, *Julius*. Prod. Arthur P. Jacobs. Assoc. Prod. Mort Abrahams. APJAC. 20th Century–Fox.

> ASSISTANT: You made it. Why can't I?
> ZIRA: What do you mean "made it"? I'm an animal psychologist, that's all. We have no authority.
> ASSISTANT: You do all right when it comes to getting space and equipment.
> ZIRA: That's because Dr. Zaius realizes our work has value. The foundations of scientific brain surgery are being laid right here in studies of cerebral functions of those animals.

1968 *2001: A Space Odyssey*. Dir. Stanley Kubrick. Scr. Stanley Kubrick and Arthur C. Clarke. Based on "The Sentinel" by Arthur C. Clarke. Perfs. Kier Dullea, *Dr. Dave Bowman*; Gary Lockwood, *Dr. Frank Poole*; William Sylvester, *Dr. Heywood Floyd*; Daniel Richter, *Moon Watcher*; Leonard Rossiter, *Dr. Andrei Smyslov*; **Margaret Tyzack, *Elena, Russian Scientist*; Irena Marr, *Russian Scientist*; Krystyna Marr, *Russian Scientist*.** Prod. Stanley Kubrick. MGM.

> RECEPTIONIST: Good morning, sir.
> Dr. FLOYD: Good morning.

RECEPTIONIST: We haven't seen you up here for a long time.

FLOYD: No. Very nice to see you again.

RECEPTIONIST: Did you have a pleasant flight, sir?

FLOYD: Yes, very nice, thanks. I think Mr. Miller of Station Security is supposed to be meeting me.

RECEPTIONIST: May I call him for you?

FLOYD: Would you, please?

1969 *Journey to the Far Side of the Sun* **(British)**. Dir. Robert Parrish. Scr. Gerry and Sylvia Anderson and Donald James. Story Gerry and Sylvia Anderson. Perfs. Roy Thinnes, *Col. Glenn Ross*; Ian Hendry, *John Kane*; Patrick Wymark, *Jason Webb*; Lynn Loring, *Sharon Ross*; **Loni von Friedl, *Lisa Hartman, Eurosec Security*.** Prod. Gerry and Sylvia Anderson. Assoc. Prod. Ernest Holding. Universal.

JASON: I want a rundown on the current security position.

LISA: Defensively?

JASON: Uh huh.

LISA: We've housed all findings, computer programs, and visual data from Sun Probe I in Vault Two.

JASON: Access?

LISA: Restricted.

1969 *Marooned*. Dir. John Sturges. Scr. Mayo Simon. Based on *Marooned* by Martin Caidin. Perfs. Gregory Peck, *Charles Keith*; Richard Crenna, *Jim Pruett*; David Janssen, *Ted Dougherty*; James Franciscus, *Clayton Stone*; Gene Hackman, *Buzz Lloyd*; Lee Grant, *Celia Pruett*; Nancy Kovack, *Teresa Stone*; Mariette Hartley, *Betty Lloyd*. Prod. M.J. Frankovich. Assoc. Prod. Frank Capra, Jr. Frankovich-Sturges Pictures. Columbia.

DOUGHERTY: No retrofire. They're still up there. It'll take a little time to psych out the engine.

MRS. LLOYD: Well, I guess it's time to go home and light the fires and mind the kids. (to Mrs. Stone) Do you need a lift?

MRS. PRUETT: Did you talk to them?

DOUGHERTY: Yes. They're fine.

MRS. STONE: For how long?

DOUGHERTY: Well, we'll be in touch Mrs. Stone.

MRS. STONE: Thank you, but I'd also like to know what's happening.

MRS. LLOYD: Teresa, Celia and I have been in this business ten years. We learned the best thing is for us girls to keep our feelings to ourselves and let the men get on with their jobs. Right, Celia?

MRS. PRUETT: Wrong. It's been fifteen years.

1969 *Moon Zero Two* **(British)**. Dir. Roy Ward Baker. Scr. Michael Carreras. Story Gavin Lyall, Frank Hardman, and Martin Davison. Perfs. James Olson, *Capt. William H. Kemp*; Catherina von Schell, *Clementine Taplin*; Warren

Mitchell, *J.J. Hubbard*; Adrienne Corri, *Elizabeth Murphy*; Ori Levy, *Korminski*; Dudley Foster, *Whitson*; Bernard Bresslaw, *Harry*. Prod. Michael Carreras. Hammer Warner Bros.-Seven Arts.

> OFFICER: We've got regular flights to Mars and Venus. What more do you want?
>
> KEMP: I'm not coming back into the corporation on passenger runs. I'm a space pilot, not a mechanically-minded wet nurse.

1970 *Beneath the Planet of the Apes*. Dir. Ted Post. Scr. Paul Dehn. Story Paul Dehn and Mort Abrahams. Perfs. James Franciscus, *Brent*; **Kim Hunter, Zira, Animal Psychologist**; Maurice Evans, *Dr. Zaius*; Linda Harrison, *Nova*; Paul Richards, *Mendez*; Victor Buono, *Fat Man*; James Gregory, *Ursus*; Jeff Corey, *Caspay*; Natalie Trundy, *Albina*; Thomas Gomez, *Minister*; David Watson, *Cornelius*; Don Pedro Colley, *Negro*; Charlton Heston, *Taylor*. Prod. Arthur P. Jacobs. Assoc. Prod. Mort Abrahams. APJAC. 20th Century–Fox.

> CORNELIUS: Dr. Zaius, how nice. We were just about to have something to eat.
>
> DR. ZAIUS: Not until I talk some sense into that headstrong wife of yours. Where is she!
>
> ZIRA: Good day, Dr. Zaius.
>
> DR. ZAIUS: Has there been an accident?
>
> ZIRA: Cornelius hit me.
>
> DR. ZAIUS: Huh?
>
> ZIRA: For my bad behavior at the meeting.
>
> DR. ZAIUS: I don't blame him.

1970 *Colossus: The Forbin Project*. Dir. Joseph Sargent. Scr. James Bridges. Based on *Colossus* by D. F. Jones. Perfs. Eric Braeden, *Dr. Charles Forbin*; **Susan Clark, Dr. Cleo Markham, Computer Scientist**; Gordon Pinsent, *The President*; William Schallert, *CIA Director Grauber*; Georg Stanford Brown, *Dr. John F. Fisher*; Marion Ross, *Angela Fields*. Prod. Stanley Chase. Universal.

> DR. FORBIN: Do you understand the meaning of the word "privacy"?
>
> COLOSSUS: Privacy. Being apart from company or observation.
>
> DR. FORBIN: Yes. Well, I need a certain amount of privacy to maintain my sanity.
>
> COLOSSUS: What kind of privacy.
>
> DR. FORBIN: Privacy in the elimination of bodily wastes, for example.
>
> COLOSSUS: No.
>
> DR. FORBIN: Privacy in sleep.
>
> COLOSSUS: No.
>
> DR. FORBIN: Uh, privacy in something you don't understand. My, my emotional life.
>
> COLOSSUS: What kind of emotional life.
>
> DR. FORBIN: My love life.
>
> COLOSSUS: There are many kinds of love.

Dr. Forbin: My, my sex life.

Colossus: How many times a week do you require a woman.

Dr. Forbin: Every night.

Colossus: Not want. Require.

Dr. Forbin: Four times a week. Listen, if you have any doubts about the need a man has for a woman, why don't you check all of your history units and all of your works of art?

Colossus: Agreed. A woman four nights a week.

1971 *The Andromeda Strain*. Dir. Robert Wise. Scr. Nelson Gidding. Based on *The Andromeda Strain* by Michael Crichton. Perfs. Arthur Hill, *Dr. Jeremy Stone*; David Wayne, *Dr. Charles Dutton*; James Olson, *Dr. Mark Hall*; **Kate Reid**, ***Dr. Ruth Leavitt, Microbiologist***; **Paula Kelly**, ***Karen Anson, Medical Technician***; Frances Reid, *Clara Dutton*; Susan Brown, *Allison Stone*. Prod. Robert Wise. Universal.

> **Dr. Hall:** Who picked Leavitt? Talk about the Odd Man Hypothesis, which we haven't yet. She's really an oddball.
>
> **Dr. Stone:** We're lucky to have her. She's the best equipped of us to double up for Kirke in microbiology.

1971 *Escape from the Planet of the Apes*. Dir. Don Taylor. Scr. Paul Dehn. Perfs. Roddy McDowall, *Cornelius*; Kim Hunter, *Zira*; Bradford Dillman, *Dr. Lewis Dixon*; **Natalie Trundy**, ***Dr. Stephanie "Stevie" Branton, Animal Behaviorist***; Eric Braeden, *Dr. Otto Hasslein*; William Windom, *The President*; Sal Mineo, *Milo*; Ricardo Montalban, *Armando*. Prod. Arthur P. Jacobs. Assoc. Prod. Frank Capra, Jr. APJAC. 20th Century–Fox.

> **Orderly:** Chow time!
>
> **Zira:** I'm not hungry.
>
> **Orderly:** Well, maybe somebody else is who can't talk yet, huh? Aw come on, ma'am. It's pure vitamin C. You better drink your soup and eat the oranges (nodding toward her pregnant belly) for the sake of that little monkey you got there...
>
> **Cornelius** (attacking him): Grrr!
>
> **Zira:** What have you done, Cornelius!
>
> **Cornelius:** Nobody makes a fool out of my wife!

1971 *The Omega Man*. Dir. Boris Sagal. Scr. John Williams and Joyce H. Corrington. Based on *I Am Legend* by Richard Matheson. Perfs. Charlton Heston, *Robert Neville*; Anthony Zerbe, *Matthias*; Rosalind Cash, *Lisa*; Paul Koslo, *Dutch*; Eric Lanueville, *Richie*; Lincoln Kilpatrick, *Zachary*. Prod. Walter Seltzer. Warner Bros.

> **Lisa** (pointing a gun at Neville): all right you son of a bitch, you just hold tight. Up against the wall, you mother. Don't turn. Just stand. When I want you to turn, I'll turn you. On or off, up or around, I'll turn you. Now cool

it! Now put your hands out. Out! Way out about shoulder high like they gonna crucify you, baby.

NEVILLE: Matter of fact, they were gonna roast me. Why'd you stop 'em?

LISA: Don't look a gift horse in the mouth. You got any more questions, fathead?

1971 *THX 1138*. Dir. George Lucas. Scr. George Lucas and Walter Murch. Story George Lucas. Perfs. Robert Duvall, *THX*; Donald Pleasence, *SEN*; Don Pedro Colley, *SRT*; Maggie McOmie, *LUH*; Ian Wolfe, *PTO*; Sid Haig, *NCH*; Marshall Efron, *TWA*; John Pearce, *DWY*; Johnny Weissmuller, Jr., *Chrome Robot*; Robert Feero, *Chrome Robot*; Irene Forrest, *IMM*; Claudette Bessing, *ELC*. Prod. Lawrence Sturhahn. Exec. Prod. Francis Ford Coppola. Assoc. Prod. Ed Folger. American Zoetrope. Warner Bros.

> **PA SYSTEM ANNOUNCEMENTS**:
> "This is City Probe Scanner. We've run across some illegal sexual activity."
> "A libido leveler has been mislaid near the pulse-buffering gate."

1972 *A Clockwork Orange* **(British)**. Dir. Stanley Kubrick. Scr. Stanley Kubrick. Based on *A Clockwork Orange* by Anthony Burgess. Perfs. Malcolm McDowell, *Alex DeLarge*; Patrick Magee, *Mr. Alexander*; Michael Bates, *Chief Guard*; Warren Clarke, *Dim*; John Clive, *Stage Actor*; Adrienne Corri, *Mrs. Alexander*; Carl Duering, *Dr. Brodsky*; Paul Farrell, *Tramp*; Clive Francis, *Lodger*; Michael Gover, *Prison Governor*; Miriam Karlin, *Catlady*; James Marcus, *Georgie*; Aubrey Morris, *Deltoid*; Godfrey Quigley, *Prison Chaplain*; Sheila Raynor, *Mum*; **Madge Ryan, *Dr. Branom, Medical Doctor***; John Savident, *Conspirator*; Anthony Sharp, *Minister*; Philip Stone, *Dad*; **Pauline Taylor, *Dr. Taylor, Psychiatrist***; Margaret Tyzack, *Conspirator*. Prod. Stanley Kubrick. Exec. Prod. Max L. Raab and Si Litvinoff. Assoc. Prod. Bernard Williams. Warner Bros.

> **ALEX**: It was around by the derelict casino that we came across Billy-Boy and his four droogs. They were getting ready to perform a little of the old in-out, in-out on a weepy young devotchka they had there.

1972 *Conquest of the Planet of the Apes*. Dir. J. Lee Thompson. Scr. Paul Dehn. Perfs. Roddy McDowall, *Caesar*; Don Murray, *Breck*; Natalie Trundy, *Lisa*; Hari Rhodes, *MacDonald*; Ricardo Montalban, *Armando*; Severn Darden, *Kolp*; Asa Maynor, *Mrs. Riley*. Prod. Arthur P. Jacobs. Assoc. Prod. Frank Capra, Jr. APJAC. 20th Century–Fox.

> **SALON MANAGER**: I'm so sorry, Mrs. Riley. I'll have someone to comb you out in just a minute.
> **MRS. RILEY**: I want to be combed out now! I have to go to a luncheon.

1972 *Frogs*. Dir. George McCowan. Scr. Robert Hutchison and Robert Blees. Story Robert Hutchison. Perfs. Ray Milland, *Jason Crockett*; Sam Elliott, *Pickett*

Smith; Joan Van Ark, *Karen Crockett*; Adam Roark, *Clint Crockett*; Judy Pace, *Bella Garrington*; Lynn Borden, *Jenny Crockett*; Mae Mercer, *Maybelle*; David Gilliam, *Michael Martindale*; Nicholas Cortland, *Kenneth Martindale*; George Skaff, *Stuart Martindale*; Lance Taylor, Sr., *Charles*; Holly Irving, *Iris Martindale*. Prod. George Edwards and Peter Thomas. Exec. Prod. Norman T. Herman. American International.

> **KAREN**: My cousin Kenneth Martindale, and Miss Bella Garrington. Pickett Smith.
> **KENNETH**: Welcome to Crockett-land.
> **BELLA** (ogling Pickett): Hi. Not quite awake yet, Mr. Pickett, but I can hardly wait to see what you look like.

1972 *Silent Running*. Dir. Douglas Trumbull. Scr. Deric Washburn, Mike Cimino, and Steve Bochco. Perfs. Bruce Dern, *Freeman Lowell*; Cliff Potts, *John Keenan*; Ron Rifkin, *Marty Barker*; Jesse Vint, *Andy Wolf*. Prod. Douglas Trumbull and Michael Gruskoff. Assoc. Prod. Martin Hornstein. Universal.

> **LOWELL**: I've spent my entire last eight years up here dedicated to this project. Now, can you think of anybody more qualified?
> **WOLF**: It's more likely they're going to announce cutbacks.
> **LOWELL**: Sorry. There's no way they're gonna announce cutbacks. Not after this amount of time.
> **BARKER**: Hey Lowell, you're dreaming.
> **LOWELL**: And you don't think it's time somebody had a dream again, huh? You don't think it's time that somebody cared enough to have a dream?

1972 *Slaughterhouse Five*. Dir. George Roy Hill. Scr. Stephen Gellor. Based on *Slaughterhouse Five Or The Children's Crusade* by Kurt Vonnegut, Jr. Perfs. Michael Sacks, *Billy Pilgrim*; Ron Leibman, *Paul Lazzaro*; Eugene Roche, *Edgar Derby*; Sharon Gans, *Valencia Merble Pilgrim*; Valerie Perrine, *Montana Wildhack*; Holly Near, *Barbara Pilgrim*; Perry King, *Robert Pilgrim*. Prod. George Roy Hill and Paul Monash. Exec. Prod. Jennings Lang. Universal.

> **VALENCIA**: Billy, you're wonderful. I'm so glad I waited.
> **BILLY**: I'm glad we waited too.
> **VALENCIA**: Otherwise, it wouldn't have seemed the same tonight.
> **BILLY**: No, it wouldn't.
> **VALENCIA**: It starts the whole marriage off on the right foot.
> **BILLY**. Yeah. Yeah.
> **VALENCIA**: I know when you were in the war you must have had experiences.
> **BILLY**: Well...
> **VALENCIA**: No, don't tell me about them. It was wartime. Anyway, it's different for a man than for a woman. I understand that. I'm just so glad we waited.
> **BILLY**: So am I.
> **VALENCIA**: And you know what? I'm gonna lose weight just for you, Billy.

See. Before, I needed a reason. And now I have one. Hey Billy, I think
we've begun the life of a new hero.

BILLY: How can you tell?

VALENCIA: Because I'm a woman.

BILLY: Huh.

1973 *Battle for the Planet of the Apes*. Dir. J. Lee Thompson. Scr. John William
Corrington and Joyce Hooper Corrington. Story Paul Dehn. Perfs. Roddy
McDowall, *Caesar*; Claude Akins, *Aldo*; Natalie Trundy, *Lisa*; Severn Darden,
Kolb; Lew Ayres, *Mandemus*; John Hustom, *The Lawwgiver*; Austin Stoker,
MacDonald; France Nuyen, *Alma*; Bobby Porter, *Cornelius*; **Heather Lowe,
Doctor**; Paul Williams, *Virgil*. Prod. Arthur P. Jacobs. Assoc. Prod. Frank Capra,
Jr. APJAC. 20th Century–Fox.

> **LISA**: Cornelius! Hasn't your father explained to you that war is not a game?
> **CORNELIUS**: Yes, Mother.
> **LISA**: And hasn't he also forbidden you to play with guns?
> **CORNELIUS**: Yes, Mother.
> **LISA**: Then you'll stop it.
> **CORNELIUS**: Yes, Mother.
> **LISA**: Now come along. Father wants us.

1973 *Invasion of the Bee Girls*. Dir. Denis Sanders. Scr. Nicholas Meyer and
Sylvia Schneble. Perfs. William Smith, *Neil Agar*; **Anitra Ford, *Dr. Susan
Harris, Entomologist***; Victoria Vetri, *Julie Zorn, Research Scientist's Assistant*; Cliff Osmond, *Capt. Peters*; Wright King, *Dr. Murger*; Ben Hammer,
Herb Kline; Anna Aries, *Nora Kline*; Katie A. Saylor, *Gretchen Grubowsky*;
Beverly Powers, *Harriet Williams*. Sequoia. Centaur.

> **AGAR**: You were the last person to see him alive, and you had dinner with
>   him on the night he was murdered.
> **ZORN**: Why do you say murdered?
> **AGAR**: Sorry.
> **ZORN**: Well, we had dinner that night. Whenever we work late, we always
>   have dinner. Gretchen knew about it.
> **AGAR**: Gretchen?
> **ZORN**: His wife.
> **AGAR**: How convenient.
> **ZORN**: all right. You might as well know. We went to dinner at the Flamingo
>   Bar & Grill. By about ten o'clock we were playing kneesies under the table
>   and having dessert like the good old days. Then we went to the motel, and
>   then it happened.
> **AGAR**: What happened?
> **ZORN**: We balled, and we balled, and we balled till he dropped dead.

1973 *Sleeper*. Dir. Woody Allen. Scr. Woody Allen and Marshall Brickman.
Perfs. Woody Allen, *Miles Monroe*; Diane Keaton, *Luna Schlosser*; John Beck,

Erno Windt; **Mary Gregory, *Dr. Melik***; John McLiam, *Dr. Agon*; Bartlett Robinson, *Dr. Orva*; Don Keefer, *Dr. Tryon*; **Marya Small, *Dr. Nero***. Prod. Jack Grossberg. Exec. Prod. Charles H. Joffe. Assoc. Pros. Marshall Brickman and Ralph Rosenblum. Jack Rollins-Charles H. Joffe. United Artists.

> LUNA: Oh, that was wonderful! I feel so refreshed. I think we should have had sex, but there weren't enough people.

1973 *Soylent Green*. Dir. Richard Fleischer. Scr. Stanley R. Greenberg. Based on *Soylent Green* by Harry Harrison. Perfs. Charlton Heston, *Thorn*; Leigh Taylor-Young, *Shirl*; Chuck Connors, *Tab*; Joseph Cotten, *Simonson*; Brock Peters, *Hatcher*; Paula Kelly, *Martha*; Edward G. Robinson, *Sol Roth*; Whit Bissell, *Santini*. Prod. Walter Seltzer and Russell Thacher. MGM.

> THORN: Detective Thorn, 14th Precinct.
> TAB: I was Mr. Simonson's bodyguard.
> THORN (looking at Shirl): Furniture?
> SHIRL: Yes.
> THORN: Simonson's? (She nods yes.) Personal or building?
> SHIRL: Building.

1973 *Westworld*. Dir. Michael Crichton. Scr. Michael Crichton. Perfs. Yul Brynner, *Gunslinger*; Richard Benjamin, *Peter Martin*; James Brolin, *John Blane*; Norman Bartold, *Medieval Knight*; Alan Oppenheimer, *Chief Supervisor*; Victoria Shaw, *Medieval Queen*; Dick Van Patten, *Banker*; Linda Scott, *Arlette*; Steve Franken, *Technician*. Prod. Paul N. Lazarus, III. MGM.

> PETER: We're paying $1,000 a day for this?
> JOHN: It's authentic. The West of the 1880s.
> PETER: Well, at least they could have made it a little more comfortable.
> JOHN: But that's the point. This is really the way it was. If you wanted comfort, you should have stayed in Chicago.
> PETER: Hey, Julie would have loved all this—poking around for hours in all those funny shops, looking for silly...
> JOHN: What the hell's wrong with you? You're a lawyer. You know better than anybody else what a ride she took you for.
> PETER: Well, the kids...
> JOHN: Fine, the kids. But here you are six months later still thinking about her.

1974 *Dark Star*. Dir. John Carpenter. Story and Scr. John Carpenter and Dan O'Bannon. Perfs. Brian Narelle, *Dolittle*; Cal Kuniholm, *Boiler;* Dre Pahich, *Talby*; Dan O'Bannon, *Pinback*; Miles Watkins, *Mission Controller*; Connie Knapp, *Computer Voice*. Prod. John Carpenter. Exec. Prod. Jack H. Harris. Bryanstor.

> DOOLITTLE: Don't give me any of that intelligent life stuff. Find me something I can blow up.

1974 *The Terminal Man*. Dir. Mike Hodges. Scr. Mike Hodges. Based on *The Terminal Man* by Michael Crichton. Perfs. George Segal, *Harry Benson*; **Joan Hackett, *Dr. Janet Ross, Psychiatrist*;** Richard Dysart, *Dr. John Ellis*; Donald Moffat, *Dr. Arthur McPherson*; Michael C. Gwynne, *Dr. Robert Morris*; William Hansen, *Dr. Ezra Manon*; Jill Clayburgh, *Angela Black*. Prod. Mike Hodges. Assoc. Prod. Michael Dryhurst. Warner Bros.

> DR. ROSS (addressing an auditorium of medical professionals): Tests showed no intracranial bleeding, and he was released from the hospital. Two months later the patient began to experience what he called blackouts. These were, in fact, periods of amnesia and were always preceded by a distinct olfactory aura. He consulted his physician, who told him that he was working too hard and recommended that he reduce his alcohol intake. The patient began to realize that the blackouts were becoming more frequent and lasting longer. Sometimes he would regain consciousness in unfamiliar surroundings.... On occasions he had torn clothes, cuts and bruises, suggesting he'd been fighting. This was subsequently proven correct. He had, in fact, attacked and tried to kill at least two people. There is an added complication. About a year ago he made what he calls a monumental discovery in his work. Benson is a computer scientist specializing in artificial life, machine intelligence. Apparently he is brilliant in his field. He claims that he discovered that machines were competing with human beings and that ultimately machines would overtake the world.... Events disturbed him sufficiently to seek psychiatric help. On the basis of his history—head injury, episodic violence, paranoia about machines—we decided that the patient is probably suffering from para-epilepsy. Unlike conventional epilepsy, the patient doesn't have physical seizures when cells of the brain misfire but instead has uncontrollable rages.... Because of the failure of drugs to control these attack rages, this neuropsychiatric unit has considered him a surgical candidate for limbic pacing by implanted computer. There is one alternative: diethylstilbestrol.

1974 *Zardoz*. Dir. John Boorman. Scr. John Boorman. Perfs. Sean Connery, *Zed*; Charlotte Rampling, *Consuella*; **Sara Kestelman, *May, Scientist of the Future*;** John Alderton, *Friend*; Sally Ann Newton, *Avalow*; Niall Buggy, *Arthur Frayn*. Prod. John Boorman. Assoc. Prod. Charles Orme. 20th Century–Fox.

> CONSUELLA: Penic erection was one of the many unsolved evolutionary mysteries surrounding sexuality. Every society had an elaborate subculture devoted to erotic stimulation. But nobody could quite determine how this (pointing to a drawing of a flaccid penis) becomes this (pointing to a drawing of an erect penis). Of course, we all know the physical process involved, but not the link between stimulus and response. There seems to be a correlation with violence, with fear. Many hanged men died with an erection. You are all more or less aware of our intensive researches into this subject. Sexuality declined probably because we no longer needed to

procreate. Eternals soon discovered that erection was impossible to achieve. And we are no longer victims of this violent, convulsive act which so debased women and betrayed men. This Brutal (indicating Zed) like other primates living unselfconscious lives, is capable of spontaneous and reflexive erection. As part of May's studies of this creature, we're trying to find, once again, the link between erotic stimulation and erection. This experiment will measure autoerotic stimulation of the cortex, leading to erection.

1975 *A Boy and His Dog*. Dir. L.Q. Jones. Scr. L.Q. Jones. Based on "A Boy and His Dog" by Harlan Ellison. Perfs. Don Johnson, *Vic*; Susanne Benton, *Quilla June Holmes*; Jason Robards, *Lou Craddock*; Tim McIntire, *Voice of Blood*; Alvy Moore, *Doctor Moore*; Helene Winston, *Mez Smith*. Prod. Alvy Moore. LQ/JAF.

> VIC: Don't give me that "I'm sorry" bullshit. You're as crazy as the rest of these damn nuts.
> QUILLA JUNE: They may be stupid, but they're not dumb like you.
> VIC: Oh no? They bring me down here to make babies and then hook me up to this stupid machine. Real smart.
> QUILLA JUNE: Population control, Vic, in case you haven't heard of it. Thirty-five girls are impregnated and then you're killed. Can't have idiots like you running around the place.

1975 *Rollerball*. Dir. Norman Jewison. Scr. William Harrison. Based on "Roller Ball Murder" by William Harrison. Perfs. James Caan, *Jonathan E.*; John Houseman, *Mr. Bartholomew*; Maud Adams, *Ella*; John Beck, *Moonpie*; Moses Gunn, *Cletus*; Pamela Hensley, *Maggie*; Barbara Trentham, *Daphne*; Ralph Richardson, *Librarian*. Prod. Norman Jewison. Assoc. Prod. Patrick Palmer. United Artists.

> MAGGIE: Look what I got for breakfast. It's a notice from the corporation.
> JONATHAN: What does it say?
> MAGGIE: That I should get out of here. Go away. Vanish. That kind of thing. Know anything about that?
> JONATHAN: Yeah, I kinda heard something about it. You knew it was coming.
> MAGGIE: We've been together six months. Didn't you even want to say good-bye?
> JONATHAN: We'll talk about it later.
> MAGGIE: You didn't, did you? You didn't even want me here when you got back.
> JONATHAN: I got to see Cletus.
> MAGGIE: What do you want me to do in the meantime?
> JONATHAN: I want you to take it easy. I want you to go in and fix us something to eat. Clete's come a long way and I'm hungry. All right?

1975 *The Stepford Wives*. Dir. Bryan Forbes. Scr. William Goldman. Based on *The Stepford Wives* by Ira Levin. Perfs. **Katherine Ross,** *Joanna Eberhart,* ***Photographer***; Paula Prentiss, *Bobby Markowe*; Peter Masterson, *Walter Eberhart*; Nanette Newman, *Carol Van Sant*; Tina Louise, *Charmaine Wimpiris*; **Carol Rossen,** **Dr. Fancher, Psychiatrist**; William Prince, *Ike Mazzard*; Carole Mallory, *Kit Sunderson*; Toni Reid, *Marie Axhelm*; Judith Baldwin, *Patricia Cornell*; Barbara Rucker, *Mary Ann Stavros*; Patrick O'Neal, *Dale Coba (Diz)*. Prod. Edgar J. Scherick. Exec. Prod. Gustave M. Berne. Assoc. Prod. Roger M. Rothstein. Fadsin Cinema Associates. Palomar Pictures International.

> JOANNA: Walter, I just want to say one thing to you. Bobby really has changed. Believe me. Everything in her house looked like a TV commercial.
> WALTER: Well, good! Good! She had to clean it sooner or later. It looked like a goddam pig sty. I mean, when are things gonna start sparkling around here? That's what I'd like to know. I mean, just look at the way the kids are dressed. Ragamuffins! Jeez, I work eighty hours a week, I live in a great house, and my kids look like they belong on welfare. Look, if you paid a little more attention to your family and a little less to your goddam picture taking...

1976 *Embryo*. Dir. Ralph Nelson. Scr. Anita Doohan and Jack W. Thomas. Story Jack W. Thomas. Perfs. Rock Hudson, *Dr. Paul Holliston*; Barbara Carrera, *Victoria Spencer*; Diane Ladd, *Martha Douglas*; Roddy McDowall, *Frank Riley*; Anne Scheeden, *Helen Holliston*; John Elerick, *Gordon Holliston*; Vincent Baggetta, *Vinnie Collier*; Jack Colvin, *Dr. Jim Winston*; **Dr. Joyce Brothers, Herself, Psychologist**. Prod. Arnold H. Orgolini and Anita Doohan. Exec. Prod. Sandy Howard. Cine Artists.

> GORDON: What are you doing?
> HELEN: It's called getting dressed.
> GORDON (patting her stomach): Get back in bed before you both catch cold.
> HELEN: Oh no, nothing doing. We have unfinished business. You know, on the way home that lookout point on Mulholland Dr. would be the perfect place to stop and...
> GORDON: Helen!
> HELEN: Well, I'm very adaptable as well as very sexy. Being pregnant does that. It makes you sexier.
> GORDON: God give me strength.
> HELEN: Don't give it a second thought, darling. It's all taken care of. You see, God is a liberated female and She is on my side.

1976 *Futureworld*. Dir. Richard T. Heffron. Scr. Mayo Simon and George Schenck. Perfs. Peter Fonda, *Chuck Browning*; Blythe Danner, *Tracy Ballard*; Arthur Hill, *Duffy*; Stuart Margolin, *Harry*; John Ryan, *Dr. Schneider*; Yul Brynner, *The Gunslinger*. Prod. Paul Lazarus, III and James T. Aubrey, Jr. Exec. Prod. Samuel Z. Arkoff. American International.

GAME SHOW HOST: Futureworld! Where you'll be transported throughout the solar system, commanding your very own rocketship and enjoying the favors of robot women of weightless beauty, soaring through space like an astronaut. All that and more is yours, Ron. Congratulations!

1976 *Logan's Run*. Dir. Michael Anderson. Scr. David Zelag Goodman. Based on "Logan's Run" by William F. Nolan and George Clayton Johnson. Perfs. Michael York, *Logan*; Richard Jordan, *Francis*; Jenny Agutter, *Jessica*; Roscoe Lee Browne, *Box*; Farrah Fawcett-Majors, *Holly*; Michael Anderson, Jr., *Doc*; Peter Ustinov, *Old Man*. Prod. Saul David. MGM.

> **LOGAN**: You know, I've been thinking. Those words we saw. "Beloved husband." "Beloved wife." What do they mean?
>
> **OLD MAN**: Oh. Well, you see, "Beloved wife" would mean my mother, and "Beloved husband" would be my father. And those words, they used those words to stay together.
>
> **LOGAN**: Stay together? They lived together all those years?
>
> **OLD MAN**: Before I was born, I don't know. But after, they did.
>
> **JESSICA**: So people stayed together for this feeling of love? They would live and raise children and be remembered?
>
> **OLD MAN**: They raised me, didn't they? (Pointing to his belly) Right in there.
>
> **JESSICA**: I think I'd like that, Logan. Don't you?
>
> **LOGAN**: Um hmm. Why not?
>
> **JESSICA**: Beloved husband.
>
> **LOGAN**: Beloved wife.

1976 *The Man Who Fell to Earth* (British). Dir. Nicholas Roeg. Scr. Paul Mayersberg. Based on *The Man Who Fell to Earth* by Walter Tevis. Perfs. David Bowie, *Thomas Jerome Newton*; Rip Torn, *Nathan Bryce*; Candy Clark, *Mary-Lou*; Buck Henry, *Oliver Farnsworth*; Bernie Casey, *Peters*. Prod. Michael Deeley and Barry Spikings. Exec. Prod. Si Litvinoff. Assoc. Prod. John Reverall. British Lion Films.

> **BRYCE**: Suddenly I got this letter from Farnsworth. Strangely after that I gradually began to lose my interest in eighteen-year-olds. I don't know what happened to me. I'm not sure. But my mind had developed a libido of its own and I didn't need the stimulation of legs and so forth. The salary was terrific too. It was three times what I'd been getting.

1977 *Demon Seed*. Dir. Donald Cammell. Scr. Robert Jaffe and Roger O. Hirson. Based on *Demon Seed* by Dean R. Koontz. Perfs. **Julie Christie, *Dr. Susan Harris, Child Psychologist***; Fritz Weaver, *Dr. Alex Harris*; Gerrit Graham, *Walter Gabler*; Berry Kroeger, *Dr. Petrosian*; **Lisa Lu, *Dr. Soong Yen, Linguist***; Larry J. Blake, *Barry Cameron*; John O'Leary, *David Royce*; Alfred Dennis, *Mr. Mokri*; Davis Roberts, *Warner*; **Barbara O. Jones, *Computer Technician***; Robert Vaughn, *Voice of Proteus Four*. Prod. Herb Jaffe. MGM.

PROTEUS: You have two alternatives, Susan. Either I complete the electro-conditioning of your brain or you must accept the inevitable. I would prefer the latter.

SUSAN: Why?

PROTEUS: You interest me.

SUSAN: Leave me my mind.

PROTEUS: You will be cooperative?

SUSAN: How can I tell you? You've not even told me how you propose to.... I want all the details.

PROTEUS: Of course. (Showing her what he has created) This is only a piece of machinery, an improvisation. I have almost completed the fabrication of this gamete, or sex cell, with which I will impregnate you.

SUSAN: What the hell is that?

PROTEUS: A cell from you, but I'm making it uniquely mine by modifying its genetic codes. In effect, it will function as synthetic spermatozoa.

SUSAN: Have you considered what it's gonna look like? No, no, you wouldn't do that. What do you need me for? You can do this on your own.

PROTEUS: I don't have the facilities here to duplicate a human womb. Tonight I will impregnate you. In twenty-eight days, you will give birth to the child.

1977 *Close Encounters of the Third Kind*. Dir. Steven Spielberg. Scr. Steven Spielberg. Perfs. Richard Dreyfuss, *Roy Neary*; François Truffaut, *Lacombe*; Teri Garr, *Ronnie Neary*; Melinda Dillon, *Jillian Guiler*. Prod. Julia and Michael Philips. Columbia.

ANNOUNCER AT THE LANDING SITE: Gentlemen, ladies, take your positions please.

1977 *Star Wars*. Dir. George Lucas. Scr. George Lucas. Perfs. Mark Hamill, *Luke Skywalker*; Harrison Ford, *Han Solo*; Carrie Fisher, *Princess Leia*; Alec Guinness, *Obi-Wan Kenobi*. Prod. Gary Kurtz. 20th Century–Fox.

LUKE SKYWALKER (to Obi-Wan Kenobi): There's nothing for me here now. I want to learn the ways of the Force and become a Jedi like my father.

1978 *Invasion of the Body Snatchers*. Dir. Philip Kaufman. Scr. W.D. Richter. Based on *The Body Snatchers* by Jack Finney. Perfs. Donald Sutherland, *Matthew Bennell*; **Brooke Adams, *Elizabeth Driscoll, Microbiology Lab Technician;*** Jeff Goldblum, *Jack Bellicec*; Veronica Cartwright, *Nancy Bellicec*; Leonard Nimoy, *Dr. David Kibner*; Kevin McCarthy, *Running Man*; Don Siegel, *Taxi Driver*. Prod. Robert H. Solo. United Artists.

ELIZABETH: You know, I actually think I found something rare,

GEOFFREY: What?

ELIZABETH: This plant. I think it's a grex.

GEOFFREY: A what?

ELIZABETH: G-R-E-X. That's when two different species cross-pollinate and

produce a third completely unique one. And listen to this. [Reading] "Epi-
lotic. From the Greek epi: upon and lobus: a pod. Many of the species are
dangerous weeds and should be avoided."

GEOFFREY: Dangerous?

ELIZABETH: In the garden. See? Look how quickly it roots. [Reading] "Their
characteristic rapid and widespread growth pattern was even observed on
many of the large, war-torn cities of Europe. Indeed some of these plants
may thrive on devastated ground."

GEOFFREY: Why don't we go up to Vail for the weekend? Fly up Friday?
Hmm? Huh? Huh?

1978 *Superman: The Movie*. Dir. Richard Donner. Scr. Mario Puzo et al.
Story Mario Puzo, Jerry Siegel, and Jerry Shuster. Perfs. Marlon Brando, *Jor-
El*; Gene Hackman, *Lex Luthor*; Christopher Reeve, *Superman/Clark Kent*;
Jackie Cooper, *Perry White*; Margo Kidder, *Lois Lane*. Prod. Pierre Spengler.
Alexander and Ilya Salkind. Warner Bros.

LOIS LANE's internal monologue while flying through the air in Superman's
arms: Here I am like a kid out of school, holding hands with a god. You
and I could belong to each other. If you need to be loved, here I am.

1979 *Alien*. Dir. Ridley Scott. Scr. Dan O'Bannon. Story Dan O'Bannon and
Ronald Shusett. Perfs. Tom Skerritt, *Dallas*; **Sigourney Weaver, *Ripley, Space
Trucker (Warrant Officer)*; Veronica Cartwright, *Lambert, Space Trucker
(Navigator)*;** Harry Dean Stanton, *Brett*; John Hurt, *Kane*; Ian Holm, *Ash*;
Yaphet Kotto, *Parker*. Prod. Gordon Carroll, David Giler, and Walter Hill.
Exec. Prod. Ronald Shusett. Assoc. Prod. Ivor Powell. Brandywine-Ronald
Shusett. 20th Century–Fox.

LAMBERT: I say that we abandon the ship. We get the shuttle and just get
the hell out of here. We take our chances and just hope that somebody
picks us up.

RIPLEY: Lambert, the shuttle won't take four.

LAMBERT: Well then, why don't we draw straws then?

PARKER: I'm not drawing any straws. I'm for killing that goddam thing right
now.

RIPLEY: Okay. Well, let's talk about killing. We know it's using the air shafts.
[Parker mutters unintelligibly.] Will you listen to me Parker! Shut up! It's
using the air shafts...

PARKER: We don't know that.

RIPLEY: It's the only way! We'll move in pairs. We'll go step by step and cut
off every bulkhead and every vent until we have it cornered and then we'll
blow it the fuck out into space.

1979 *Star Trek: The Motion Picture*. Dir. Robert Wise. Scr. Harold Livingston.
Story Alan Dean Foster. Perfs. William Shatner, *Captain Kirk*; Leonard Nimoy,
Mr. Spock; DeForest Kelley, *Dr. McCoy*; James Doohan, *Scotty*; George Takei,

Sulu; **Nichelle Nichols, *Uhura, Communications Officer.*** Prod. Gene Roddenberry. Paramount.

> **V'Ger's Probe**: V'Ger and the Creator will become one.
> **Spock**: Who is the Creator?
> **Probe**: The Creator is that which created V'Ger.
> **Kirk**: Who is V'Ger?
> **Probe**: V'Ger is that which seeks the Creator.

The Outliers

The following contains production data for science fiction films from 1963 to 1978 that I excluded from my canon of Post–Fifties, 1968, Middle Period, and Revitalization films. Each film had an element or elements that qualified it for inclusion. However, these elements were ultimately subsumed by other characteristics. Entries contain excerpts taken directly from the films to indicate various characteristics: expressions of scientific authenticity, comments on concerns of the day, representations of women, and finally, just silliness. Information was obtained, confirmed, and compiled from a variety of sources including the films themselves, *Variety's Complete Science Fiction Reviews* (1985), and the Internet Movie Database.

1963 *Monstrosity* (*aka The Atomic Brain*). Dir. Joseph Mascelli. Scr. Vy Russell, Sue Dwiggins, and Dean Dillman, Jr. Perfs. Marjorie Eaton, *Hetty March*; Frank Gerstle, *Dr. Otto Frank*; Frank Fowler, *Victor*; Erika Peters, *Nina Rhodes*; Judy Bamber, *Beatrice 'Bea' Mullins*; Lisa Lang, *Anita Gonzalez*; Xerxes, *Xerxes the Cat*. Prod. Jack Pollexfen and Dean Dillman, Jr. Assoc. Prod. Vy Russel and Sue Dwiggens. Cinema Venture. Emerson.

> **Narrator**: The brain cells are being reactivated by an atomic fission produced in the cyclotron.

1963 *These Are the Damned*. Dir. Joseph Losey. Scr. Evan Jones. Based on *The Children of Light* by H.L. Lawrence. Perfs. Macdonald Carey, *Simon Wells*; Shirley Anne Field, *Joan*; Viveca Lindfors, *Freya Neilson*; Alexander Knox, *Bernard*; Oliver Reed, *King*. Prod. Anthony Hinds. Assoc. Prod. Anthony Nelson Keys. Hammer. Columbia.

> **Bernard**: To survive the destruction that is inevitably coming we need a new kind of man.

1967 *Blood Beast from Outer Space* (aka *Night Caller*). Dir. John Gilling. Scr. Jim O'Connolly. Based on *The Night Callers* by Frank Crisp. Perfs. John Saxon, *Dr. Jack Costain*; Maurice Denham, *Dr. Morley*; **Patricia Haines, *Ann Barlow, Analysis Expert***; Alfred Burke, *Det. Supt. Hartley*; Robert Crewdson, *Medra*.

Exec. Prod. John Philips. Prod. Ronald Liles. New Art Productions. Armitage Films.

> ANN BARLOW: We've carried out x-rays, spectrometer, and routine radiation tests. We find the sphere is made of an undetermined silicon type material. This forms an exterior protective shell of three millimeters thick. It's not radioactive.

1968 *The Power*. Dir. Byron Haskin. Scr. John Gay. Based on *The Power* by Frank M. Robinson. Perfs. George Hamilton, *Prof. Jim Tanner*; **Suzanne Pleshette, *Prof. Margery Lansing, Geneticist***; Richard Carlson, *Prof. Norman E. Van Zandt*; Yvonne De Carlo, *Mrs. Sally Hallson*; Earl Holliman, *Prof. Talbot Scott*; Gary Merrill, *Mark Corlane*; Barbara Nichols, *Flora*; Arthur O'Connell, *Prof. Henry Hallson*; Michael Rennie, *Arthur Nordlund*; Vaughn Taylor, *Mr. Hallson*. Prod. George Pal. MGM.

> LANSING: I never should have told you.
> TANNER: What?
> LANSING: What wine does to me.
> TANNER: Let's see what it does.
> LANSING: Jim...
> TANNER (kissing her): We can always talk.
> LANSING: I can't get it out of my mind.
> TANNER (continuing to kiss her): Try.
> LANSING: I've been thinking.
> TANNER: You can always think.
> LANSING: No really. As a geneticist, I know that there is no limit to the variables of gene frequency.
> TANNER (somewhat taken aback): What?
> LANSING: Genetically speaking, it's entirely possible to produce a man of tomorrow right now.
> TANNER (playfully): Right now?
> LANSING: One extraordinary combination of genes like four royal flushes in a row ... do you understand?
> TANNER (continuing to kiss her): Yeah, we're dealing with the four flushes.
> LANSING: Oh, Jim. I'm serious.
> TANNER (handing her a glass of wine): Drink. Drink your wine. Drink, drink, drink.

1971 *Glen and Randa*. Dir. Jim McBride. Scr. Lorenzo Mans, Rudolph Wurlitzer, and Jim McBride. Perfs. Steven Curry, *Glen*; Shelley Plimpton, *Randa*; Woodrow Chambliss, *Sidney Miller*; Garry Goodrow, *Magician*. Exec. Prod. Sidney Glazier. UMC Pictures.

> GLEN: Maybe you're gonna have some babies. Well, we can put 'em in a sack. Put 'em in it and take it to the city with us.
> RANDA (crying): What are we gonna make a sack out of?

GLEN: Well, why don't you have it now while they're small? I can carry 'em in my pocket.

RANDA (still crying): I can't do that. I don't know how to do that.

1975 *Bug*. Dir. Jeannot Szwarc. Scr. William Castle and Thomas Page. Based on *The Hephaestus Plague* by Thomas Page. Perfs. Bradford Dillman, *James Parmiter*; Joanna Miles, *Carrie Parmiter*; Richard Gilliland, *Gerald Metbaum*; Jamie Smith Jackson, *Norma Tacker*; Alan Fudge, *Mark Ross*; Jesse Vint, *Tom Tacker*; Patty McCormack, *Sylvia Ross*. Prod. William Castle. Paramount.

CARRIE PARMITER: Ooh. Ah. Owww. Aaaah!
NORMA TACKER: Aaaaaaahhhhhhh! Aaaaaaahhhhhhh!
JAMES PARMITER: Aaaah! Aah aah. Aaah!

1976 *The Food of the Gods*. Dir. & Scr. Bert I. Gordon. Based on a portion of *The Food of the Gods* by H.G. Wells. Perfs. Marjoe Gortner, *Morgan*; **Pamela Franklin, *Lorna Scott, Bacteriologist***; Ralph Meeker, *Jack Bensington*; Jon Cypher, *Brian*; Ida Lupino, *Mrs. Skinner*; Belinda Balaski, *Rita*; Tom Stovall, *Thomas*. Exec. Prod. Samuel Z. Arkoff. Prod. Bert I. Gordon. American International.

MORGAN: My father used to say, "Morgan, one of these days the Earth will get even with Man for messing her up with his garbage. Just let Man continue to pollute the Earth the way he is and nature will rebel. It's gonna be one hell of a rebellion."

1976 *Rattlers*. Dir. John McCauley. Scr. Jerry Golding and John McCauley. Perfs. Sam Chew, *Dr. Tom Parkinson*; **Elisabeth Chauvet, *Ann Bradley, Photographer***; Dan Priest, *Colonel*; Ron Gold, *Captain Delaney*; Al Dunlap, *General*; Dan Balentine, *Pilot*; Gary Van Orman, *Woodley*; Darwin Jostin, *Palmer*; Cary Pitts, *Sergeant*; Eric Lawson, *Guard*; Tony Ballen, *Sheriff Gates*. Prod. John McCauley. Boxoffice International Pictures.

DR. PARKINSON: I can't take that girl out there. I've got to have somebody that can at least take care of themselves.
SHERIFF GATES: Tom, I know how you feel, and I agree with you, but this is the only way I could swing it. Look, you know we're short on funds, and every damn women's lib group is on our backs about job equality. This girl has worked for us before, and she's really strictly a pro. Look, she spent two years in Vietnam as a press photographer, and she'll be able to handle herself, okay?
DR. PARKINSON: Yeah, well I hope you're right.
SHERIFF GATES: Believe me, she's a better photographer than most of the men we've used and a hell of a lot prettier.

1977 *Empire of the Ants*. Dir. Bert I. Gordon. Scr. Jack Turley and Bert I. Gordon. Based on "Empire of the Ants" by H.G. Wells. Perfs. Joan Collins, *Marilyn*

Fryser; Robert Lansing, *Dan Stokely;* John David Carson, *Joe Morrison;* Albert Salmi, *Sheriff Art Kincade;* Jacqueline Scott, *Margaret Ellis;* Pamela Shoop, *Coreen Bradford;* Robert Pine, *Larry Graham.* Prod. Bert I. Gordon. Exec. Prod. Samuel Z. Arkoff. Cinema 77. MGM.

> **OPENING VOICEOVER:** This is the ant. Treat it with respect, for it may very well be the next dominant life form of our planet. Sound incredible? Impossible? Have you ever taken a good close look at what the ant is all about? Like these Atta Cephalotes (sic), one of the fifteen thousand different species inhabiting our planet. This one cultivates crops of fungus for food. Others herd aphids, just as man herds cattle. And what about the warriors, the builders of bridges, roads, tunnels? Frightening isn't it that a creature as small as an ant is able to have a fair claim to rank next to man in the scale of intelligence. They have a sophisticated communication system. Specific messages are transmitted from one ant to another through the use of a chemical substance called pheromones. It causes an obligatory response. Did you hear that? Obligatory. Pheromones give an order that cannot be disobeyed. It's a mind bending substance that forces obedience. But we don't have to worry about it. That's business better left to the ants.

1977 *The Incredible Melting Man.* Dir. & Scr. William Sachs. Perfs. Alex Rebar, *Steve West;* Burr DeBenning, *Dr. Ted Nelson;* Myron Healey, *Gen. Michael Perry;* Michael Alldredge, *Sheriff Neil Blake;* Ann Sweeny, *Judy Nelson;* Lisle Wilson, *Dr. Loring.* Prod. Samuel W. Gelfman. A Rosenberg-Gelfman Production. American International.

> **HOUSTON CONTROL:** Thirty seconds and counting. Astronauts report conditions good. T-minus twenty-five seconds. Twenty seconds and counting. Fifteen seconds. Titan's internal. Twelve. Eleven. Ten. Nine. Ignition sequence occurs. Six. Five. Four. Three. Two. One. Lift off. We have a lift off. Saturn lift off on Scorpio Five. Saturn clear. Roger and out.
> **WEST:** Scorpio Five to Houston Control. Good at forty seconds.
> **HOUSTON CONTROL:** Scorpio Five from Houston Control. Good at one minute. Roger.
> **WEST:** Shut down two-ten by three-oh-five point six. Entering rings.
> **HOUSTON CONTROL:** Roger. We copy. All's confirmed. Lose contact through Saturn's rings. Pick up ten five point eight. Good luck.
> **WEST:** Thank you. Roger out.

1977 *Kingdom of the Spiders.* Dir. John "Bud" Cardos. Scr. Richard Robinson and Alan Caillou. Story Jeffrey M. Sneller and Stephen Lodge. Perfs. William Shatner, *Rack Hansen;* **Tiffany Bolling, *Diane Ashley, Arachnologist;*** Woody Strode, *Walter Colby;* Altovise Davis, *Birch Colby.* Assoc. Prod. J. Bond Johnson. Exec. Prod. Henry Fownes. Prod. Igo Kantor and Jeffrey M. Sneller. Arachnid Productions Ltd. Dimension Pictures.

HANSEN: I gotta tell you, I'm still a little skeptical about this spider theory of yours.

BOLLING: Would you be less skeptical if a man had told you?

HANSEN: Hey, the only person who's uptight about you being a woman is you.

1978 *The Swarm*. Dir. Irwin Allen. Scr. Stirling Silliphant. Based on *The Swarm* by Arthur Herzog. Perfs. Michael Caine, *Brad Crane*; **Katharine Ross, *Dr. Helena Anderson, Medical Doctor;*** Richard Widmark, *Gen. Slater*; Richard Chamberlain, *Dr. Hubbard*; Olivia de Havilland, *Maureen Schuester*; Ben Johnson, *Felix*; Lee Grant, *Anne MacGregor*; Jose Ferrer, *Dr. Andrews*; Patty Duke Astin, *Rita*; Slim Pickens, *Jud Hawkins*; Bradford Dillman, *Major Baker*; Fred MacMurray, *Clarence*; Henry Fonda, *Dr. Krim*; Cameron Mitchell, *General Thompson*. Prod. Irwin Allen. Warner Bros.

HELICOPTER PILOT: Oh my god! Bees! Bees! Millions of bees! Air Search 28 to base! Bees! Millions of bees!

GEN. SLATER: Bees?

Appendix I:
The Outer Limits Actors

Outer Limits Actors Who Worked in Fifties Science Fiction Films

EPISODE	ACTOR—FIFTIES MOVIE
The Children of Spider County	Dabbs Greer—*Invasion of the Body Snatchers*
The Inheritors I & II	Dabbs Greer—*It! The Creature from Beyond Space*
Behold Eck!	Douglas Henderson—*King Dinosaur*
The Chameleon	Douglas Henderson—*Invasion of the Saucer Men*
The Brain of Colonel Barham	Douglas Kennedy—*The Alligator People*
	Douglas Kennedy—*The Amazing Transparent Man*
	Douglas Kennedy—*The Land Unknown*
Nightmare	Ed Nelson—*Attack of the Crab Monsters*
	Ed Nelson—*Invasion of the Saucer Men*
	Ed Nelson—*The Brain Eaters*
The Invisibles	George MacReady—*The Alligator People*
The Production and Decay of Strange Particles	George MacReady
The Brain of Colonel Barham	Grant Williams—*The Incredible Shrinking Man*
	Grant Williams—*The Leech Woman*
	Grant Williams—*The Monolith Monsters*
The Chameleon	Henry Brandon—*The Land Unknown*
Don't Open Till Doomsday	John Hoyt—*The Time Travelers*
I, Robot	John Hoyt—*Attack of the Puppet People*
	John Hoyt—*When Worlds Collide*
Specimen: Unknown	Russell Johnson—*Attack of the Crab Monsters*
	Russell Johnson—*It Came from Outer Space*

(Episode)	(Actor—Fifties Movie)
	Russell Johnson—*This Island Earth*
Keeper of the Purple Twilight	Warren Stevens—*Forbidden Planet*
The Probe	Warren Stevens
Nightmare	Whit Bissel—*Creature from the Black Lagoon*
	Whit Bissel—*I Was a Teenage Frankenstein*
	Whit Bissel—*I Was a Teenage Werewolf*
	Whit Bissel—*Monster on the Campus*
	Whit Bissel—*Target Earth*

Appendix II:
The Outer Limits Women

Episode	Actress	Character—Role
Architects of Fear	Geraldine Brooks	Yvette Leighton—Wife
Behold, Eck!	Joan Freeman	Elizabeth Dunn—Optometrist's secretary
Behold, Eck!	Marcel Herbert	Miss Willet—Scientist's secretary
*Bellero Shield	Sally Kellerman	Judith Bellero—Wife
*Bellero Shield	Chita Rivera	Mrs. Dame—Servant
Borderland	Nina Foch	Eva Frazer—Mathematician, wife
Borderland	Gladys Cooper	Mrs. Palmer—Medium
Brain/Barham	Elizabeth Perry	Jennifer Barham—Wife
Chameleon	No women	
Children/County	Bennye Gatteys	Anna Bishop—Girlfriend, daughter
Cold Hands	Geraldine Brooks	Ann Barton—Wife
Controlled	Grace Lee Whitney	Carla Duveen—Girlfriend
Controlled	Linda Hutchins	Arleen Schnabel—Girlfriend
Corpus Earthling	Salome Jens	Laurie H. Cameron—Wife
Counterweight	Jacqueline Scott	Dr. Alicia Hendrix—Anthropologist
Cry of Silence	June Havoc	Karen Thorne—Wife
Demon/Hand	Arline Martel	Consuela Bieros—Garment worker
*Don't Open	Melinda Plowman	Vivia H. Balfour—Newlywed
*Don't Open	Miriam Hopkins	Mrs. Mary Kry—Spinster
Don't Open	Nellie Burt	Wife
Duplicate Man	Constance Towers	Laura James—Wife
Duplicate Man	Ivy Bethune	Miss Thorson—Receptionist
Expanding Human	Barbara Wilkin	Susan Wayne—Wife
Expanding Human	Mary Gregory	Mrs. Merrill—Manager

(EPISODE)	(ACTRESS)	(CHARACTER—ROLE)
Expanding Human	Shirley O'Hara	Receptionist
*Feasibility Study	Phyllis Love	Andrea Holm—Wife
*Feasibility Study	Joyce Van Patten	Rhea Cashman—Wife
*Forms/Unknown	Barbara Rush	Leonora Edmond—Mistress
*Forms/Unknown	Vera Miles	Kassia Paine—Mistress
Forms/Unknown	Madeline Holmes	Old widow
Forms/Unknown	Gabrielle Rossillon	Young woman
Fun and Games	Nancy Malone	Laura Hanley—Divorcee
*Galaxy Being	Jacqueline Scott	Carol Maxwell—Wife
*Galaxy Being	Allyson Ames	Loreen—Girlfriend
Guests	Luana Anders	Tess Ames—Girlfriend
Guests	Gloria Graham	Florida Patton—Older actress
Guests	Nellie Burt	Ethel Latimer—Wife
Human Factor	Sally Kellerman	Ingrid Larkin—Psychiatrist's assistant
Human Factor	Jane Langley	Nurse
Human Factor	Shirley O'Hara	Dr. Soldini—Doctor
Hundred Days	Joan Camden	Ann Pearson—Wife
Hundred Days	Nancy Rennick	Carol Selby Conner—Daughter
I, Robot	Marianna Hill	Nina Link—Niece
I, Robot	Christine Matchett	Evie Cooper—Girl
I, Robot	Mary Jackson	Mrs. MaCrae—Housekeeper
Inheritors (I)	Linda Hutchins	Nurse
Inheritors (II)	Jan Shutan	Mrs. Subiron—Young widow
Inheritors (II)	Joanne Stewart	Miss Steen—Social worker
Inheritors (II)	Suzanne Cupito	Minerva Gordon—Girl
Inheritors (II)	Paulie Clark	Nurse
Invisible Enemy	No women	
Invisibles	Dee Hartford	Mrs. Clark—Wife
It Crawled	Joan Lamden	Stephanie Linden—Research scientist
It Crawled	Barbara Luna	Gaby Christian—Girlfriend
It Crawled	Lea Marmer	Cleaning lady
Keeper/Twilight	Gail Kobe	Janet Lane—Wife
Man/Never Born	Shirley Knight	Noelle Andersen—Fiancée
Man/Power	Priscilla Morrill	Vera Finley—Wife
Man/Power	Ann Loos	Emily Radcliffe—Wife
Man/Power	Diane Strom	Secretary
Man/Power	Jane Barclay	Nurse
Mice	Diana Sands	Dr. Julia Harrison—Doctor

(Episode)	(Actress)	(Character—Role)
Moonstone	Ruth Roman	Prof. Diana Brice—Lunar scientist
Mutant	Betsy Jones Moreland	Julie Griffith—Biochemist
Nightmare	Lillian Adams	Mother
Nightmare	Lisa Mann	Governess
O.B.I.T.	Joanne Gilbert	Barbara Scott—Wife
Premonition	Mary Murphy	Linda Darcy—Wife, mother
Premonition	Emma Tyson	Janie Darcy—Daughter
Probe	Peggy Ann Garner	Amanda Frank—Fiancée
*Production/Decay	Signe Hasso	Laurel Marshall—Wife
*Production/Decay	Allyson Ames	Arndis Pollard—Girlfriend
Second Chance	Janet DeGore	Mara Matthews—Artist
Second Chance	Mimsy Farmer	Donise Ward—Girlfriend
Second Chance	Angela Clark	SueAnn Beasley—Wife
Soldier	Catherine McLeod	Abby Kagan—Wife
Soldier	Jill Hill	Toni Kagan—Daughter
Soldier	Mavis Neal	Woman
Sixth Finger	Jill Haworth	Cathy Evans—Girlfriend
Sixth Finger	Constance Cavendish	Gert Evans—Shopkeeper
Sixth Finger	Nora Marlowe	Mrs. Ives—Housekeeper
Special One	Marion Ross	Aggie Benjamin—Wife
Specimen Unknown	Gail Kobe	Janet Doweling—Wife
Tourist Attraction	Janet Blair	Lynn Arthur—Mistress
Wolf 359	Sarah Shane	Ethel Meredith—Wife
Zanti Misfits	Olive Deering	Lisa Lawrence—Girlfriend
*ZZZZZ	Joanna Frank	Regina—Entomologist's assistant
*ZZZZZ	Marsha Hunt	Francesca Fields—Wife

The * indicates that women were paired in an episode, a relatively rare occasion. For example, the older, traditional wife is threatened (and rightfully so) by the younger woman in "ZZZZZ." The older, traditional wife serves as an example to follow for the younger woman in "The Production and Decay of Strange Particles." One wishes the long-suffering wife in "The Galaxy Being" would be as pleasant to her husband as the young girlfriend is to her mate (or, depending on where one's sympathies lie, that the impractical husband would be as realistic as his unmarried cohort). In "A Feasibility Study," one woman doesn't let being a wife stop her from being who she wants to be, and the other woman is desperately unhappy. In "The Forms of Things Unknown," one woman is timid, and the other is dominating. They play off of each other. You get the picture.

Appendix III: Women in Science Fiction Films (1964–1979)

FILM	ACTRESS	CHARACTER	ROLE
Alien	Sigourney Weaver	Ripley	Space trucker
	Veronica Cartwright	Lambert	Space trucker
Andromeda	Kate Reid	Dr. Ruth Leavitt	Microbiologist
	Paula Kelly	Karen Anson	Technician
	Midori	Bess	Lab technician
Around the World	Shirley Eaton	Dr. Maggie Hanford	Marine biologist
Barbarella	Jane Fonda	Barbarella	Astronavigatrix
Battle/Apes	Heather Lowe		Medical doctor
Beneath/Apes	Kim Hunter	Zira	Animal psychologist
Charly	Claire Bloom	Alice Kinian	Doctoral student
	Lilia Skala	Dr. Anna Straus	Psychologist
Clockwork	Madge Ryan	Dr. Branom	Medical doctor
	Pauline Taylor	Dr. Taylor	Psychiatrist
Colossus	Susan Clark	Dr. Cleo Markham	Computer scientist
Crack/World	Janette Scott	Dr. Sorenson	Scientist
Demon Seed	Julie Christie	Dr. Susan Harris	Psychologist
	Lisa Lu	Dr. Soong Yen	Linguist
	Barbara O. Jones		Technician
Destination/Space	Sheree North	Dr. Rene Peron	Marine biologist
	Wende Wagner	Sandra Welles	Photographer
Dr. Black	Rosalind Cash	Dr. Billie Worth	Medical doctor

(FILM)	(ACTRESS)	(CHARACTER)	(ROLE)
Embryo	Dr. Joyce Brothers	Herself	Psychologist
Escape/Apes	Natalie Trundy	Dr. Branton	Animal psychiatrist
Fantastic Voyage	Raquel Welch	Cora Peterson	Technician
Invasion/Bee Girls	Anitra Ford	Dr. Susan Harris	Entomologist
	Victoria Vetri	Julie Zorn	Research assistant
Invasion/Snatchers	Brooke Adams	Elizabeth Driscoll	Technician
Mars/Women	Yvonne Craig	Dr. Marjorie Bolen	Space geneticist
Mutiny/Outer Space	Dolores Faith	Faith Montaine	Biochemist
	Pamela Curran	Lt. Connie Engstrom	Communications officer
Journey/Sun	Loni von Friedl	Lisa Hartman	Security
Planet/Apes	Kim Hunter	Zira	Human psychologist
Sleeper	Mary Gregory	Dr. Melik	Doctor
	Marya Small	Dr. Nero	Doctor
Star Trek	Nichelle Nichols	Uhura	Communications officer
Stepford Wives	Katherine Ross	Joanna Eberhart	Photographer
	Carol Eve Rossen	Dr. Fancher	Psychiatrist
Terminal Man	Joan Hackett	Dr. Janet Ross	Psychiatrist
They Came	Jennifer Jayne	Lee Mason	Assistant
Time Travelers	Merry Anders	Carol White	Technician
	Joan Woodbury	Gadra	Future scientist
2001	Margaret Tyzack	Elena	Russian scientist
	Irena Marr		Russian scientist
	Krystyna Marr		Russian scientist
Women/Planet	Merry Anders	Lt. Karen Lamont	Communications officer
	Suzie Kaye	Ens. Stevens	Communications officer
Zardoz	Sara Kestelman	May	Future scientist
Zontar	Colleen Carr	Louise	Technician

Appendix IV:
Spouses (1964–1979)

FILM	ACTRESS—WIFE	ACTOR—HUSBAND
Andromeda	Susan Brown—Allison	Arthur Hill—Dr. Jeremy Stone
	Frances Reid—Clara	David Wayne—Dr. Charles Dutton
Beneath/Apes	Kim Hunter—Zira	David Watson—Cornelius
Countdown	Joanna Moore—Mickey	James Caan—Lee Stegler
	Barbara Baxley—Jean	Robert Duvall—Chiz Stewart
Close Encounters	Teri Garr—Ronnie	Richard Dreyfuss—Roy Neary
Crack/World	Janette Scott—Dr. Sorenson	Dana Andrews—Dr. Sorenson
Demon Seed	Julie Christie—Dr. Harris	Fritz Weaver—Dr. Harris
Embryo	Anne Scheeden—Helen	John Elerick—Gordon Holliston
Escape/Apes	Kim Hunter—Zira	Roddy McDowall—Cornelius
Fahrenheit	Julie Christie—Linda	Oskar Werner—Guy Montag
Fail-Safe	Hildy Parks—Katherine	Dan O'Herlihy—Gen. Black
	Janet Ward—Mrs. Grady	Ed Binns—Col. Grady
Frogs	Lynn Borden—Jenny	Adam Roark—Clint Crockett
Bee Girls	Anna Aries—Nora	Ben Hammer—Herb Kline
	Katie A. Saylor—Mrs. Grubowsky	Deceased
Body Snatchers	Veronica—Nancy Cartwright	Jeff Goldblum—Jack Bellicec
Journey/Far Side	Lynn Loring—Sharon	Roy Thinnes—Col. Glenn Ross
Marooned	Lee Grant—Celia	Richard Crenna—Jim Pruett
	Nancy Kovack—Teresa	James Franciscus—Clayton Stone
	Mariette Hartley—BettyBuzz	Gene Hackman—Lloyd

(FILM)	(ACTRESS—WIFE)	(ACTOR—HUSBAND)
Mission Mars	Heather Hewitt—Edith	Darren McGavin—Col. Blaiswick
	Shirley Parker—Alice	Nick Adams—Nick Grant
Seconds	Frances Reid—Emily	John Randolph—Arthur Hamilton
Slaughterhouse	Sharon Gans—Valencia	Michael Sacks—Billy Pilgrim
	Holly Near—Barbara	Perry King—Robert Pilgrim
Stepford Wives	Katherine Ross—Joanna	Peter Masterson—Walter Eberhart
	Paula Prentiss—*Bobby*	Simon Deckard—Dave Markowe
	Nanette Newman—Carol	Josef Somer—Ted Van Sant
	Tina Louise—Charmaine	Franklin Cover—Ed Wimpiris
	Toni Reid—Marie	George Coe—Claude Axhelm
Zontar	Susan Bjurman—Anne	John Agar—Dr. Curt Taylor
	Patricia Delaney—Martha	Anthony Huston—Keith Ritchie

Chapter Notes

Preface

1. Haskin also directed six episodes of *The Outer Limits*—"The Hundred Days of the Dragon," "The Architects of Fear," "A Feasibility Study," "Behold Eck!," "Demon with a Glass Hand," and "The Invisible Enemy."

2. This description and the ones that follow in this paragraph were taken from MoviesUnlimited.com. (The entry for *Seconds* has since been removed from the site.)

3. Unless otherwise noted, dialogue is quoted directly from the films.

Chapter 1

1. Unless otherwise noted, all quotes were taken directly from the episodes and films.

2. Macready also acted in two episodes of *The Outer Limits*: "The Invisibles" and "The Production and Decay of Strange Particles."

3. Agar's previous science fiction films included *Revenge of the Creature* (1955), *Tarantula* (1955), *The Mole People* (1956), *The Brain from Planet Arous* (1957), *Attack of the Puppet People* (1958), *Invisible Invaders* (1959), and *Journey to the Seventh Planet* (1962).

4. Hoyt also acted in *The Outer Limits* episode "Don't Open Till Doomsday."

5. Duncan also wrote *The Outer Limits* episode "The Human Factor."

Chapter 2

1. Even though I was there for all of it, commentary on the period was corroborated by perusing Judith Goldsmith's *A Timeline of the Counterculture* (http://www.well.com/~mareev/TIMELINE/), Hip Inc.'s *Hippy Timeline* (http://www.hippy.com/timeline.htm), and Bonnie K. Goodman's *The 60's: A Journey Through the Decade* (http://www.ronaldreagan-web.com/thesixties/index.htm).

2. *They Came from Beyond Space*, a UK Amicus production, had been released in May 1967, but it represented really the last gasp of the old order. Featured performers included Jennifer Jayne of *The Crawling Eye* (1958) and Robert Hutton of *Colossus of New York* (1956), *Invisible Invaders* (1959), and *The Slime People* (1963).

3. Unless otherwise noted, all quotes were taken directly from the films.

4. *Sibonetics: The Application of Logic to Electronics* is the full title of one of Walgate's books. *The Energy of Thought* and "The Principles of Thought Control" are other of his titles noted in the film.

5. According to accounts of Anna Freud's life—Elisabeth Young-Bruehl's *Anna Freud: A Biography* (New York: Summit, 1988) and Robert Coles' *Anna Freud: The Dream of Psychoanalysis* (Reading, MA: Addison-Wesley, 1992)—she did not live her life without a significant relationship. Her longtime companion and colleague was Dorothy Burlingham.

6. My *Women Scientists in Fifties Science Fiction Films* (Jefferson, NC: McFarland, 2005) includes an extensive note on the scene with the Russian scientists, 208–209.

7. Quotations from Grant's work have been taken from the version of that paper he presented at the conference, a copy of which he graciously provided me. Grant's essay has since been published in Grant's *Shadows of Doubt: Negotiations of Masculinity in American Genre Films* (Detroit: Wayne State University Press, 2010).

8. See Chapter 5, "Cinematically Representing a Heteroglot World" in *Women Scientists in Fifties Science Fiction Films* for a thorough discussion of the contribution of the female lead's character in *Kronos*.

Chapter 3

1. The *Wikipedia* entry "Shirley Thomas (USC professor)" gives an overview of Thomas's impressive career.

2. Unless otherwise noted, all quotes were taken directly from the films.

3. Many thanks to my research assistant Corneisha McCorckle for the insightful work she did delineating the differences between Peter and Ruth Leavitt. Her research report was titled "How Can One Person Be So Different?"

4. When I was a freshman at Louisiana State University in 1967–1968, female students were permitted to smoke, but not when walking lest we be mistaken for prostitutes, we were told.

5. *Marooned* was released November 10, 1969. The Apollo 13 event occurred in April 1970.

6. Esteemed artist Claude Renoir is credited as the film's director of photography.

7. From A. Ellis and A. Abarbanel, eds., *Encyclopedia of Sexual Behavior* (New York: Hawthorn, 1961).

8. A note on the vaginal orgasm: Millet clarifies, "While there is no 'vaginal orgasm' per se, there is of course orgasm in vaginal coitus (and probably one of different experiential character than that produced by exclusively clitoral stimulation)," an orgasm that so many women clearly enjoy. Nonetheless, Millet is emphatic that "the clitoris is the organ specific to sexuality in

the human female, the vagina being an organ of reproduction as well as of sexuality, and possessing no erogenous tissue save in the lower third of the vaginal tract, the nerve endings in these cells all deriving from and centering in the clitoris" (117).

9. *Marooned, Colossus, Invasion of the Bee Girls, Sleeper, Futureworld, Demon Seed, Westworld.*

10. *Rollerball.*

11. *Marooned, Escape from the Planet of the Apes.*

12. *Escape from the Planet of the Apes, Soylent Green, Conquest of the Planet of the Apes.*

13. *Colossus, The Andromeda Strain, Escape from the Planet of the Apes, Invasion of the Bee Girls.*

14. *Escape from the Planet of the Apes, Embryo.*

15. *Escape from the Planet of the Apes, Sleeper.*

16. *Westworld, Futureworld.*

17. *The Man Who Fell to Earth.*

18. *The Terminal Man, Sleeper, The Andromeda Strain.*

19. As another accomplishment in her illustrious and varied career, Mercer was one of the producers of the extraordinary documentary film *Angela Davis: Portrait of a Revolutionary* (1972).

20. Even though I was there for all of it, thanks to the following sites for jogging my memory: http://www.well.com/~mareev/TIMELINE, http://en.wikipedia.org/wiki/1968_flu_pandemic, http://www.nydailynews.com/archives/news/meatless-boycotting-butchers-april–1973-article-1.920373, http://www.econreview.com/events/wageprice1971b.htm, and http://en.wikipedia.org/wiki/Zero_population_growth.

21. Why no one realizes this charade is perplexing. There are no people older than thirty among any of the inhabitants. At one point, Logan even asks his friend Francis, "Did you ever see anybody renew?" Francis evades the question.

22. Mind you, even back in the day, I thought Firestone was pretty extreme. Yes, she was right that biology is in large part destiny when it comes to bearing children, but the idea of the complete abolishment of the family unit did not and, in my opinion, is not going to happen, nor is the eradication of sex differences. How-

ever, who would have thought, even in the Seventies, that rich women would eventually be able to pay working women to carry their babies in their wombs for them? Who would have thought that males identifying and altering their bodies to female and females identifying and altering their bodies to male would have become more or less commonplace?

23. Steven Jay Schneider, ed., *101 Sci-Fi Movies You Must See Before You Die* (Hauppauge, NY: Barron's Educational Series, 2009),138.

24. Brian Attebery, *Decoding Gender in Science Fiction* (New York: Routledge, 2002), 174.

25. Vivian Sobchack, *Screening Space: The American Science Fiction Film* (New Brunswick: Rutgers University Press, 1987), 81.

26. Lisa Nocks, "'That Does Not Compute': The Brittleness Bottleneck and the Problem of Semantics in Science Fiction," in David Ferro and Eric Swedin, eds., *Science Fiction and Computing: Essays on Interlinked Domains* (Jefferson, NC: McFarland, 2011), 118.

27. Hunter Heyck, "Embodiment, Emotion, and Moral Experiences The Human and the Machine in Film," in Ferro and Swedin, eds., 237.

28. Sobchack, 239.

29. Rick., *Variety*, April 1, 1970.

30. *Demon Seed*, Internet Movie Database.

31. Both the decision and the dissent were found on "*Roe v. Wade* Supreme Court Decision," Women's History, About.com.

32. Madden (naturally) includes a computer from a *Star Trek* episode in his comments regarding HAL, Colossus, and Proteus. He writes, "I'm thinking specifically of 'The Ultimate Computer.' In this episode, Dr. Richard Daystrom, inventor of the original Starship computer system, has come up 'with a whole new approach' to computing. Like HAL, the new computer installed on the Starship Enterprise is meant to replace humans in order 'to free them for other activities.' However, like HAL, the new computer has been programmed by humans and turns out to be not particularly benevolent. It seems that Dr. Daystrom has implanted his brain 'ingrams' on the new computer and it now

shares Daystrom's innate fear and insecurity. Ultimately, Kirk, Spock and Daystrom must defeat the new computer, as Dave had to defeat HAL, in order to survive."

Chapter 4

1. The fundamental definition Sobchack ultimately formulates is as follows: "The SF film is a film genre which emphasizes actual, extrapolative, or speculative science and the empirical method, interacting in a social context with the lesser emphasized, but still present, transcendentalism of magic and religion, in an attempt to reconcile man with the unknown" (63).

2. Unless otherwise noted, dialogue is quoted directly from either the films or their trailers.

3. Of course there is an exception to this statement—in particular, *Café Flesh* (1982), an X-rated film ending with the typical money shot, but nonetheless a film with a fascinating dramatic premise, set in an original post-apocalyptic world of the future.

4. If you care to know the solution to the mystery of the children, here it is. Bernard, the project's director, explains to the artist Freya, his lover, that the children "were born radioactive. Their mothers were exposed to an unknown kind and level of radiation by an accident." "To survive the destruction that is inevitably coming," he continues, "we need a new kind of man. My children are the buried seeds of life. When that time comes the thing itself will open up the door and my children will go out to inherit the earth." The project is working to produce even more children like these. "What earth will you leave them," Freya asks, "after all that man has made and still has to make?" and then Bernard, in order to protect the project, kills her.

5. The *Wikipedia* entry "*The Damned* (1963 film)" cites Michael Hagging and Phil Hardy, *The Aurum Film Encyclopedia: Science Fiction* (London: Aurum Press, 1984), reprinted as *The Overlook Film Encyclopedia: Science Fiction* (Woodstock, NY: Overlook Press, 1995), as the source for this information.

6. The *Wikipedia* entry "*The Damned* (1963 film)" provides the following information about the film's release: "The film

was made in May–June 1961 but, due perhaps to political considerations, was not released in Britain until 1963. Even then it was subject to several cuts, from 96 to 87 minutes in Britain and 77 minutes in America where it was released as *These Are the Damned* in 1965. A complete print was released in arthouse cinemas in 2007. On 15 January 2010, it was released on DVD as part of the Icons of Suspense Collection from Hammer Films."

7. Of course there's an exception. Tone. in *Variety* describes *Glen and Randa* as "sluggish," "with as much interest and pace as pouring concrete." In a July 2006 IMDB post, however, author roblins describes it as "just plain brilliant."

8. If *The Power* had been released in, say, 1965, who knows? We might have liked it.

9. In a contemporary review of *Logan's Run*, Murf. did not see any problems with Logan and Jessica's "exhilarating" escape into nature and reliance on a doddering old man for survival. Some of the words Murf. used to describe the film are "rewarding," "philosophical," and "compelling."

10. Twenty-first century films such as *Another Earth*, *The Sound of My Voice*, and *Take Shelter*, however, have been employing science fictional elements not as their primary components but rather as foundational premises, further expanding the characteristics of the genre.

11. I am aware that more and more explicit gore has been included in the science fiction film genre as audiences have become progressively desensitized to violence, requiring increasingly extravagant filmic experiences.

Conclusion

1. Unless otherwise noted, all quotes were taken directly from the films.

2. "National Maximum Speed Limit Law," *Wikipedia*, 2014.

3. "Statement on Proposed Statehood for Puerto Rico—December 31, 1976," *Presidency.ucsb.edu*, The American Presidency Project, UC Santa Barbara, 1999–2015.

4. "Presidential Key Events—Jimmy Carter," *Millercenter.org*, University of Virginia, 2015.

5. "Ronald Reagan for President 1980 Campaign Brochure—Let's make America great again," *4.President.org*, 4President Organization, 2000–2009.

6. "October 28, 1980—The Carter-Reagan Presidential Debate," *Debates.org*, Commission on Presidential Debates, 2012.

7. Peter Kramer, "Ronald Reagan and Star Wars," *HistoryToday.com*, History Today Ltd., 1999.

8. "'Evil Empire' Speech (March 8, 1983)," *Millercenter.org*, University of Virginia, 2015.

9. The remake of *Invasion of the Body Snatchers* includes two direct references to the original 1956 film: cameo appearances by Don Siegel, the film's director, and Keven McCarthy, its male lead.

10. These similarities between *Star Trek: The Motion Picture* and *2001: A Space Odyssey* are not surprising, considering that Douglas Trumball worked on special photographic effects on both films.

11. The *Wikipedia* entry "Scotty (Star Trek)" cites Anthony Hayward, "Obituary: James Doohan," *The Independent*, July 22, 2005, as the source for this information.

12. The *Wikipedia* entry "Hikaru Sulu" cites "Takei on how Sulu got his name," Archive of American Television 2004 interview, as the source for this information.

13. The *Wikipedia* entry "Star Trek: The Original Series," cites Lee Spiegel "Nichelle Nichols on Having First Major Black Female TV Role and That First Interracial Kiss on 'Star Trek,'" *The Huffington Post*, February 6, 2012, as the source for this information.

Bibliography

Adler, Renata. "Science + Sex = *Barbarella.*" Rev. of *Barbarella*. NYTimes.com. The New York Times Company, 12 Oct. 1968. Web. Feb. 2012.

"Alexis Carrel." *Wikipedia*. Wikimedia Foundation, June 2014. Web. June 2014.

Als, Hilton. "The Theatre: Playing to Type." Rev. of *By the Way, Meet Vera Stark* by Lyn Nottage. *The New Yorker* 23 May 2011: 86–87. Print.

"*The Andromeda Strain:* Making the Film." Dir. Laurent Bouzereau. *The Andromeda Strain*. Dir. Robert Wise. Universal, 2001. DVD.

Attebery, Brian. *Decoding Gender in Science Fiction*. New York: Routledge, 2002.

Barr, Marleen S. "'All At One Point' Conveys the Point, Period: Or, Black Science Fiction Is Bursting Out All Over." Preface. *Afro-Future Females: Black Writers Chart Science Fiction's New-Wave Trajectory*. Ed. Barr. Columbus: Ohio State University Press, 2008. ix-xxiv. Print.

Baudry, Jean-Louis. "The Apparatus: Metapshychological Approaches to the Impression of Reality in Cinema." *Camera Obscura* 1 (Fall 1976). Trans. Jean Andrews and Bernard Augst. Rpt. in *Film Theory and Criticism: Introductory Readings*, 6th ed. Ed. Leo Braudy and Marshall Cohen. New York: Oxford University Press, 2004. 206–239. Print.

"Bechdel test." *Wikipedia*. May 2014. Web. May 2014.

Bolt, Richard H. "Machines Are 'Talking Back.'" *The Christian Science Monitor* 20 July 1967: 9. Rpt. as "The Man-Machine Partnership." *Computers and Society*. Ed. George A. Nikolaieff. New York: H.W. Wilson, 1970. 54–60. Print. The Reference Shelf Series.

Browne, Nick. "The Spectator-in-the-Text: The Rhetoric of *Stagecoach.*" *Film Quarterly* 34.2 (1975–76). Rpt. in Braudy and Cohen. 118–133. Print.

Brownmiller, Susan. *Against Our Will: Men, Women and Rape*. New York: Fawcett Columbine, 1975. Print.

Brzezinski, Zbigniew. "The Search for Meaning Amid Change." *New York Times* 6 Jan. 1969: C141+. Rpt. Nikolaieff. 190–196. Print.

Burck, Gilbert H. "The Boundless Age of the Computer." *Fortune* Mar. 1964: 101–10+. Rpt. as "The Boundless Potential." Nikolaieff. 17–38. Print.

Burner, David. Introduction. *Making Peace with the Sixties*. Princeton: Princeton University Press, 1996. 3–12. Print.

Caldwell, Gail. *A Strong West Wind: A Memoir*. 2006. New York: Random House Trade Paperbacks, 2007. Print.

"Charly." *Wikipedia*. May 2014. Web. May 2014.

Coles, Robert. *Anna Freud: The Dream of Psychoanalysis*. Reading, MA: Addison-Wesley, 1992.

Collins, Gail. *When Everything Changed: The Amazing Journey of American Women from 1960 to the Present*. New York: Little, Brown, 2009. Print.

Corrington, Joyce. Personal interview. Aug. 2011.

Crichton, Michael. *The Andromeda Strain*. New York: Harper, 1969. Print.

"Department of Defense Directive 5120.36." *The Secretary of the Army's Senior Review Panel Report on Sexual Harassment Volume One July 1997*. F-3. *DITC Online*. Defense Technical Information Center, n.d. Web. Feb. 2013.

"Destination: Mars." Dir. Michael Lennick. *Robinson Crusoe on Mars*. Dir. Byron Haskin. The Criterion, 2007. DVD.

Diski, Jenny. *The Sixties*. New York: Picador, 2009. Print.

Donalson, Melvin. Introduction. *Masculinity in the Interracial Buddy Film*. Jefferson, NC: McFarland, 2006. 3–12. Print.

Donne, John. "A Valediction: Forbidding Mourning." *poetryfoundation.org*. Poetry Foundation, 2014. Web. July 2014.

Dreitzel, Hans Peter. Introduction. *Family, Marriage, and the Struggle of the Sexes*. New York: Macmillan, 1972. 5–20. Print. Recent Sociology Series.

"Dudley Dickerson." *Wikipedia*. Feb. 2012. Web. Feb. 2012.

Dworkin, Andrea. *Woman Hating*. New York: Plume, 1974. Print.

Ebert, Roger. "Reviews." Rev. of *Change of Mind*. RogerEbert.com. Ebert Digital, LLC, 27 Oct. 1969. Web. Jan. 2015.

Editors of *Bride's Magazine*. *The Bride's Reference Book: A Guide for Young Marrieds*. New York: Essandess Special Editions, 1956. Print.

Firestone, Shulamith. *The Dialectic of Sex: The Case for Feminist Revolution*. New York: William Morrow, 1970. Bantam rev. ed., 1971.

Franklin, H. Bruce. "Don't Look Where We're Going: Visions of the Future in Science Fiction Films. 1970–82." *Science-Fiction Studies* 29 (Mar. 1983): 70–80. Print.

Freedman, Carl. *Critical Theory and Science Fiction*. Hanover, NH: Wesleyan University Press, 2000. Print.

_____. "Kubrick's *2001* and the Possibility of a Science-Fiction Cinema." *Science-Fiction Studies* 25 (1998): 300–318. Print.

Freud, Sigmund. "Humour (1927)." *International Journal of Psychoanalysis* 9: 1–6. Scribdwww. Scribd., 2015. Web. June 2014.

Friend, Tad. "Funny Like a Guy: Anna Faris and Hollywood's woman problem." *The New Yorker* 11 Apr. 2011: 52–61. Print.

Friedan, Betty. Epilogue. 2001. *The Feminine Mystique*. 1963. New York: Norton, 2001. 513–532. Print.

_____. Introduction to the Tenth Anniversary Edition. 1973. *The Feminine Mystique*. 1963. New York: Norton, 2001. 43–48. Print.

Gibron, Bill. Rev. of *The Man Who Fell to Earth*. *DVD Verdict*. Verdict Partners LLC, 2005. Web. May 2014.

Gielow, Fred C. Jr. *Introducing ... the Computer*. White Plains, NY: IBM, n.d. 3–10. Rpt. as "What Is a Computer?" Nikolaieff. 69–77. Print.

Gilligan, Carol. *In a Different Voice: Psychological Theory and Women's Development*. 1982. Cambridge: Harvard University Press, 1993. Print.

Gornick, Vivian. *Women in Science: Portraits from a World in Transition*. New York: Simon & Schuster, 1983. Print.

Grant, Barry Keith. "*2001: A Space Odyssey*, Feminism, and Science Fiction." Popular Culture Association. San Antonio, TX. April 2004. Panel presentation.

Greene, Eric. *Planet of the Apes as American Myth: Race and Politics in the Films and Television Series*. Jefferson, NC: McFarland, 1996. Print.

Haigh, Thomas. "Technology's Other Storytellers: Science Fiction as History of Technology." *Science Fiction and Computing: Essays on Interlinked Domains*. Ed. David L. Ferro and Eric G. Swedin. Jefferson, NC: McFarland, 2011. 13–37. Print.

Her. Dir. and scr. Spike Jonze. Perfs. Joaquin Phoenix, Amy Adams, Scarlett Johanssen. Prods. Megan Ellison, Spike Jonze, and Vincent Landay. Warner Bros., 2013. DVD.

Heyck, Hunter. "Embodiment, Emotion, and Moral Experiences: The Human and the Machine in Film." Ferro and Swedin. 210–248. Print.

"Hikaru Sulu." *Wikipedia*. Dec. 2014. Web. Jan. 2015.

"*The Incredible Melting Man*." *Wikipedia*. June 2014. Web. June 2014.

"Inside the Making *of Dr. Strangelove or: How I Learned to Stop Worrying and Love the Bomb.*" Dir. David Naylor. *Dr. Strangelove or: How I Learned to Stop Worrying and Love the Bomb.* Dir. Stanley Kubrick. Columbia, 2001. DVD.

"Introduction by Joyce Corrington (Screenwriter), Paul Koslo ('Dutch'), and Eric Laneuville ('Richie')." *The Omega Man.* Dir. Boris Sagal. Warner Bros., 2003. DVD.

Kael, Pauline. "The Current Cinema: A Fresh Start." Rev. of *Barbarella.* New Yorker.com. Conde Nast, 2 Nov. 1968. Web. Feb. 2012.

Kaiser, Charles. *1968 in America: Music, Politics, Chaos, Counterculture, and the Shaping of a Generation.* New York: Grove, 1988. Print.

Kuhn, Annette. "Cultural Theory and Science Fiction Cinema." Introduction. *Alien Zone: Cultural Theory and Contemporary Science Fiction Cinema.* Ed. Kuhn. New York: Verso, 1990. 1–12. Print.

Lanier, Jaron. "It's Not a Game." *MIT Technology Review* 19 Apr. 2011. Web. July 2014.

Levinson, Harry. *The Exceptional Executive: A Psychological Conception.* 1968. New York: New American Library, 1971. Print.

The Longest Trek: Writing the Motion Picture. Star Trek: The Motion Picture. Dir. Robert Wise. Paramount, 2013. DVD.

Luciano, Patrick. *Them or Us? Archetypal Interpretations of Alien Invasion Films.* Bloomington: Indiana University Press, 1987. Print.

Menville, Douglas. *A Historical and Critical Survey of the Science-Fiction Film.* June 1959. Rpt. New York: Arno Press, 1975. Print.

Millett, Kate. *Sexual Politics.* 1969. Urbana: University of Illinois Press, 2000. Print.

Modell, Arnold H. "Humiliating Fantasies and the Pursuit of Unpleasure." *On Freud's "A Child Is Being Beaten."* Ed. Ethel Spector Person. New Haven: Yale University Press, 1997. Print. Contemporary Freud: Turning Points & Critical Issues Series.

Mulvey, Laura. "Visual Pleasure and Narrative Cinema." *Screen* 16.3 (1975). Rpt. in Braudy and Cohen. 837–848. Print.

Nama, Adilifu. *Black Space: Imagining Race in Science Fiction Film.* Austin: University of Texas Press, 2008. Print.

Nikolaieff, George A. Preface. Nikolaieff. 3–6. Print.

Nocks, Lisa. "'That Does Not Compute': The Brittleness Bottleneck and the Problem of Semantics in Science Fiction." Ferro and Swedin. 117–130. Print.

Noonan, Bonnie. *Women Scientists in Fifties Science Fiction Films.* Jefferson, NC: McFarland, 2005. Print.

The Outer Limits: The Original Series. Vol. 1. 1963–1964. MGM, 2003. DVD.

The Outer Limits: The Original Series. Vol. 2. 1964–1965. MGM, 2003. DVD.

Pak, Chris. "Computers in Science Fiction: Anxiety and Anticipation." Ferro and Swedin. 38–53. Print.

"Radio Spot #1." *The Stepford Wives.* Dir. Bryan Forbes. Paramount, 2004. DVD.

Schneider, Steven Jay, ed. *101 Sci-Fi Movies You Must See Before You Die.* Hauppauge, NY: Barron's Educational Series, 2009. Print.

Schow, David J., and Jeffrey Frentzen. *The Outer Limits: The Official Companion.* New York: Ace Science Fiction Books, 1986. Print.

"Scotty (Star Trek)." *Wikipedia.* Jan. 2015. Web. Jan. 2015.

Shirey, Eric. "Astronauts 'Marooned' in Space Foreshadow Real-Life Disaster." *Yahoo! Contributor Network.* Yahoo! Inc., 10 Nov. 2011. Web. July 2013.

Sklar, Robert. *Film: An International History of the Medium.* Upper Saddle River, NJ: Prentice Hall, 1993. Print.

Smith, William D. "Computer Business Races On." *New York Times* 6 Jan. 1969: C85. Rpt. as "The Overnight Success." Nikolaieff. 39–40. Print.

Sobchack, Vivian. *Screening Space: The American Science Fiction Film.* New Brunswick: Rutgers University Press, 1987. Print.

"Star Trek." *Wikipedia.* June 2013. Web. July 2013.

"Star Trek: The Original Series." *Wikipedia.* Jan. 2015. Web. Jan. 2015.

The Stepford Life. Dir. David Gregory. *The Stepford Wives.* Dir. Bryan Forbes. Paramount, 2001. DVD.

"*The Stepford Wives* (1975 film)." *Wikipedia.* July 2013. Web. July 2013.

Stone, Robert. *Prime Green: Remembering*

the Sixties. New York: Harper Perennial, 2007. Print.

Telotte, J.P. *Science Fiction Film*. Cambridge: Cambridge University Press, 2001. Print. Genres in American Cinema Series. Ed. Barry Keith Grant.

"Theatrical Trailer." *Barbarella: Queen of the Galaxy*. Dir. Roger Vadim. Paramount, 1999. DVD.

Thomas, Shirley. *Computers: Their History, Present Applications and Future*. 61–73. New York: Holt, 1965. Rpt. as "Modern Computers." Nikolaieff. 125–139. Print.

Thompson, Hunter S. *Fear and Loathing in Las Vegas: A Savage Journey to the Heart of the American Dream*. New York: Popular Library, 1971. Print.

U.S. Supreme Court. *ROE v. WADE*, 410 U.S. 113 (1973). FindLawwww. Thomson Reuter, 2014. Web. June 2014.

Variety's Complete Science Fiction Reviews. Ed. Donald Willis. New York: Garland, 1985. Print.

Warren, Bill. *Keep Watching the Skies! American Science Fiction Movies of the Fifties*. The 21st Century Edition. Jefferson, NC: McFarland, 2010. Print.

Woodward, C. Vann. "Clio with Soul." *Black Studies: Myths & Realities*. Washington, D.C.: A. Philip Randolph Educational Fund, 1969. 16–31. Print.

Wright, Brian. "Movie Review: Colossus, The Forbin Project (1970)." TheCoffeeCoasterwww. WordPress, 18 Sept. 2013. Web. July 2014.

Young-Bruehl, Elisabeth. *Anna Freud: A Biography*. New York: Summit, 1988.

Zimmerman, Bonnie. "What Has Never Been: An Overview of Lesbian Feminist Literary Criticism." *Feminisms: An Anthology of Literary Theory and Criticism*, rev. ed. Ed. Robyn R. Warhol and Diane Price Herndl. New Brunswick: Rutgers University Press, 1997. 76–96. Print.

Index

Numbers in **_bold italics_** indicate pages with photographs.